I0819170

ALSO BY FERGUS M. BORDEWICH

Klan War:
Ulysses S. Grant and the Battle to Save Reconstruction

Congress at War:
How Republican Reformers Fought the Civil War, Defied Lincoln, Ended Slavery, and Remade America

The First Congress:
How James Madison, George Washington, and a Group of Extraordinary Men Invented the Government

America's Great Debate:
Henry Clay, Stephen A. Douglas, and the Compromise That Preserved the Union

Washington:
The Making of the American Capital

Bound for Canaan:
The Underground Railroad and the War for the Soul of America

Killing the White Man's Indian:
Reinventing Native Americans at the End of the Twentieth Century

My Mother's Ghost:
A Courageous Woman, a Son's Love, and the Power of Memory

Cathay:
A Journey in Search of Old China

CENTENNIAL

CENTENNIAL

THE GREAT FAIR *of* 1876 *and the* INVENTION *of* AMERICA'S FUTURE

* * * * * * *

FERGUS M. BORDEWICH

ALFRED A. KNOPF
New York
2026

A BORZOI BOOK

FIRST HARDCOVER EDITION
PUBLISHED BY ALFRED A. KNOPF 2026

Published by Alfred A. Knopf, a division of Penguin Random House LLC,
1745 Broadway, New York, NY 10019.

Knopf, Borzoi Books, and the colophon are registered trademarks of
Penguin Random House LLC.

Photograph on insert page 2 is courtesy of the Hagley Museum. Machinery Hall. Interior of transept from north end, with Corliss Engine and Baldwin Locomotive. Hagley ID: AVD_2003_255__03_B_31A_01. Centennial Exhibition Photograph and Ephemera Collection. Online. Hagley Museum and Library, Wilmington, DE 19807.
Photograph of John Kehoe on insert page 6 is courtesy of
Anne Flaherty, Kehoe Foundation.

Library of Congress Cataloging-in-Publication Data
Names: Bordewich, Fergus M. author
Title: Centennial : the Great Fair of 1876 and the invention of America's future / Fergus M. Bordewich.
Description: First hardcover edition. | New York : Alfred A. Knopf, 2026. | Includes bibliographical references and index.
Identifiers: LCCN 2025053807 | ISBN 9780593803363 (hardcover) | ISBN 9780593803370 (ebook)
Subjects: LCSH: Centennial Exhibition (1876 : Philadelphia, Pa.) | Technological innovations—United States—History—19th century | Republican Party (U.S. : 1854–) | United States—Politics and government—1869–1877 | United States—Social conditions—1865–1918
Classification: LCC T825.B1 B67 2026
LC record available at https://lccn.loc.gov/2025053807

penguinrandomhouse.com | aaknopf.com

Printed in the United States of America
1st Printing

The authorized representative in the EU for product safety and compliance is Penguin Random House Ireland, Morrison Chambers, 32 Nassau Street, Dublin D02 YH68, Ireland, https://eu-contact.penguin.ie.

For Chloe and Basheer,
who cast their light on different histories

Everybody is Centennializing.

—MACON WEEKLY TELEGRAPH

We sail a dangerous sea of seething currents, cross and under-currents, vortices—all so dark, untried—and whither shall we turn?

—WALT WHITMAN

Contents

Preface

This book began as the story of the greatest cultural event of America's Gilded Age, the spectacular Centennial Exhibition of 1876, an extravaganza concocted to celebrate the nation's first century. It quickly grew beyond the fair's confines to become a book about America itself. Although still rooted in Philadelphia, it travels as far as the Montana prairie, beleaguered hamlets in Reconstruction South Carolina, coalfields and railroad yards, conclaves of politicians and plutocrats, an inventor's laboratory, and even, briefly, the salons of Rome. The story it tells is peopled with power brokers, rebels, presidential aspirants, terrorists, artists and writers, moguls, engineers, defiant women and patriotic zealots, and both winners and losers in the great American struggle for survival and success. In the triumphs and unfolding crises of 1876, it is possible to see the birth pangs of the modern United States, as the old politics and moral consciousness of prewar America was replaced by a new sense of what it was to be American, and by a renewed, if flawed, promise of greatness to come.

In the eyes of both its promoters and ordinary Americans, the Centennial stood as a self-conscious metaphor for the nation. It bore testimony to their surging faith in its moral exceptionalism, its glowing future, its industrial might, its new wealth, its sense of cultural superiority, and an unquestioning belief in its destiny. A memorable poster created for the great fair presented a swaggering Uncle Sam bestriding North America and dandling the earth in his hands. A century and a half later, the Centennial offers a panoramic window onto the United States at a watershed in its history, indeed a more revealing one than Americans of that day realized. Unlike most of them, we can also see the darker landscape of social inequities, deepening class conflict, racial shame, and sometimes delusional self-confidence that lay beneath all the triumphalism and hoopla. The Centennial year was only the beginning of an extended period of social and cultural upheaval that would stretch deep into the twentieth century. Beyond the brass bands, bunting, and soaring oratory lay pressing questions about the direction of the country. What was the United States to be in the century ahead? Would its Centennial herald an era of expanding freedom, or the triumph of white supremacy? Would government be cleansed of corruption, or continue to succumb to it? Would resurgent Native tribes succeed in fending off encroaching settlement on the Great Plains? Would the rising tide of workers' agitation force corporate power to the bargaining table? Would the once-ascendant Republican Party go down to humiliating defeat barely a decade after its triumph in the Civil War?

I tell the story of that watershed year primarily through four individuals whose lives embodied different facets of the transformation that was taking place in the nation: the rising presidential contender Rutherford B. Hayes, the governor of Ohio; Tom Scott, president of the nation's largest corporation, the Pennsylvania Railroad, and one of the most powerful industrial moguls of the day; the flamboyant Black sculptor Edmonia Lewis, the most controversial figure to show her work at the Centennial Exhibition; and Alexander Graham Bell, whose new invention, a "speaking device," was demonstrated publicly for the first time there. The Centennial year included a critical, fiercely contested national election, exposed shocking evidence of collusion between corporate power brokers and public officials, and witnessed the final act of Reconstruction, renewed Indian war in the West, and deepening, soon-to-be explosive labor strife. Seen through the lens of the Centennial, these events form both a rich tapestry of the Gilded Age and a window onto the birth pangs of modern America.

In 1876, America was still discovering itself. Eighty-five years earlier, Patrick Henry, fearing for the future of the newly born United States, opined to his protégé James Monroe, "Altho' the

Form of Governmt into which my Countrymen determined to place themselves had my Enmity, yet as we are one & all embarked, it is natural to care for the crazy Machine, at least so long as we are out of Sight of a Port to refit." Since 1791, the nation had changed dramatically. The pastoral world of small farms and isolated hamlets was rapidly evolving into a modern industrial society where factories produced a dizzying panoply of consumer goods, standards of living had dramatically increased, and railroads were reinventing the speed of people's lives. But the "crazy machine" was still running stronger than ever, its once-fragile gears now firmly meshed, its output more multitudinous than Henry or any of the other Founders had ever imagined. Roiling, tumultuous, and contentious, it was hurtling on toward a future that the men and women of 1876, optimistic as they so often were, could only hazily see.

CENTENNIAL

CHAPTER 1

THE GREAT FAIR

★ ★ ★ ★ ★

Well, Moon, see that the bill is passed;
the Centennial must be made a great success.

—THOMAS A. SCOTT

On the morning of May 10, 1876, Ulysses S. Grant stepped from his overnight quarters on Walnut Street in downtown Philadelphia to be greeted by an escort of brass bands, massed sailors and soldiers, cavalry in horse-tailed helmets, admirals and beribboned major generals, state governors, members of the U.S. Supreme Court, magnates of industry, politicians of every rank and stripe, foreign ambassadors, and the president's guest of honor, the emperor of Brazil, Dom Pedro II. They were the advance guard of the most spectacular public extravaganza to be mounted in Gilded Age America, the long-anticipated celebration of the nation's first Centennial a figurative stone's throw from Independence Hall, where the Founding Fathers had signed the Declaration of Independence. In carriages, on horseback, and on foot the festive cavalcade processed along streets festooned with patriotic bunting and the flags of all nations, through roaring crowds of men, women, and children to Fairmount Park, two miles to the north, which a year's labor had transformed into a phantasmagorical theater of national glory, vaster and grander than anything ever before seen in America.

At the park, Grant and his entourage mounted a giant stage to face a crowd that numbered at least 100,000 and perhaps twice that, packed so densely that it was difficult to move without the aid of police. Boys slack-jawed with excitement perched on statues of the Muses. Bishop Matthew Simpson of the Methodist Church offered thanks to God for the nation's prosperity and progress, for the courage of its Founding Fathers, and for the labor-saving machinery that eased the lives of the toiling masses. An orchestra of 150 musicians played “La Marseillaise,” “God Save the Queen,” the anthems of Brazil, Germany, Russia, the Netherlands, Spain, and a dozen other powers, followed by a specially commissioned march composed for the occasion by Richard Wagner. A thousand-voiced chorus next sang the official “Centennial Hymn” penned by the aged John Greenleaf Whittier, dedicated to “Our fathers' god, from whose hand the centuries fall like grains of sand”:

Oh! Make Thou us, through centuries long,
In peace secure, in justice strong.

Then, the popular Quaker poet Bayard Taylor recited his “Song of 1876,” a paean to sectional reconciliation—a vital national concern barely a decade after the Civil War, when the ghosts of 650,000 dead stalked the hearts of Americans North and South:

Waken voice of the Land's Devotion!
Spirit of Freedom, awaken all!
North and South, we are met as brothers!

At last, the president rose. Grant was a man of modest height, more portly than when he ascended to his office seven years earlier, his chestnut hair beginning to go gray. In big gatherings he was stiff, even shy, his voice difficult to hear from a distance. He gripped his speech in his clenched fist. He felt more beleaguered than ever before, shackled to the country's wounded economy, grimly watching his effort to save Reconstruction sputter for lack of

Northern support, embarrassed by the exposure of venality among his trusted advisors, belittled by defectors from his own party, who sneered at him as incompetent or worse. Wherever he turned some new sump of trouble seemed to be concealed. But he never lacked dignity or sincerity, and he soldiered on.

"One hundred years ago, our country was new and but partially settled," he began, in that soft voice. To Grant, the frontier, now unfolding far west of the Missouri River, was no abstraction. He was born in an Ohio cabin in 1822, when settlement extended only in patchwork west of the Appalachians and most of the Midwest was still woodland, from which towns were being hacked by main force. "Our necessities have compelled us to chiefly expend our means and time in felling forests, subduing prairies, building dwellings, factories, ships, docks, warehouses, roads, canals, machinery. Most of our schools, churches, libraries & asylums have been established within a hundred years. Burthened by these great primal works of necessity which could not be pretermitted"—that is, delayed—"we yet have done what this exhibition will shew in the direction of rivalling older and more advanced nations in law, medicine, and theology—in science, literature, philosophy, and the fine arts. And now fellow citizens, I hope careful examination of what is about to be exhibited to you will not only inspire you with a profound respect for the skill and taste of our friends from other nations, but also satisfy you with the attainments made by our own people during the past one hundred years."

He then declared the Centennial officially open. Cannon boomed. Tens of thousands of voices cheered. As the presidential party descended from the stage, the great choir roared out Handel's "Hallelujah Chorus." With Dom Pedro and his family at his side, and senators and congressmen in tow, Grant made his way through the palatial, glass-roofed Machinery Hall, to the foot of the Corliss Engine, the most powerful piece of machinery in the world. At the direction of its inventor, the famous engineer George Corliss, Grant grasped one lever and Dom Pedro the other. In unison, they pulled and the immense iron walking beams began to move and the great wheel began to spin, setting in motion eight miles of shafts, belts, and spindles connected to the hundreds of lesser machines throughout the hall. Gongs clanged, steam whistles shrilled, cannon again boomed, and church bells rang across the city. Those who were there felt that the wheel of history itself had turned before their eyes. A reporter for the *Philadelphia Times* strained for words: "The obedient looms began their round of six months like an ark of machinery set afloat for a voyage to preserve the creations of man."

THE CENTENNIAL EXHIBITION—sometimes called the Exposition, but most often simply the Centennial—was the most ambitious public event in the nation's history up to then: a spectacle of industrial might, America's first World's Fair, an "Arabian Nights of Modern Times," as one magazine effusively termed it, evoking an almost magical experience that innumerable visitors would struggle to describe. *Harper's Bazaar* quipped that Philadelphia "appears for the nonce to have thrown off her sombre Quaker apparel, and to have ushered in the Centennial with much the air of a venerable old lady endeavoring to execute some difficult steps in the can-can." Showmanship aside, it marked the country's first century with an epic celebration of its past and the promise of its future. The roar of the engines and innovations that packed its halls proclaimed that the country could now not only manufacture for itself everything it needed but also sell its burgeoning surpluses to all the world. The Exposition's menagerie of new farming equipment—giant tractors, harvesters, mechanical planters—foretold the ecological future of the as yet barely settled West, as well as the fate of the still potent Native tribes that blocked the way. A plenitude of works by the nation's artists challenged the world to take American art seriously. A pavilion designed, built, and staffed entirely by women hoped to upend society's most basic gendered conventions. Colossal displays of new consumer goods teased the eye and tantalized desire.

Apart from its dazzling exhibits, the Centennial embodied a stock-taking of the nation's past as it charged toward new existential challenges. Throughout its first century the nation had labored to knit together its disparate, mutually distrustful parts, fissured by slavery and bitter disagreement over the powers of the central government. Only with the Civil War's end could Americans begin to feel assured that republican government would truly prevail. That the United States would survive as a nation no one but the most unforgiving former Confederates now doubted; slavery was gone and states' rights had (or so it seemed to victorious Yankees) been consigned to the dustbin of lost causes.

If triumphalism was the Centennial's dominant idiom, beneath its glittering surface it served as a giant kaleidoscopic lens that revealed much about America at one of its most transformative moments, as big money infiltrated government, technology reshaped everyday American life, Black Americans struggled to exercise their hard-won freedom, feminists demanded rights for women, and Native tribes went to war to repel advancing settlement in the West. Although the Centennial celebrated the spread of mechanization in all aspects of American life, it did so in the midst of massive poverty and unemployment, in the third year of the worst economic depression the United Sates had yet experienced. With the bloody violence of the 1871 Paris Commune still stark in Americans' memories, fear of what people were beginning to call "communism" entered popular speech for the first time. Even as Bishop Simpson spoke in the opening ceremony of the improved lives of working men, in Chicago mobs of bricklayers armed with clubs and pistols were marching for higher wages, miners were striking in Ohio, and less than a hundred miles north of Philadelphia, Irish American labor leaders were on trial for their lives.

Everyone knew that the future of the country lay at stake in the coming presidential election, barely six months away. The parties readied themselves for what promised to be an epic battle, with the resurgent Democrats pitted against the scandal-ridden Republicans. Even as Americans proclaimed the superiority of their democracy, they felt the country's political culture and private morality corroding with a new, hustling greed that infected the very institutions that the Centennial celebrated. Describing one notoriously shameless magnate, the society reporter Emily Briggs wrote, "Floating in Congressional waters at all hours of the legislative day may be seen the burly form of [Collis] Huntington, the great, huge devil-fish of the railroad combination. He plows the Congressional main, a shark in voracity of plunder, a devil-fish in tenacity of grip. At the beginning of every session, this representative of the great Central Pacific comes to Washington as certain as a member of either branch of Congress. Every weakness of a Congressman is noted, whilst the wily Huntington decides whether the attack shall be made with the weapon of the male or the female kind." Revelations of shocking self-dealing tarred prominent members of the administration and Republicans in Congress. Lobbyists handed out wads of cash on the floor of Congress. In Mark Twain's satirical 1873 novel *The Gilded Age,* a practiced lobbyist complains, "The fact is that the price is raised so high on a United States Senator now, that it affects the whole market; you can't get any public improvement through on reasonable terms."

America also stood at what a later era would call a racial inflection point. The fate of Reconstruction and of the four million Black Americans also hung precariously in the balance. The previous decade had brought them freedom, citizenship, enfranchisement, and new opportunity. But their future depended on the unlikely possibility of a Republican victory at the polls. Unless Republicans somehow overcame the odds, worried John Sherman, brother of General William Tecumseh Sherman and one of the most consequential men in the U.S. Senate, the Southern states would "soon be organized, by violence and intimidation, into a compact political power"—a solid South—that could dominate the national government for generations to come.

THE CENTENNIAL EXHIBITION was conceived as a kind of grand theater of national harmony where Americans could come together again in a performance of patriotic self-affirmation. Its promoters predicted that Shiloh, Antietam, and Gettysburg would be forgotten in the remembrance of Lexington, Concord, and Bunker Hill, and visions of a common future. The Exhibition's organizers paired retired Union and Confederate generals at gala events, and named a relative of Robert E. Lee to read the Declaration of Independence on the Fourth of July. African Americans, too, initially had high hopes: A Black member of Congress, Josiah Walls of Florida, effusively declared that the Centennial would undoubtedly "strengthen the bonds which can unite freemen to their native land, and kindle a blaze of patriotic feeling in whose dazzling light all questions of minor differences and all hurtful recollections of past disagreements will be blotted out."

But evidence of the shifting public sentiment on race was visible even at the Centennial. Despite plentiful official references to emancipation and equality, Black Americans had been excluded from the Exhibition's planning and from nearly all the jobs it generated, with the ambiguous, at best, exception of a Southern-themed restaurant, which advertised a band of "old-time darkies" strumming banjos and where Black waiters impersonated slaves. Perhaps significantly, it was the most popular eatery at the Centennial. Frederick Douglass, although invited to sit among the dignitaries on opening day—but not to speak—was initially refused entry to the stage until a U.S. senator personally intervened. Although it was not widely publicized, nativist violence also erupted on opening day, when several Japanese were physically attacked and a Chinese official was nearly stripped of his robes.

In all, some ten million Americans visited the Centennial, about 20 percent of the country's population, most of them expecting to be inspired by the country's achievements and hoping to be uplifted by evocations of its history. There were ordinary Americans of all kinds, war veterans from both North and South, presidential candidates, celebrities ranging from P. T. Barnum to Henry Wadsworth Longfellow and Mark Twain. Foreign visitors numbered in the hundreds of thousands, most famous among them Emperor Dom Pedro II of Brazil, the first foreign head of state ever to visit the United States, who loved the Exposition so much that he often wandered among the crowds in disguise. Most visitors were dazzled with what they found. "We are lost in bewilderment," exclaimed one thrilled young Philadelphian. "The wealth of the world is before us. Where shall we go first? What shall we do? These are the questions one hears on every side."

ONE AMERICAN WAS notably omitted from the Centennial's opening-day lineup: Walt Whitman, in whose pulsating voice the

American multitude lived more vividly than in the stanzas of any other poet of the time. His absence was all the more glaring since he lived just three miles from Fairmount Park, across the Delaware River in New Jersey, close enough that from his home near the Camden waterfront he could hear the boom of cannon and the thundering chords of Wagner's march. Chronically short of money, Whitman had prayed with at least a trace of desperation that official recognition by the Centennial would win him renewed attention and a substantial honorarium. He had submitted to the judging committee a soaring ode, titled "Song of the Exposition," which he hoped would be read at the opening ceremony:

Here shall you trace in flowing operation,
In every state of practical, busy movement, the rills of civilization . . .
In large calm halls, a stately museum shall teach you the infinite lessons of minerals,
In another, woods, plants, vegetation shall be illustrated—in another animals, animal life and development.
One stately house shall be the music house,
Others for other arts—learning, the sciences, shall all be here,
None shall be slighted, none but shall be here honor'd, help'd, exampled.
(This, this and these, America, shall be your pyramids and obelisks,
Your Alexandrian Pharos, gardens of Babylon . . .)

The lines were lovely but uninspired. Whitman was striving for respectability. But he was shunted aside anyway in favor of more popular poetic voices whose work was easier for the public to digest than the sometimes disturbing poetry of *Leaves of Grass,* which continued to define his reputation for most Americans who were aware of him at all. The commission in charge of such selections had chosen hackneyed voices of the romantic sort that Whitman deplored.

At fifty-seven, Whitman was admired by a few, ignored by most, and living in straitened circumstances if not in the penury that he sometimes claimed. White-haired, his beard as bushy as a patriarch's, he no longer looked the cocky boulevardier of his early photographs. Often he could not even write because of paralysis. No major house would publish his books. He had hoped that a new Centennial edition of his work would make him independent of his brother's support, but it flopped. He was a kind of one-man subtext to the Centennial, a sharer in its thrilled celebration of the nation's history and future, and also a lonely retort to its chest-thumping self-confidence.

The Centennial embodied all that Whitman loved about America—its muscular optimism, its enthusiasm for experimentation and its aspiration to empire, its celebration of the mechanical and the commercial, and above all its relentless democratizing spirit. In 1871, in a dense, strangely equivocal essay he titled *Democratic Vistas,* he predicted that before the nation's next Centennial, in 1976, there would be "forty or fifty great states," Canada and Cuba among them, with a population of sixty or seventy million. "The Pacific will be ours, and the Atlantic mainly ours. There will be electronic communication with every part of the globe." But an undertow of doubt had infected his thinking. He was disheartened by his country's "crudeness, vice, and caprices," by the "depravity of the business classes," by a government "saturated in corruption," by Americans' "almost maniacal" appetite for wealth. Still, he concluded that democracy was an unstoppable tide, "filling the world with effulgence and majesty," and would yet be sustained by the birth of a "New Man" whose robust individuality would be, like a well-crafted tool, the "compensating balance-wheel of the successful working machinery of aggregate America."

AMONG THE DIGNITARIES who joined Ulysses Grant on the Centennial's opening day, wearing a gleaming silk hat and regal black broadcloth, sat the man millions of Americans expected to become the next president of the United States, New York's governor, Samuel J. Tilden. Since 1861, the Democrats had been hobbled first by the defection of their Southern members to the Confederacy, and after the war by their premature welcome of former Confederates back into the party fold. They were an ungainly but potent alliance of urban immigrants, small-government Jacksonians, and Southern whites desperate to recapture their states from biracial Republican rule. In this Centennial year, with its lusty extolling of sectional reconciliation, the Democrats expected to finally shed the albatross of their past. Tilden was not a perfect candidate. He was introverted and unmarried, and he lacked the common touch. But all America knew him as the dragon-slayer who had brought down New York's notorious Tweed ring. He was insulated from manipulation by his party's bosses by his personal fortune, which he earned as a corporate lawyer in New York, and he was a champion of clean government at a time when the Republicans seemed to be drowning in the political quicksand of corruption.

All but the most partisan Republicans—and many of them too—feared disaster in the November elections. Having enjoyed a monopoly of power for fifteen years, the onetime party of Lincoln had grown rich and complacent, and was shot through with self-dealing appointees, contractors, and moneymen on whom they fed. The party was dangerously split between stalwart but beleaguered defenders of the administration and disgruntled reformers who were threatening to bolt. In the South, Republican governments in state after state were falling to white supremacist "Redeemers" as terrorism drove Black voters—virtually all of them Republican—away from the polls. In the final year of his presidency, Grant seemed isolated and exhausted. With the Democrats now in control of the House of Representatives, investigations erupted on every side. No one doubted Grant's personal probity. But his minister to Britain, Robert Schenck, was revealed to have promoted a worthless mining stock and defrauded British investors. Secretary of War William Belknap was found to be selling Indian trading post concessions to the highest bidder and living grandly on the profits. Grant's personal secretary, Orville Babcock, was entangled in a sordid collaboration with a ring of whiskey distillers, who paid him off with diamonds and cigar boxes stuffed with cash. The Republicans' woes were compounded by the lingering effects of the catastrophic financial panic that began in 1873, which brought ruin to thousands of businesses and banks, destroyed farm prices, and led to mass unemployment, malnutrition, and homelessness. Democrats smelled blood. "The whole government of the nation has been corrupt—desperately corrupt—and the honor and glory of applying the antidote will belong to you," General Joseph Hooker encouragingly wrote to Tilden that spring.

Tilden's most likely opponent was also sitting on the dais: James G. Blaine of Maine, the combative and charismatic former Speaker of the House of Representatives, who hungered openly for the nation's highest office. Blaine had rivals, of course. Indiana Senator Oliver P. Morton, a physical wreck but still volcanic with political energy, was an outspoken Radical fiercely supportive of the rights of newly enfranchised Southern Black Republicans. Former Solicitor General Benjamin Bristow of Kentucky was popular with the party's reform wing for exposing many of the administration's most venal appointees. Blaine's most potent challenger, however, was the preening New York spoilsman, Senator Roscoe Conkling, the only one among them who could match Blaine's magnetism. Mainly in the Midwest, a few politicos were also talking about the well-liked but little-known governor of Ohio, Rutherford B. Hayes, a former Union general and model of teetotaling probity. All were members of a rising generation of Republican leaders who were replacing fiery crusaders like Thaddeus Stevens and Charles Sumner, both now dead, and Ben Butler and Benjamin F. Wade, who had been pushed from office by voters looking for new men to lead the party into the uncertain postwar age. (In Wade's case, the Democrats had captured the state legislature, which at that time still elected U.S. senators.)

They operated at a new intersection of power and wealth that was transforming the Republican Party into a machine that barely resembled the idealistic coalition that had captured the White House under Abraham Lincoln in 1860. Republicans were now the party of power. For most of the nineteenth century, the Democrats had dominated all three branches of government. That abruptly ended in 1861, when almost the entire contingent of Southern Democrats decamped to the Confederacy, leaving the fledgling Republicans with enormous majorities in both houses, total control of government patronage, and sudden responsibility for waging a war they hadn't prepared for.

Prodigious amounts of money had to be found to sustain the war effort. The army demanded arms, food, uniforms, tents, draft animals, and cavalry horses. Millions of soldiers had to be paid. Entire fleets had to be built for the navy. New industries came into being and old ones metastasized. Railway networks expanded. The production of iron ore doubled. Steel plants proliferated. New oilfields opened in Pennsylvania, and new silver mines in Nevada. The war fostered a new symbiosis between business and government as Congress approved contracts, subsidies, grants, new banking regulations, and tariffs that poured federal largesse into Northern industry and, in return, corporate money into the pockets of pliable legislators and officials.

Republican policymaking increasingly reflected the interests of industry and Wall Street. Members of Congress became eager partners in investment schemes and were rewarded with bonds and stocks that they were free to sell to their political friends for fabulous profits. In return, moguls and contractors were required to contribute lavish sums for the party's coffers if they wanted to enjoy friendly legislation. During the 1872 campaign, the Philadelphia financier Jay Cooke complained that he was being ridden "like a free horse" by demands for campaign contributions.

No industry was more central to the emerging new political dynamic than railroads: They were ever-expanding, incredibly profitable, and glamorous. In less than a generation they had transformed the way Americans lived, traveled, did business, built cities and towns, settled the frontier, and waged war. Countless popular prints celebrated them as the quintessential agents of civilization spreading across the continent in the image of a steaming train, with woodlands, wilderness, and Indians fleeing before it, and farms springing up in its wake.

The federal entanglement with railroading began with the building of the transcontinental line that, with its completion in 1869, bound California to the rest of the country. Private capital alone was insufficient to shoulder the costs. Legislation granted the railroads a vast amount of land along the right-of-way—eventually 127 million acres—which they were free to sell to settlers, and provided for government loans up to $48,000 per mile, inventing what historian Richard White has termed "hothouse capitalism" by nursing private investment and protecting it from risk. By the 1870s, railroad tycoons were welding together networks of iron that spread weblike across vast regions of the country, employing battalions of lobbyists to squeeze subsidies from Congress. Rival capitalists battled ceaselessly for political advantage, government charters, federal land grants, rights-of-way, and other benefits, transforming party politics as dynamically as it was altering the nation's physical landscape.

Amid the constellation of such men, one of the most pitiless was Tom Scott of the Pennsylvania Railroad, godfather to the Centennial, who in the 1860s and 1870s soared like a human meteorite through the expanding universe of railroading. Orphaned at the age of ten, with little formal education, he essentially invented himself through a combination of charm, tireless work, and a genius for mathematics. Scott joined the Pennsylvania Railroad as a local manager at twenty-seven and became the road's general superintendent at thirty-five. Two years later, he was its vice president and a director, and in 1874 its president. In 1872, he was even mentioned as a putative presidential candidate for the breakaway reformist Liberal Republican movement. (Despite its name, it was actually conservative in orientation.) Scott built on the early expansion of the railroad's longtime president John Edgar Thomson, his mentor and then close ally and partner. Thomson, a brilliant manager, was an introverted Quaker, whose cautious nature was overmatched by Scott's magnetism and boiling energy. It was Scott who maintained a private office in the state capitol building at Harrisburg, next to the legislative chamber, and Scott who perfected the art of strategic bribery, leaving packets of cash for politicians invited to his hotel room.

Under the leadership of Thomson, and increasingly Scott, the road underwent a massive expansion from the Delaware River to the Mississippi to form the largest, most efficient, and richest railroad network in the world. Scott had flooded the Pennsylvania legislature with applications for state charters for at least a dozen (and likely more) vaguely named holding companies, a Scott innovation, all of them supposedly headed by placeholding incorporators connected with the Pennsylvania Railroad's management—including two of Scott's personal secretaries. The applications were carefully written to conceal the new companies' real purpose, which was to build and acquire rail lines, though the word "railroad" rarely appeared in their documentation. (Had it done so, it would have required state approval for the issuance of bonds and the approval of routes.) Scott's subterfuge also enabled the Pennsylvania to amass vast swathes of real estate without provoking speculation and higher prices. One was a fictional cover for the construction of a railroad between Denver, Colorado, and the Rio Grande, another for a new connecting line in Illinois, another for a line through the Shenandoah Valley of Virginia, part of Scott's scheme to expand the Pennsylvania Railroad's power through the South. By leveraging the railroad's immense borrowing power along with its political muscle, Scott planned ultimately to reach the Pacific Ocean.

Tall, blond, and boyish-looking even in middle age, Scott had, *The New York Times* wrote of him, "an exhaustless flow of animal spirits combined with extraordinary mental energy." He inspired superlatives. His ally, Lincoln's first secretary of war, Simon Cameron, called him "the greatest railroad master that ever lived." Andrew Carnegie, whom Scott plucked from obscurity to work for the Pennsylvania Railroad, regarded him as a political genius. Scott's bitter rival John D. Rockefeller considered him the most unscrupulous man he had ever met.

The Civil War turned Scott from talented corporate star into a legend. In the war's first days, offering his services to the government gratis, he created order out of panic. When pro-Confederate saboteurs broke the railway lines around Washington, he quickly figured out how to reroute troop trains from Pennsylvania via Annapolis to save the capital from capture. He then dispatched his own telegraph operators to Washington to create a single national network for the army, and pioneered the rapid construction of rail lines to follow the federal armies as they advanced into Confederate territory. In 1862, he daringly took personal charge of an ammunition train to speed it to troops waiting near the battlefield at Antietam, roaring into the federal camp enveloped in clouds of smoke from the train's overheated axles. In yet another extraordinary feat, in 1863, he hastened the transfer of reinforcements from the East to relieve the beleaguered federal garrison at Chattanooga. (Although Scott's commitment to the Union was unbending, he ensured that, whenever possible, federal troops, materiel, and provisions were carried in the Pennsylvania's cars, at as much as a 40 percent markup over commercial shippers.)

In 1876, Scott was at the peak of his power. The Pennsylvania Railroad controlled more than 6,500 miles of track, earned annual profits of $25 million, employed a workforce of 20,000, and carried as many as 145,000 passengers daily. It seemed to more than a few Americans that the entire Centennial Exhibition was just another grandiose extension of the Pennsylvania Railroad. Scott was one of the Centennial's most vigorous boosters, recognizing it as a golden opportunity to promote the railroad and the wealth that it had drawn to Philadelphia. The Pennsylvania donated hundreds of thousands of dollars' worth of stock to the organizers, invested considerable resources in the fair's development, mounted numerous exhibits extolling the railroad's achievements, and carried vast numbers of visitors to its gates.

The idea for a national celebration arose, humbly enough, with a professor at Wabash College in Indiana, J. L. Campbell, who suggested it in a letter to the mayor of Philadelphia, who eagerly endorsed it and won backing for it from members of the city's social elite and its political class, and eventually from Pennsylvania's state legislature, where Tom Scott's openhanded largesse played a significant role in winning support.

In 1871, the idea reached Congress. Some members objected to the creation of a federally authorized Centennial commission that would amount to a "vast corporation" for which no basis existed in the Constitution. But the fair's supporters won out, arguing persuasively, in the words of Pennsylvania Senator Simon Cameron, that the fair offered an unparalleled opportunity "to show the world what influence and what power free institutions had had upon the human race." Brushing off the naysayers, Congress authorized the Exhibition to celebrate the nation's history, industry, resources, and achievements in the arts. Several cities aspired to serve as host, but the logical choice was always Philadelphia, the patriots' Revolutionary War capital, and home to such hallowed sites as Independence Hall, Benjamin Franklin's grave, and the house where Thomas Jefferson penned the Declaration of Independence. Commissioners were appointed from each state, with Joseph R. Hawley, a Hartford newspaperman and former Union general, as overall president, and Alfred T. Goshorn, a Cincinnati lead manufacturer, as the fair's director-general. The commission confidently predicted that the Centennial would be an engine of national renewal, where Americans would come together "around the old family hearthstone" of national independence. Goshorn, who traveled around Europe recruiting foreign exhibitors, promised that the Centennial would open vast new markets for American investment as it inspired "a stronger confidence at home and abroad in the peaceful endurance of our free institutions." Declared one Philadelphia newspaper, it would be "a popular museum, a training school, an academy of design, a vast study for the common people."

Turning ambitions for the Centennial into concrete reality of course demanded massive investment. Congress authorized a quasi-independent board of finance—dominated by the Pennsylvania Railroad—to sell $10 million in shares to the public. The federal government subscribed $1.5 million. Various states guaranteed another $2.5 million, and $500,000 was raised from the sale of ice cream, soda water, and other concessions. Surprisingly, the Pennsylvania state legislature hesitated, however, when it was asked for a commitment of $1 million. Scott thereupon ordered his men in Harrisburg to "alter the vote." He told his chief lobbyist, Samuel S. Moon, "Well, Moon, see that the bill is passed; the Centennial must be made a great success." The bill was.

The railroad stood to benefit handsomely from the Centennial, of course. The vast majority of the Exhibition's eight million visitors would travel to Philadelphia on Tom Scott's lines or those of their affiliates—a greater volume of traffic than was ever handled by any other country during a six-month period. The Pennsy lavishly advertised itself as the only line running direct to the Centennial buildings, boasting of its "luxurious night cars," "unsurpassed eating stations," and "magnificent scenery" all the way. Scott's crews laid new track, developed a state-of-the-art safety signaling system, introduced elegant "drawing room sleeping cars," and added a hundred new gaslit parlor cars with individual cushioned swivel chairs and velvet hassocks. Scott also directed a special branch line to be built right to the Centennial's gates, where travelers disembarked at the railroad's new multitowered Tudoresque depot just steps from the exhibition's Main Building, a dazzling confection of iron and glass designed by the railroad's chief architect, which spectacularly captured not just the muscular triumphalism of the Centennial but also the soaring ambitions of the Pennsylvania Railroad's chief executive. When thousands of shipments from around the world overwhelmed the commission's staff, Scott ordered the railroad's personnel to step in: 16,039 cars of building materials and 4,116 cars of exhibits were unloaded, sorted, and distributed with exemplary efficiency.

One week after Opening Day, *The Atlantic Monthly*'s editor, William Dean Howells, a man of high principle and often severe judgment, descended from one of Tom Scott's luxury coaches to take stock of the Centennial. Of "that wonderful Pennsylvania Railroad," Howells enthused, "I have heard Mr. Scott spoken of as a railroad despot, and I have felt it my duty to hate him. I now make him my apology. Such a man has the right to enslave the public, and I wish that all the conductors and brakemen throughout the land might go and sit at the feet of his employees."

CHAPTER 2

THE BEAT CONVULSIVE

★ ★ ★ ★ ★

Columbia has got her high heeled shoes on, as you may say, and is showin' off, tryin' to see what she can do.

—MARIETTA HOLLEY

To visit the Centennial with William Dean Howells is to simultaneously tour the American mind of the time. Howells's very presence at the great fair was an event of cultural significance. Although little read today, he was deemed a prodigy in his own day. He began literary life as a precocious printer's devil; while still young, he awed the Eastern literary, and he would rule over highbrow taste for a generation from his throne as editor of *The Atlantic Monthly*. Novelist, poet, fluent in several languages, he was a friend to Mark Twain, Nathaniel Hawthorne, Henry David Thoreau, Ralph Waldo Emerson, Oliver Wendell Holmes Sr., and the James brothers, William and Henry. Lofty of expression, the paradigm of sophistication, he was a walking compendium of the received wisdom, prejudices, aspirational ideals, and cultural assumptions of middle-class Americans, for whom he saw himself as a self-conscious surrogate.

Howells was a living bridge between the conservative sensibilities of midcentury America and the tumultuous unpredictability of the new. Although rooted in the post-frontier Midwest—he lived his early years in an Ohio log cabin—he faced forward toward the twentieth century, simultaneously reflecting the self-restraint of a fading conservatism and embracing the onrush of new technology, as well as changing racial mores, women's rights, and the dawn of modern literature. His review of *The Adventures of Tom Sawyer* in the current issue of *The Atlantic Monthly* would make Twain famous. In later life, he would befriend and champion Edith Wharton, Theodore Dreiser, Robert Frost, Sinclair Lewis, and Willa Cather, and he would live on into the era of automobiles, air travel, and silent films, which he worried might one day be exploited for political propaganda.

Although he grew up in a home saturated with radical politics, Howells was less a natural political animal than a humanist who wore the garments of progressive reform. His father, a printer and later a newspaper editor, was a passionately partisan Whig and later Republican, a lifelong friend of future President James A. Garfield, and a supporter of John Brown and the Underground Railroad. In 1860, at the age of twenty-four, Howells authored Abraham Lincoln's official campaign biography, his first book, which won him appointment as wartime American consul in Venice, a sinecure that kept him far from the front lines even though he was of prime military age. Long after the abolitionist impulse dissipated for most Northerners, Howells continued to defend civil rights for Black Americans and even interracial marriage in the unfriendly climate of Jim Crow. Related through his wife to Ohio Governor and putative presidential candidate Rutherford B. Hayes, he would soon play a modest but significant role in the coming presidential contest.

HOWELLS WAS FAR from alone on that dank and drizzly morning in May. Trains were disgorging passengers every few minutes in front of the Centennial's gates. Others came on streetcars from downtown that arrived in an unending stream, with sixty or more packed into cars designed for twenty-four, climbing and clinging inside and out like a human swarm wherever they could find a fingerhold. Others strolled over from one of the new hotels that had been thrown up just outside the gates, amid the tawdry pop-up midway of waffle stands, beer halls, pie stalls, sausage vendors, lemonade hawkers, and sideshow attractions promoting "wild men of Borneo" and Fijian "unadulterated man-eaters." "The most striking feature of this whole Centennial business is the 'get up and git' you see all about everything and everybody," wrote a reporter from Georgia. "Move! Go! You catch it from the peanut and popcorn sellers on the sidewalk. You hear it and feel it in the jostling, wrestling crowd. The only question is, how much of it can you stand?"

Once inside the gates, Howells was confronted by a spectacular ensemble of architectural confections that tested even his capacious appetite for a banquet that mingled the exotic and the mundane in seemingly endless profusion. For him, as for most visitors, the sheer *too-muchness* of it all was an essential part of the experience.

The Main Building, at 1,880 feet long by 464 feet wide, was the largest man-made structure in the world, glisteningly translucent like one of the new steel-and-glass-sheathed railroad stations of Europe; to its right, in Machinery Hall, visitors found the most intriguing inventions; farther on, Renaissance-inspired Memorial Hall showcased the art of the world; Moorish-influenced Horticultural Hall was "as entrancing as a poet's dream"; and the towered Agricultural Hall nodded to the Gothic. Scattered through the park stood seventeen state buildings, nine sponsored by foreign governments, assorted annexes, restaurants, a photographic gallery, a quartz mill, a glass-making pavilion, a model school, a Tunisian bazaar in a Bedouin tent, comfort stations equipped with the novelty of flush toilets, buildings devoted exclusively to the works of women, to leatherware, to the Bible, to luxury coffins—some two hundred buildings in all, interlaced with flowerbeds, ponds, fountains, waterfalls, and ornamental trees.

There were statues everywhere, a pantheon in marble and bronze of the figures that loomed transcendently in the public imagination: Washington and Franklin over and over, Moses perched atop the "Total Abstinence" fountain as if upon the crown of Mount Sinai, grandiose images of "Columbia," of the English historian Thomas

Carlyle, the inventor Elias Howe, a memorial to Presbyterian proselytizer John Witherspoon, an immense, thirty-ton rendering of "the American soldier," and the rather startlingly detached arm of Frédéric Bartholdi's proposed "Statue of Liberty." (Visitors could ascend to the torch for a small charge.)

Although vendors hawked guidebooks long and short, and in almost every language, for a few cents, Howells, like most visitors, preferred to wander from building to building as the spirit moved him. For ladies and the infirm—Walt Whitman among them—wicker chairs on wheels were stationed at each of the principal buildings, renting for the shocking rate of sixty cents per hour, with attendant. Alternatively, a narrow-gauge railway—constructed, of course, by the Pennsylvania Railroad—hooted in a circle around the Exposition grounds, for a fare of five cents. There were Yankees ceaselessly chewing tobacco, dandies from New York, loping Westerners from beyond the Appalachians, promenading women nibbling ice cream and sandwiches, companies of uniformed West Point cadets, contingents of university students, excursions of workers hosted by their factories, 4,000 from a single Baltimore cotton mill, a thousand from upcountry Pennsylvania sponsored by a coal company. A reporter reveled in the "modern Babel" of languages, "from our own familiar and vigorous Anglo-Saxon to the guttural of our barbaric Aboriginese [*sic*], or the singsong jargon of the 'heathen Chinese.'"

"Columbia has got her high heeled shoes on, as you may say, and is showin' off, tryin' to see what she can do," exclaimed the eponymous title character of *Samantha at the Centennial,* a satirical novel by Marietta Holley, the country's first female humorist, who outsold Mark Twain in his lifetime. "Why, a hull Dictionary couldn't begin to tell my feelins as I stood there a lookin' round on each side of me, down that broad majestic, glitterin' street full of folks and fountains and glitterin' stands, and statutes [*sic*], and ornaments, with gorgeous shops on each side containin' the most beautiful beauty, the sublimest sublimity, and the very grandest grandeur the hull world affords." Holley, or at least her avatar "Samantha," was the antithesis of Howells. Where he was bent on setting the standard of respectable taste, the unsophisticated

Samantha responded to whatever and whomever she encountered with hungry curiosity, wide-eyed spontaneity, and bold innocence. Taken together, they were the flip sides of Gilded Age sensibility.

AMERICANS IN 1876 were living in a time of dynamic economic and technological growth that had already wrought dizzying change within a single lifetime. As the economic historian Robert J. Gordon has put it, "A newborn child in 1820 entered a world that was almost medieval: a dim world lit by candlelight, in which folk remedies treated health problems and in which mobility was no faster than that possible by hoof or sail." By the 1870s, railroads, steamships, and the telegraph had already revolutionized travel and communications. Yet 75 percent of the nation's forty million inhabitants still lived on farms or in rural communities, many of them very isolated. Few survived much beyond the age of sixty-five, while infant mortality stood at a cruel rate of 175 per 1,000 births, leavening every family with an almost constant sense of loss and grief. Food was at best boring, heavily weighted toward pork, which could be easily preserved by salting, and often very unsafe, especially in cities, where meat was commonly contaminated—"absolutely poisonous," in the words of a New York inspector—and such fruit as existed was often sold half-rotten. (The recent invention of canning was not yet widespread.) Horses were ubiquitous—an average of 700 per square mile in Boston, for example—and streets were filthy and odorous with prodigious quantities of their manure. Except for the upper classes, clothing was basic, often homemade, and rarely washed. Dwellings lacked electricity, central heating, and indoor toilets; many city-dwellers still relied on chamber pots and open windows. For most Americans, there was virtually no entertainment available except what families provided for themselves, and the occasional traveling circus or tent revival. Probably the most popular form of entertainment of all was the political campaign, with its speechmaking, rallies, marching bands, rabble-rousing, thrilling competition, and suspense.

Relatively few Americans had ever seen a museum or a department store, or even imagined such a teeming multiplicity of things all in one place, from titillating European art to gargantuan engines, such as the Corliss, that dwarfed locomotives. Never had Americans, or most Europeans, experienced such a disorienting collision of demands on their attention. Many visitors uninhibitedly plopped themselves on pieces of priceless furniture, and poked paintings with their canes, and allowed their small children to crawl into the mouths of cannons. The exotic scents, the unending chatter of the crowds, the continuous sound of music from bandstands and organs dazed the brain and numbed the senses. The pulsating hagiography of technology, invention, and capitalism promised to all a future of endless prosperity and progress. Alexander Graham Bell, entering the Exhibition for the first time, was stunned. "It is wonderful!" he wrote to his fiancée, Mabel Hubbard. "You can have no idea of it until you see it. It is so prodigious and wonderful that it absolutely staggers one."

The confusing variety of the Centennial overwhelmed even the skeptical French journalist Louis Simonin, who reported to his readers, "Do you love disorder? You will find it everywhere." There were astonishing displays cheek by jowl: domed and pinnacled vitrines, like miniature palaces, stuffed with dizzying geometric displays of toys, ivory-work, false teeth, corsets, bolts and screws, wax, hats, silks, pottery, gas fixtures, iron weights, bank ledgers, corsets, suspenders, colored sewing thread, stoves, tinware, drills, saws, silks and woolens in every imaginable color, grains, preserved fruits, oysters and lobsters; there were buttons fashioned into monuments as intricate as rococo shrines, Gatling guns, fleets of plows and carriages, fire engines with boiler drums that looked like giant milk bottles. An entire annex was devoted to nothing but hydraulic machinery: whole forests of vertical pumps—500 of them manufactured by a single Connecticut company—rams, nozzles, blowers, and devices from dainty water buckets on wheels to be used by ladies for watering their flowers, to monsters that spewed water 200 feet at a rate of 30,000 gallons per minute.

The foreign pavilions drew Howells's particular scrutiny. The Swedes erected huge columns and pyramids of iron and steel bars and pipes towering nearly to the lofty roof of their building, festooned in a sort of industrial fantasy with tires, bars, ingots, cases of nails, railway axles, and a reindeer made of spikes. The French emphasized embroideries and lace, bibelots for the boudoir tables, ornate clocks, musical instruments, Aubusson carpets, Gobelin tapestries, stained glass that would later grace St. Patrick's Cathedral, and, a bit oddly, an entire annex devoted solely to brick. Brazil's glittering "Moorish palace" shimmered with strange birds and insects, gold, and diamonds. Mexico, barely emerged from ruinous civil war, displayed a 4,059-pound lump of silver, the largest ever found, and stupendous blocks of onyx and colored marble. In the popular Turkish café, patrons were served coffee in tiny cups and could try smoking a *narguile.*

Howells did not admit of befuddlement, much less of unhealthy reactions, as some apparently did at a Tunisian boîte, where an Algerian girl performed "voluptuous dances, to the great disgust of certain devout persons, who finally caused the closing of this place of perdition," caustically noted the worldly Frenchman Louis Simonin. Howells extolled displays of hams from Cincinnati cocooned in crimson and gold silk, pyramids erected by Louisville tobacco dealers who artistically arranged their wares by the colors of their leaves, six-foot-high glass cylinders filled with examples of Iowa's varied soils, Indian cotton "with its satisfying Hindoo names," a "bacchanal show" of Rhenish wines, the whimsy of an Oswego starch manufacturer who turned corn and its stalks into an artful display, "airily-pretty" silverwork from Norway, a New York firm promoting three hundred varieties of potatoes, entire avenues that sported mowing and reaping machines resplendent in varnished woods and burnished steel, parked on imported carpets and attended by agents "each more zealous than another in the faith that his machine was the last triumph of invention." Among the state buildings, his favorite was Mississippi's, constructed with seventy kinds of native wood and gables decked with streamers of Spanish moss, where a "typical Mississippian," "young in years but venerable in alligator-like calm," sat on the porch with his boots on the railing and his hat pulled down over his eyes, "sheltering his slowly moving jaws as they ruminate the Virginian weed."

Howells took pride in his biases. He complained about an ill-proportioned sculpture of Washington perched atop an eagle. He found "the gross and boastful vanity, the exultant snobbishness" of the German paintings intolerable, particularly a portrait of the kaiser and Chancellor Otto von Bismarck "swollen with prodigious majesty and self-satisfaction," epitomizing "the singularly offensive despotism from which it comes." On the other hand, Horticultural Hall charmed him with its "light arabesque forms," but, he carped, one "soon wearies of palms and cactuses and unattainable bananas." He found the Italian exhibits "a rather poverty-stricken effort of bric-a-brackishness," and thought the French too much characterized by "shoppiness." In Machinery Hall, there were too many sewing machines. "A whole half-mile of sewing machines seems a good deal; and is there so very much difference between them?" He was disappointed that he saw so few "exotics": a single Turk "in most consoling bagginess of trousers, crimson jacket, and white stocking"; and a "still, sphinx-eyed young Egyptian" who "scorning our recentness from a remote antiquity wore a fez. But a fez is very little." He spied one "Jap" in his national costume: "a small, lady-handed [male] carpenter, who wrought with tools of eccentric uses upon one of the showcases, and now and then darted a disgusted look through his narrow eye-slits at the observer."

Many other visitors were enchanted by the elegance of the Japanese pavilion and its formal garden, where they might have noticed a small ornamental plant with tiny purple flowers that would one day devour entire swathes of America: kudzu. But they were perplexed by the Japanese themselves, "with their shambling gait, their eyes set awry in their head, and their grave and gentle ways," one tourist exclaimed. "How can it be in them to make such wonderful things?" *The New York Times* solemnly pronounced the Japanese to be similar to southern Europeans. "Both are essentially people who live for the present; both prefer the bright side of the mirror of life to the duller but truer; both are epicurean in their tastes, habits and customs; to both is luxury delightful, and exertion detestable, without being slothful, as the Italians."

Feelings were icier toward the Chinese, who were known to Americans mostly through highly racist reports on white workers' often bloody persecution of them on the West Coast. In their pavilion, the first Chinese one ever at an international exhibition, visitors saw an entire procession of mandarins carved from ivory, a seven- or eight-story tiered pagoda festooned with bells, hand-carved mahogany furniture, an abundance of Chinese maritime products—dried squid, sharks' fins, desiccated shrimp and sea slugs—along with perplexing pharmaceuticals that included dried snakes and tiny, mystifying pills adorned with minute Chinese ideographs. Bigotry was nothing to be embarrassed about: Of the Chinese, asserted *The Philadelphia Inquirer,* "their very presence spreads a moral and physical leprosy, contaminating everything it touches, and corrupting the very air with the poison of a loathsome disease?" Whenever they dared to appear in their national dress, Chinese visitors and staff were dogged by crowds of idle boys and men, who hooted and yelled at them as if they were alien creatures. Howells, uncharacteristically short of opinions, merely remarked on the "bedeviled arts of theirs, [which] affected one like the things of a capricious dream." Alexander Graham Bell was more generous, telling his fiancée, Mabel, "I am surprised to see what a splendid show the Chinese are making. How presumptuous of us to think ourselves so far superior to them."

Howells experienced the Centennial primarily as a great spectacle of American nationalism, proof in steel, marble, and glass that the United States had come proudly of age. In the several large American exhibits, he admired new modes of illumination for lighthouses, models of arsenals, collections of the continent's fur-producing animals and its whale fishery, a stunning array of 408 painted plaster models of American fish, and the Meteorological Bureau's sophisticated instruments, a profusion of maps, models, and statistics so vast and refined that they astonished even the cynical Simonin. Howells was not entirely without wit. "The bribes almost sprang from one's pocket at the sight of the neat perfection with which the Revenue Department was represented," he remarked, and of the army's extensive displays, he dryly admired "the varied ingenuity and beautiful murderousness of the weapons of all kinds, the torpedoes with which alone one could pass hours of satisfaction, fancifully attaching them to the ships of enemies."

Americans in 1876 were more universally and publicly patriotic than they would be in the twenty-first century. History, at least as white Americans recounted it, was something to be loudly extolled and saturated with sentiment. There was no space in official memory for the savagery of a revolution that had torn apart towns and families in what historians today often regard not as a triumph of unity but as America's *first* civil war, in some ways even more divisive than the one just ended. Yet, even as dark truths about the Revolutionary War were overlaid with simplifying myth, the nation's birth for many still possessed a remarkable sense of immediacy. Countless visitors to the Centennial could still recall members of the founding generation as living men and women: John Quincy Adams had died only in 1848, James Madison in 1836 and his widow, Dolley, in 1849, and Thomas Jefferson and John Adams in 1826, while a few veterans of the Revolutionary War had lived even into the 1870s. Northerners, moreover, had just fought a war for the Union that took more than 400,000 Yankee lives in order to preserve the government that the Founders had wrought. The maimed and shell-shocked remained a common sight in every American town, a constant reminder of the price paid for saving the republic. (Possibly another 350,000 died for the Confederacy.) Marietta Holley, in the voice of her fictional Samantha, eschewing satire, expressed the thrill with which Americans commonly responded to "The Star-Spangled Banner":

> Hearin' that soul stirrin' music, and seein' that very banner a wavin' and floatin' out, as if all the blue sky and rainbows sense Noah's rainbow was cut up into its glorious stripes, with the hull stars of heaven a shinin' on 'em,—why, as my faculties come back to me, a seein' what I see—and hearin' what I heerd, I thought of my 4 fathers, them 4 old fathers, whose weak hands had first unfurled that banner to the angry breeze, and thinks'es I, I would be willin' to change places with them 4 old men right here on the spot, to let 'em see the bright sunshine of 1876, what they done in the cloudy darkness of 1776.

Allusions to the nation's history were ubiquitous at the Centennial. Massachusetts presented a log home meant to replicate life in the Plymouth Colony, furnished with relics of Puritan days—John Alden's writing desk, a spinning wheel, an ancient Bible, pewter spoons—tended by ladies clothed in the style of their forebears. In the U.S. government's building, visitors saw portraits of remarkable men, the uniforms of soldiers and marines since 1776, and, most memorably, a collection of George Washington's relics, which were treated with religious awe: his coat, vest, and buckskin breeches, his camp bed, table furniture, sword, and pistols. Manifestations of Washington, in particular, served as visual shorthand for the nation's hopes and ideals. He was everywhere, in portraits, statuary large and small, and most impressively suspended, along with Benjamin Franklin, an iconic figure of an "Indian maiden," and images of corn and buffalo, over one of the entrances to the Main Building, in a forty-foot-high construction of painted wood and papier-mâché. (Similar constructions over the other entrances represented Europe with Charlemagne and Shakespeare, Asia with Confucius and Mohammed, and Africa with an Egyptian pharaoh and—tellingly—a slave girl.) There was even a peculiar nine-foot-high working model of Washington's tomb, from which the great man seemingly rose from the dead to be saluted by mechanical soldiers standing guard.

AS EMOTIVE AS appeals to history were, they were often overshadowed by the extravagant displays of the new. To see the emerging future was to become part of it. In a sense, that was the point of the Exposition—to demonstrate that the surging tide of American greatness resided in the thousands of dazzling vitrines, the opulence of consumer goods, and the countless pulsating engines that embodied the industrial behemoth the country was fast becoming.

The greatest invention of the nation's first century was America itself, the astonishing machinery of the federal government, the first republican organism in modern history, the fruition of the Enlightenment in departments, bureaus, agencies, committees, legislatures, the intricate web of obligations and laws of citizenship, the legal restraints of the leviathan of power, the "crazy machine," as Patrick Henry had called it. The machine of government was now complete, so most Americans believed, but for minor tinkering. The franchise had now been extended to former slaves; there was increasing talk, this election year, of reforming the civil service to eliminate corruption. What more was there to do but to organize more states to fill out the continent and plug them into the perfected system?

The American lust for invention remained, but its energies and talents had now turned to literal machinery. The federal Patent Office, an astonished reporter found, was issuing about a hundred patents a day "to a nation, each inhabitant of which appears to be an inventor." Indeed, it was in this aspect of the Centennial, perhaps more than any other, that Americans saw what they considered the real inspiration of their civilization. Wrote Howells, "on every side the thousand creations of American inventive genius were in operation, with an exhilaration and impressiveness in the whole effect which can in no wise be described." In the realm of industry, the contributions of all other nations seemed to him insignificant compared to the American. "The superior elegance, aptness, and ingenuity of our machinery is observable at a glance. Yes, it is still in these things of iron and steel that the national genius most freely speaks."

Icons of Tom Scott's Pennsylvania Railroad's far-flung empire loomed large among the industrial exhibits. Visitors marveled at working models of a grain elevator, a steamship, bridges, and an oil well replete with pipelines, and technical advances such as newly invented air brakes and refrigeration processes, all representing the railroad's diverse enterprises. And they saw bold proof of the stunning advances in railroading that had taken place in a bare generation, comparing the oldest steam engine of all—the dinky *John Bull,* built in 1831, which first chugged along a one-mile track in New Jersey—to the immense new locomotives on display, several of them just purchased by Emperor Dom Pedro for shipment to Brazil. Just months earlier, Whitman had penned "To a Locomotive in Winter," a rapturous ode that must have cheered Tom Scott's heart, if he ever read it:

Thee in thy panoply, thy measur'd dual throbbing and
thy beat convulsive,

The black cylindric body, golden brass, and silvery steel,
Thy ponderous side-bars, parallel and connecting rods,
gyrating, shuttling at thy sides,
Thy metrical, now swelling pant and roar, now tapering
in the distance,
Thy great protruding headlight fix'd in front,
The dense and murky clouds out-belching from thy
smoke-stack . . .
Type of the modern—emblem of motion and power—
pulse of the continent.

Many of the machines on display, locomotives included, were essentially refinements of existing ones. Others were utterly new. Samantha, awestruck like so many, gaped at "jewelers a jewelin', rubber shoemakers a rubbin', weavers a weavin', bobbins a bobbin', rock-crushers a crushin', lacers a lacin', silk worms a silkin', paper-makers a paperin', elevators a elevatin', pumpers a pumpin.'" Howells, the father of two small children, saw particular genius in an "automaton baby-tender that attached the cradle to the parental bed," enabling drowsy parents to start the cradle rocking and to put even "the most refractory baby" to sleep without having to get up or "lose your temper."

The ponderously named George Grant Difference Engine—a distant ancestor to the computer—performed up to twenty complex calculations per minute, powered by hand-cut gears driven by an external motor. (Insurance companies used it to calculate actuarial tables.) A portable bathtub made of rubberized cloth doubled as a suitcase when it was folded up—useful indeed in an era when many hotels did not provide private baths. There were several progenitors of the typewriter, including a "Typographic Machine" exhibited by a doctor from West Troy, New York, whose revolving disk carrying type-arms printed a letter each time a key was pressed; and the "Sholes & Glidden Typing Machine," which typed only capital letters and introduced the QWERTY keyboard still in use today. A "printing telegraph," with a piano-like keyboard, enabled a typist to print letters on a strip of paper. The Western Electric Manufacturing Co. exhibited a self-correcting "automatic printer" that printed out its messages in letters whether any operator was present or not. Another Western Electric device—a "mercurial bulb"—set off a startling noise when the atmosphere around it overheated: in short, a fire alarm, coupled with an "electric annunciator" to indicate where the fire was. Another exhibitor presented a battery-driven "Electro-Magnetic Mallet" for use by dentists to fill teeth, delivering "from 500 to 3,000 blows a minute, and as easily controlled as the telegraph." Its manufacturer declared promisingly that it could also be converted to an "autographic pen," and that "the sculptor too can make it serviceable."

The industrial star of the Centennial, however, was the great Corliss Engine, which visitors typically perceived as a manifestation of the muscular dynamism of America itself: stupendous and hard driving, a perfect metaphor in forged steel for the mighty future of the entire nation. America, inspired visitors might well imagine, would one day become the great machine that drove the world. This behemoth was technically known as a "walking-beam" engine, meaning that the motion of vertical pistons was converted into circular motion by an oscillating crossbeam, connecting rod, and crank arm; remarkably, it operated with no vibration and was calibrated, it was said, as precisely as the mechanism of a clock. It weighed 1,320,000 pounds and had required sixty railcars to transport its parts to Philadelphia from Providence, Rhode Island, where it was built by the self-taught engineer George Corliss, whose foundry had built the turret for the first ironclad warship, the *Monitor,* which during the Civil War had altered the course of naval history. With its majestic pulse, the Corliss Engine powered a universe of machines that made cigars, hand soap, and chocolate, manufactured paper, powered whirring brigades of sewing machines and printing presses that every morning vomited out *The New York Herald* and *New York Times* at a rate of eight copies per second, printed wallpaper, smelted ores from the Sierra Nevada to produce refined silver ingots, rifled gun barrels, wove silk, drove piles, milled sugarcane, made glue, baled cotton, pared peaches, ground needles, blew glass busts of the Founding Fathers, and turned rough stones into gleaming garnets, rubies, and sapphires.

* * *

NEVER BEFORE HAD so many innovations been brought together in one place. However, early visitors to the Centennial could not see what would be the Exhibition's single most transformative invention of all, which in less than a lifetime would revolutionize daily life, the course of business, the speed of public communication, and personal relationships. Of all the inventors whose work debuted there, none better embodied the conjunction of imagination, entrepreneurship, big business, and social impact than Alexander Graham Bell. Like Tom Scott of the Pennsylvania Railroad, Bell was both a product and driver of the industrial age, who turned machinery into dynamic commercial empire. Born in Scotland, in 1847, Bell—slender, handsome, self-effacing—spoke with a British accent that softened his native burr, befitting the scion of a family of former actors devoted to the spoken word. His father, Alexander Melville Bell, well known in his own right as an "elocutionist"—essentially a speech pathologist—was already famous for inventing a system of visual symbols, known as "Visible Speech," to show deaf students how to activate their vocal organs to shape sounds. The "Bell Method," as it was also called, was already in wide use in Britain when the Bells moved to Ontario in 1870, hoping to introduce it in North America.

Alexander Graham seemed destined from an early age to follow in his father's footsteps. Endowed with a sensitive ear for pitch and tone, he proved a brilliant and popular teacher. As his reputation spread, he was invited to teach at the Boston School for the Deaf, then to lecture at MIT and, in 1873, to accept appointment as professor of "Vocal Physiology and Elocution" at the new School of Oratory at Boston University, a remarkable accolade for a twenty-six-year-old with no university education. Adults and children alike found him warm and empathetic; however, his poise concealed a deeply passionate nature and an intellect supercharged with ideas that seemed to erupt uncontrollably from his brain.

The impulse to invent came naturally to Bell, as it did, it seemed, to countless young men who percolated with ambitious ideas for new mechanical gadgets, electrical devices, and chemical processes. He had long evinced a profound curiosity about the mechanics of language. When he was a teenager, he and a brother built a "speaking machine" of sorts, using rubber, wood, tin, and wire to replicate the human vocal organs, which emitted the sound of a crying baby when air was blown through a tube into its mouth. He later taught the family dog to "talk" by gently manipulating its throat until it could articulate a series of sounds that in combination sounded like "grandma." Alone in his family, he taught himself to communicate with his deaf mother by speaking close to her forehead so she could hear the vibrations of his voice.

Bell, although not a natural businessman, understood that his invention would remain stillborn without investment capital. He was canny enough to accept the financial support of Gardiner Greene Hubbard, a wealthy Boston patent attorney and investor whom he came to know as the father of one of his pupils, and his future wife, Mabel Hubbard. Bell's main goal in the early 1870s was the development of a "multiple telegraph" that could transmit several messages at once over a single wire, thereby sharply reducing the cost per message. Telegraphy, dominated by Western Union, was a national business, and the market potential for innovations that improved service was immense. Bell saw his work in electronics as more than a mere hobby, but it was primarily a means to raise funds for the promotion of Visual Speech. He wrote hopefully to his father in October 1874, "Should I be able to make any money out of the idea—we shall have Visible Speech put before the world in a more permanent form."

Bell was not alone in his ambitions. In Germany, Dr. Philipp Reis had invented a device that could carry sounds over telegraph wires but could not actually produce different degrees of loudness or transmit different frequencies. Thomas Edison claimed to be at work on a "speaking telegraph" that sounded worrisomely like a telephone. But Bell's most potent rival was an Ohio electrician named Elisha Gray, who had already patented a number of improvements in telegraphy and had now managed to transmit simple chords, but not speech or multiple messages. "It is a neck and neck race between Mr. Gray and myself who shall complete our apparatus first," Bell wrote to his father. "He has the advantage over me in being a practical electrician—but I have reason to believe that I am better acquainted with the phenomenon of sound than he is." Bell also suspected, rightly, that Western Union with all its wealth was in league with Edison to co-opt both his own and Gray's research. Timing was critical. If one of the rivals preceded him, even by a few months, the difficulty of raising capital would probably force him to sell off his invention to others for a relative pittance.

In November, Bell cautiously informed his father of an idea "that I have scarce dared to breathe to anybody for fear of being thought insane . . . an instrument by which the human voice might be telegraphed" by using the principle of electromagnetism. He conceived inducing a current of electricity by placing a magnet with one of its poles near the pole of an electromagnet and generating an oscillating current in the electromagnet's coils. "I feel as if I were in a dream," he added a few days later. "The iron core of the electromagnet of the receiving instrument emits the sound *without any armature at all*!!" Bell knew, as experimenters had since the eighteenth century, that electric current generates a magnetic field about itself, and that the stronger the current, the stronger the field it produces, and that if a current was made to vary in strength and at sufficient speed it would be possible to convey any kind of sound, including the human voice. Put simply, he was in the process of making the first telephone. (The term itself was not new: Since the eighteenth century it had referred to a speaking tube for the hard of hearing.)

Bell devoted every available moment of his time to electricity and experiments, straining to keep up his teaching, which he still thought of as his true vocation. He worked intensely, usually at night, accompanied by a young machinist named Thomas Watson, in a laboratory set up at a boardinghouse a few blocks from Boston Common. He was tortured by insomnia and by the early months of 1876 he felt close to nervous breakdown. "I am disheartened and almost in despair at my inability to *think* properly," he wrote to Mabel Hubbard in January. "I feel as if there is something wrong about [my] mental machinery—my whole *method* of thought seems to be disarranged." It only got worse. By the beginning of April, he had tried every expedient he could think of to sleep. "But no—it won't come," he confided to Mabel. "I close my eyes, but I can see with them shut! I try to stop thinking but it's of no use—I cannot get the reins of my mind! There is a picture before my eyes—a moving picture—a little lead-pencil vibrating in mercury! From which you will understand that I am suffering tonight from a severe attack of telegraph on the brain!"

Thanks to the efforts of Mabel's father, who also happened to be one of the three Massachusetts commissioners to the Centennial, on March 7, two days after Bell's twenty-ninth birthday, the U.S. Patent Office in Washington formally approved the first patent ever issued for a telephone. Mabel, who was deeply devoted to his cause, expressed amazement that he had triumphed over the power of Western Union, which, she wrote, had been "willing to spare no expense, honest or dishonest, to conquer you. Just now too when [Secretary of War] Belknap's iniquity, coming after all those other stories and scandals, makes us feel as if there were no justice in such a sink of corruption as Washington."

Bell was experimenting intensely with undulatory currents, using a [copper] reed as a "receiver" and a tuning fork as a "transmitter," while causing the fork to vibrate near successive electromagnets of different resistances. When he immersed the fork at an angle in the water and made it vibrate, he heard a faint but indistinct sound. When he added acid to the water, the sound became louder, and still louder yet when he inserted a ribbon of brass in the water. He then tried placing a horizontal diaphragm over the water with a needle suspended from it, and after that a box with the diaphragm serving as its floor. When Watson talked through a hole in the top of the box, they heard something that seemed like mumbling. On March 10, Bell extended a brass pipe into the water with a platinum needle dipping into it from the diaphragm. And in place of the box, Bell substituted the mouthpiece of a speaking tube. He sent Watson to a room down the hall, out of earshot.

Bell described what happened next, in an excited letter to his father: "I called into the Transmitting Instrument, 'Mr. Watson—come here—I want to see you'—and he came!" Watson had heard each word with perfect clarity come from the electromagnet at his end. The two men then exchanged places. “Mr. Watson sang an air. Every note was audible. He then read from a book and the voice came from the electro-magnet in a curious half-muffled way. The last sentence, however, I heard very plainly and distinctly. It was ‘Mr. Bell, do you understand what I say?’” With an undisguised sense of the gravity of the moment, he added, “This is a great day for me. I feel that I have at last struck the solution of a great problem—and the day is coming when telegraph wires will be laid on to houses just like water or gas—and friends will converse with each other without leaving home.”

CHAPTER 3

WILDFIRE

⋆ ⋆ ⋆ ⋆ ⋆

What she undertakes to do she will do, though she has to cut through the heart of a mountain with a pen knife.

—LYDIA MARIA CHILD

William Dean Howells naturally deemed himself an arbiter of serious art in all its forms. Acres of the Centennial were allocated to creative work, in monumental, Renaissance-inspired Memorial Hall and its overflow annex, and in canvas- and sculpture-stuffed galleries in most of the national buildings. Nationalist though Howells was, he nonetheless scorned many of the American entries as "loud and bad." Among these were fashionable literary and classical themes: Ophelia with her dress filled with flowers, *Circe and the Companions of Ulysses,* the death of Caesar, Adam and Eve lamenting over the dead Abel, *The Christian Martyrs Under Nero.* (Compared to the European galleries, nudes were uncommon. Of one American group of statuettes, Marietta Holley's "Samantha" dryly commented, "They all had clothes on, which was a surprise to me, and indeed a treat.") Statues of children were especially popular: children laughing, crying, sulking, feeding birds, playing hide-and-seek, getting ready for bed, saying prayers, emerging from seashells, making faces at a teacher. There was a study of a young girl shrinking from exposing herself in the studio of an artist, a painting of boys digging for a rat, an embarrassed girl with two perplexed suitors. There were figures from American folklore and history: Rip Van Winkle, General George G. Meade, the Battle of Gettysburg, a Minuteman, a Black family resting after the day's labors, a spirited "Yankee Doodle" that was deemed "peculiarly attractive" to everyone, according to a commemorative guide.

Remarkably, Howells missed the most remarkable, and most controversial, American work of all: *The Death of Cleopatra,* by the flamboyant expatriate sculptor Edmonia Lewis. Raved one viewer, the work "excites more admiration and gathers larger crowds than any other work of art in the vast collection of Memorial Hall." As inspiring as the sculpture—and to some much more disturbing—was Lewis herself. In the minds of countless white Americans—and for that matter, many Black Americans too—she ought not even to exist. She was the only "colored" American female sculptor in the United States, and at the age of just thirty-one she was also an astonishing international success.

AFRICAN AMERICANS were nearly invisible at the Centennial. One Black tourist, visiting from Georgia, reported to his chagrin that he "could not discover among all that mass of people one single Negro in the discharge of any duty save as restaurant waiters and barbers in the hotels." It was a sadly ironic comment on such a celebration of the nation's founding values in the city that had spawned the abolitionist movement. In fact, by the 1870s Philadelphia was as infested with as much tacit and overt racism as any Northern city. On election days, whites sometimes rioted against Black voters, driving them away from the polls while the police passively looked on, and in 1871, when the city's most prominent Black leader, Octavius Catto, was murdered in broad daylight, no one was prosecuted. In 1874, a middle-class Black couple was robbed and evicted bodily from a fund-raiser for the Centennial for which they had bought tickets. It would take them six years of litigation to recover their money.

Early hopes for a prominent Black role in the Centennial went unfulfilled. "We have been hypocrites and liars with respect to our real history long enough," wrote the Black Philadelphian Robert Purvis in 1873, calling futilely for the inclusion of Black history in the celebrations, particularly the role of Black soldiers in the Revolutionary War. (The role of African Americans in that conflict was tangled. Approximately 5,000 may have joined the patriot army, gambling that the liberty and equality the Revolution promised might apply to them too, and fighting bravely from the Battle of Bunker Hill to the British surrender at Yorktown. Among such men, however, some were actually *lent* to the army by their enslavers, and expected to return home to continued slavery after the war. But probably three times as many fled their bondage to seek freedom with the British and fight against their former "masters.")

Despite Philadelphia's high Black unemployment, very few were hired to work on the construction of the Centennial's grounds and buildings, and none in positions of responsibility. The *Chicago Inter-Ocean* reported that when a Centennial commissioner from Iowa proposed that Black security officers be recruited for the Exposition's police force "nearly every one of the Southern members was on his feet, [and] canes and umbrellas were flourished," rejecting a direct appeal from Frederick Douglass. "This is to be a great Centennial year of jubilee but according to the Confederate notion," the paper scornfully declared. "The black men are to be left to peek through the knot-holes." Black women tried to collaborate in the Women's Pavilion, but were rudely shunted aside. The Republic of Liberia, founded by former slaves, sponsored a modest display, but Black Americans were rare among the exhibitors.

One of the few whites who protested was Colonel John W. Forney, the editor of Philadelphia's leading newspaper, a staunch abolitionist, and one of the Centennial's most active promoters. In a flaming editorial in *The Philadelphia Press,* he accused the "great show" of the American people's industry, achievement, and independence of scandalously omitting the role played by its Black citizens. "Although the chains of slavery have been broken from the limbs of an entire race in the blaze and fire of our advancement, and the negro stands before the law a freeman, covered with the habiliments of citizenship, yet, the prejudice against him, the results of his previous condition, have prevented him from taking any part in this marvelous undertaking in celebration of one hundred years of American independence, save that of a menial, the water-drawers and hat-takers to the assembled races to be found there."

Black visitors were encouraged and sometimes apparently required—accounts differ—to attend the Centennial only on segregated visiting days. Mention of African Americans in official materials was fleeting and ambivalent: Joaquin Miller's "Song of the Centennial" dispensed with race in two patronizing lines: "A new and black brother, half troubadour / a stray piece of midnight comes grinning on deck." Uglier yet, a popular satirical account of the Centennial included a "humorous" cartoon of the "Boo Choo," a fictional "African" delegation, on parade: loose-limbed, fat-lipped Black men in grass skirts, beating drums and waving spears, with skewers stuck in their mountainous hair. Serious works of art with Black themes were often mocked. Of a statue titled *L'Africaine,* sculpted by an Italian, an American critic scoffed, "Africa—stagnant, blind and neglected among the countries of the earth! Whose vast desert is but the outward symbol of the desolation beyond . . . where man is alike uncultured and unconscious; sunk, alas! in that most melancholy degradation." Even the liberal-minded Howells denounced a bronze statue titled *Emancipation,* which depicted "a most offensively Frenchy negro, who has broken his chain, and spreading both his arms and his legs abroad is rioting in a declamation of something; one longs to clap him back into hopeless bondage."

AMID THE WIDESPREAD RACISM of the 1870s, Edmonia Lewis was an avatar of a new and promising future that growing numbers of African Americans shared. Like countless aspiring Americans both white and Black, she believed that her talent and determination would enable her to cut her own way through Gilded Age America, break boundaries, defy expectations, and prevail. It was a heady time even for the less privileged. A racial revolution was underway, offering immense promise and hope and possibility. Slavery had been destroyed. Racial discrimination was being challenged in Congress, in hotels and restaurants, on trains and steamboats. Black Americans were flocking to schools and gaining literacy; Black churches were springing up everywhere; Black men were joining the Republican Party and voting in prodigious numbers. Thousands held public office in the Southern states, including the U.S. Senate and House.

Revolution bred reaction, however. As former slaves and their allies in the South claimed political rights and public respect, ex-rebels turned to savage violence. From modest origins in Tennessee, the Ku Klux Klan rapidly spread across the former Confederacy, and by the early 1870s had murdered at least two thousand people, the vast majority of them Black, and many with unspeakable cruelty. Organized massacres of freed people were carried out in New Orleans, Memphis, and elsewhere. Black schools and churches were burned, teachers terrorized, and Black voters driven away from the polls. By 1873, President Grant had suppressed the worst of the violence and launched the prosecutions of thousands of Klansmen. But the Republican Party, and the political power of the former slaves, had been severely damaged by the years of intimidation. Insurgent reactionaries—"Redeemers," in their own parlance—were organizing to recapture power in the former Confederate states, and by 1876 had already succeeded in all but three. Attitudes that had once seemed vanquished by the Civil War were once again percolating into public life. Some Southerners were even talking once again about slavery as a "divine institution."

Ominously, Northern public opinion was also shifting. Growing numbers of Northerners were losing patience with the South's problems and, in truth, with "the Negro." Most white Northerners' concern for racial justice had ended with the demise of slavery and the passage of the Thirteenth, Fourteenth, and Fifteenth Amendments, which on paper converted former slaves into full-fledged citizens. Northerners were coming to feel that Black Southerners ought to be able to take care of themselves, without any special federal protections or guarantees. Senator Carl Schurz, once among the most clear-eyed of Radicals, now advocated restoring the franchise to former Confederates and opposed federal protection for civil rights. Walt Whitman, too, mirrored the slackening of support for Black

Americans. Once he had welcomed the democratic mingling of the races, and during the war had admired the sight of Black recruits marching through Washington on their way to the battlefront. Now he disparaged Black appeals for suffrage and equality as mere sentimentality. If "Negroes" were to survive at all, he believed, they must develop the "mental and moral qualities" of the "leading and dominant race." In a letter to his mother, he described with unadulterated racism a Black political demonstration as "comical, yet very disgusting & alarming in some respects—they were very insolent, & altogether it was a strange sight—they looked like so many wild brutes let loose." Even the *New York Tribune,* once among the most outspoken Republican newspapers in the country, now advocated a white supremacist line and told its wide national readership that outrages against Southern Black voters were mere "myths."

In a last radical gasp before its new Democratic majority took over, Congress had passed a broad civil rights act banning discrimination in jury selection, public accommodations, theaters, restaurants, transportation, and schools. In truth, it was less a triumph than an epitaph for the cause of civil rights since it was almost universally disregarded and hard to enforce, where there was a will to enforce it at all. Just three weeks after its enactment, a federal judge in Memphis contemptuously scoffed that the new law embodied an "almost grotesque exercise of national authority," and ruled it unconstitutional. (In 1883, the Supreme Court would agree and declare it void.) The Court, despite its nominal Republican majority, was already a nursery of revived states' rights jurisprudence that undermined the safety of Black Americans. The Fourteenth Amendment had been crafted specifically to protect the constitutional rights of freed people. But by 1876 it was being treated as a "Magna Charta of accumulated wealth and organized capital," in the words of one historian. In a series of decisions, the Court had reinterpreted the amendment to protect businesses from state interference while crippling the federal government's ability to overrule state laws in civil rights cases. In a recent ruling, the Court declared that the Bill of Rights was not enforceable within the states as long as state courts were functioning, meaning that victims deprived of the most basic constitutional rights had no alternative but to seek redress in state courts, which rarely even pretended to punish crimes against African Americans. The mass of Northern public opinion didn't seem to care. Pontificated *The Nation,* the Court deserved praise for "recovering from the war fever" and "abandon[ing] sentimental canons of constitutional interpretation."

The Republican Party was no longer an engine of reform. The plutocrats who now steered it saw the South more as a lucrative field for investment than as a battleground of racial politics. The Pennsylvania Railroad's Tom Scott was but one of many investors who were happy to make pragmatic peace with Southern white supremacists. Scott had once been an abolitionist. Now, of course, his primary interest was increasing the railroad's power. For years, he had been acquiring Southern routes, sometimes openly and sometimes through shell companies, ultimately bundling them together under the financial aegis of a holding company named the Southern Railway Security Company. Scott remained a Republican, but he was quite willing to work with pliable "Redeemer" Democrats, using company funds to bribe local politicians and to exploit the Pennsylvania Railroad's influence on Capitol Hill to moderate the federal government's efforts to enforce civil rights. The battle for influence was ruthless; Scott bought up control of many of the South's leading newspapers, and was even accused of ruining innocent Southern girls by prostituting them for politicians. Nor was he beyond fanning racial resentment in order to win federal support for his financially unstable Texas & Pacific Railway as a matter of "justice" for the South. For Scott, the outcome was nearing a crisis. More broadly, however, his political gyrations vividly illustrated the party's accelerating transformation as the pursuit of corporate profit and personal power ate away at the reputation for high-minded rectitude that had once defined it.

As its nominating convention approached, the Republican Party was in grave and perhaps fatal disarray. Even as it endured unrelenting attack as the party of alleged "tyranny" from the resurgent Democrats, elites within its own ranks—Liberal Republicans, as they called themselves—damned the Grant administration as incompetent and corrupt. Many Americans of all political stripes blamed the government for the lingering economic effects of the financial panic of 1873, which shuttered thousands of businesses and threw hundreds of thousands out of work. The voters had already shown their anger in 1874, when the Democrats captured the House of Representatives, ending the Republicans' monopoly of power. Control of the House put the Democrats in charge of the Ways and Means Committee, which originated federal spending bills, and they had already made it clear that they would no longer provide new funds to maintain more than the barest minimum of federal troops in the South or enough prosecutors to complete the Justice Department's cases against the Ku Klux Klan. Everyone knew that the presidential campaign would be a referendum on Reconstruction. With Grant set to retire and no obvious and untainted champion to carry the party forward, Republican leaders feared a debacle.

NONE OF THIS directly touched Edmonia Lewis, who was preoccupied with her hopes for the Centennial. She had been thinking about the fair for years, telling an interviewer as early as 1872, "I intend to make a beautiful statue, as beautiful as I can, and send it to the Philadelphia Exposition anonymously. I do this in order that it may be judged fairly and without favor or prejudice." In March 1875, the Centennial's roving commissioner John Forney, a well-connected Republican, turned up at Lewis's studio in Rome, prospecting for American artists to submit their works for exhibit. In an editorial in *The Philadelphia Press,* he offered her as an urgent symbol for the nation, declaring that her presence would show that the gains of Reconstruction had not been defeated. She didn't need to be asked twice. She was already engaged on what she knew was her masterwork, something that she hoped would stun critics and the public alike.

In the nineteenth century, the death of Cleopatra was a popular subject that enthralled viewers with its titillating mixture of the erotic and the transcendental. Lewis's project was fraught with risk. She envisioned something more expressive than she had previously attempted and that, if she succeeded, could place her in the first rank of American sculptors. It would require a piece of marble larger than any she had worked before, and demand an outlay of at least several thousand dollars, not to mention the cost of shipping it more than 4,000 miles to Philadelphia. Several of her friends were also submitting works for the Centennial and the competitive pressure she felt was intense.

LEWIS'S *carte de visite* shows a woman with large, warm, pensive eyes seated in an elegant fringed chair, wearing a shimmering wrap half draped over her shoulders, a silk necktie, and an exotic sort of cap pitched rakishly over her striking wavy hair. Superficially, Lewis could hardly have been more different from the aggressive Tom Scott and the self-effacing Alexander Graham Bell. But she was no less an expression of the new America that was coming into being in the year of the Centennial. Like them, she embodied the spirit of a rapidly changing America that celebrated self-invention, unshackled entrepreneurship, and creative individualism. Scott and Bell were of course pioneers in the spheres of industry and innovation; Lewis was a frontierswoman of the art world, who invented a life as bold and adventurous as any woman or man of her time. There were other successful female artists and writers. Some were Lewis's friends, others rivals. But she was in one respect utterly unique among them: race. Despite a complex heritage, she was most often referred to by those who met her as "the negro sculptress."

A pamphlet titled *How Edmonia Lewis Became an Artist,* probably written at her request, provided a romanticized version of her biography:

> Edmonia Lewis was born in a wigwam, her mother being an Indian and her father a negro. When little Edmonia was only three years old her mother died, leaving her to the care of her Indian relatives; and at the grave of her dear mother she kissed her father good-by, and has never seen him since. With the Indians she had a happy life—which was indeed a wild, roving one—hunting, fishing and making moccasins. Her brother,

> who was at a school for Indian boys, soon finished his studies and went to California, where he was able in a few years to send money to his little orphan sister, that she might be sent to school. A few years were spent at school; from there she went to Boston, Massachusetts, wishing to study music; but one day as she was walking through School Street, her eye caught sight of the statue of Benjamin Franklin. This was the first time in her life that she had ever seen anything in the line of sculpture. She said to herself: "Oh, how I should like to make something like that man standing there!" She asked questions and found out that statues were first made out of clay. She got some clay from a very kind sculptor, and then she made some sticks and went to work on a little foot. Next thing was a lady's hand that she made a study from. After this, she made a bust of Voltaire; this being finished, Edmonia received a commission to do a medallion for which she received twenty dollars. Three years from the time that she made the little foot, she had received orders enough to enable her to go to Italy. In Rome she opened a studio, and began to study from life.

Recent research by Lewis's biographer Kirsten P. Buick has revised this quasi-mythical account. Lewis was born with the baptismal name Maria Ignatia at Greenbush, New York, near Albany, in 1844. Her father was most likely Haitian and worked as a valet, and abandoned the family in her infancy. Although she always described her mother as Chippewa, that tribe lived far to the west, in Michigan and beyond. She spent her early girlhood at least partly in one of the Catholic Iroquois Native communities near the Canadian border, where she would have seen religious statuary in local churches. At the age of eight, she was enrolled in New York Central College, a Baptist abolitionist school in central New York with a racially mixed student body and several Black professors. Lewis claimed that she left the school because she was declared to be "wild—they could do nothing with me." Buick has shown, however, that she earned near-perfect grades in every class, including Latin, art, mathematics—and conduct. Her school fees were paid by her older brother, who achieved success as a Gold Rush pioneer, and later as a businessman in the Montana Territory. In 1859, Lewis went on to Oberlin College, in Ohio, one of more than thirty "colored" students, where she revealed a startlingly mature talent for drawing and painting, and doubtless learned something about sculpture. At Oberlin, she was also noticed by prominent abolitionists, who would continue to play a significant role in her life and career.

In 1862, Lewis found herself at the center of a disturbing event. That winter, she was arrested on a charge of feeding two female fellow students, both white, an aphrodisiac colloquially known as "Spanish Fly," during an excursion that also involved two young men. Whether she was a complete innocent unjustly blamed for her friends' misbehavior, or had herself instigated an "adventure" that spun out of control, remains a mystery. Before the case went to court, Lewis was kidnapped, taken to a field, and stripped and beaten by men who were never identified. Although the story certainly suggests that she may have been raped, that cannot be documented. At her trial, where she was represented by John Mercer Langston, the first Black lawyer in Ohio, Lewis was acquitted for lack of evidence. A year later, however, she was accused of stealing art materials from one of her professors. She was again acquitted, but the odor of impropriety that now clung to her made it impossible for her to continue at Oberlin.

Strikingly, in an era when pious chastity and decorum were ostentatiously prized, the scandal didn't hobble Lewis's budding career. Her supporters at Oberlin clearly considered her innocent of all the charges against her, since they provided her with personal letters to William Lloyd Garrison and others in Boston, where she was immediately introduced into that city's vibrant antislavery community, which embraced her wholeheartedly. The sculptor Edward Brackett took her on as a pupil—her bust of Voltaire was copied from one in his studio—and in less than a year she was brashly proclaiming herself an artist. For a young woman of her patchwork background, it was an extraordinary declaration of independence. At the same time, she began crafting her persona as a child of nature, with a quintessentially American zeal for self-reinvention. She told the author Lydia Maria Child in February 1864 that her creative impulse derived from her mother, who "was always inventing new patterns for moccasins, and other embroidery, and I went into the cities with my mother's people to sell them." When Child asked if she enjoyed that kind of life, Lewis pertly replied, "Oh, yes, I liked it a great deal better than I do your civilized life. There is nothing so beautiful as the free forest. To catch a fish when you are hungry, cut the boughs of a tree, make a fire to roast it, and eat it in the open air, is the greatest of all luxuries. I would not stay a week pent up in cities, if it were not for my passion for art."

The challenges were formidable. The United States then had no arts schools, no easy access to sculptural materials, no professional stoneworkers, no models, much less ones who might pose in the nude, and no place for a woman to study anatomy. Working in clay and marble was also considered too physically demanding for women, most certainly for one as small as Lewis, who may have stood less than five feet in height. Nevertheless, before the year was out, she had acquired a studio, opened it to the public, and staged a solo show, where she exhibited busts and plaster medallions of Garrison, John Brown, and the locally famous young officer Robert Gould Shaw, who died leading his Black regiment in its brave but tragic assault on Confederate-held Fort Wagner in 1863. Of this work, the poet Anna Quincy Waterston wrote in an eponymous poem "Edmonia Lewis," "She has wrought well with her unpracticed hand / The mirror of her thought reflected clear, / This youthful hero-martyr of our land." Although she never spoke directly about politics, she told an interviewer years later that she hoped "to do something for the race—something that will excite the admiration of the other races of the earth."

Lewis quickly revealed entrepreneurial talent. She began selling her work at antislavery meetings. Then, with the approval of the young colonel's abolitionist family, she made a hundred plaster casts from the Shaw bust and sold them at fifteen dollars apiece—earning enough to set off for Rome, the prime destination for any sculptor who wanted to build a reputation. There, marble was easy to obtain, stonecutters could be cheaply hired, models were plentiful. It would become her home for the next twenty years. She sailed for Europe on August 26, 1865. "My enthusiasm increased day by day," she later recalled, "and I began to feel that I was going to enter the sphere for which I was designed." There was also a darker subtext to her departure from America. "I was practically driven to Rome, in order to obtain the opportunities for art-culture, and to find a social atmosphere where I was not constantly reminded of my color," Lewis told *The New York Times* in 1878. "The land of liberty had no room for a colored sculptor."

In Rome, Lewis found a teeming, tolerant, and seedily picturesque city of 100,000, in which beggars, soldiers, monks, long-robed priests, ladies with lace-fringed parasols, chestnut roasters, cigar vendors, girls with pitchers on their heads, and ragged urchins jostled among deep-shadowed narrow streets, scarred monuments, rococo churches, fountains trailing maidenhair moss, mysterious stairways, vaulted ruins, weedy piazzas, laundry lines, and mounds of horse dung, in an atmosphere redolent of orange blossoms, simmering spaces, and overflowing privies. Artists and writers submerged themselves in the study of art, copying and sketching, and soaking up the vestiges of the "classical" at a time when the civilizations of the ancient world were considered the apogee of aesthetic achievement. Some expatriate sculptors, Nathaniel Hawthorne caustically remarked, spent their entire careers "making Venuses, Cupids, Bacchuses, and a vast deal of other marble progeny of dream-work, or rather frost-work"—a "vapoury exhalation out of the Grecian mythology." Most, both male and female, embraced Roman life with relish. Of Lewis's contemporary and friend, the talented young American sculptor Harriet Hosmer, Elizabeth Barrett Browning wrote, "She lives here all alone; dines and breakfasts at the cafes precisely as a young man would; works from six in the morning till night, as a great artist must." Browning's words might as easily have applied to Edmonia Lewis.

Lewis soon found a welcoming home among a group of resident female artists, among them Anne Whitney, Emma Stebbins, Louisa Lander, and Hosmer, most of them American or British, centered around the celebrated Boston-raised actress Charlotte Cushman. Henry James, who knew many of them well, condescendingly described Cushman's circle as a "strange sisterhood of American 'lady sculptors' who at one time settled upon the seven hills in a white marmorean flock." Many though not all were lesbian. Onstage, Cushman specialized in male roles; a witness to her performance of Hamlet remarked that her love scenes were "of so erotic a character that no man would dare indulge in them." Magnetic, intense, and mercurial, she lived openly in Rome with a series of partners, Hosmer and Stebbins among them, and generously took newcomers like Lewis under her wing, providing them with a place to stay in her palatial dwelling, lending them money, and helping them find buyers for their work.

Although she sometimes wore a gold ring to discourage male advances, Lewis never married or had children, and was not known to be romantically associated with either men or women. If her relationships with anyone in Cushman's group went beyond friendship, there is no record of it. She may of course have concealed her intimacies: Even in tolerant Rome, she was always more vulnerable to damaging smears and insinuations than were her white peers, especially in the ever-appraising eyes of the American clientele upon whom she mainly depended. Whatever her erotic attachments, if she had any, what most stands out about Lewis was her determination, at any cost, to live with complete commitment the life that she had chosen. She was, in the end, an island unto herself, taking her freedom and opportunity for granted, guided by her own sense of unique destiny. In an era when few women had careers of any kind or even owned property, when dependence on men was the norm, and even something as quotidian as attending the theater or a restaurant alone was unthinkable, it was a heroic choice. "What she undertakes to do," Lydia Maria Child wrote of her, "she will do, though she has to cut through the heart of a mountain with a pen knife."

By 1870, Lewis had become *fashionable*. That year, she reported property worth $20,000, making her one of the wealthiest Black Americans of her time. When work was pressing, she hired as many as half a dozen Italian stoneworkers to carry out her orders. Newspapers from Leipzig to California published articles about her—"Colored Genius at Rome," ran a typical one from Philadelphia. The *San Francisco Elevator,* a Black paper, declared her work to be "strong evidence of the capacity of our race for the highest reaches of art, and a refutation of the slanders of our natural inferiority." King Victor Emmanuel II awarded her a gold medal for a sculpture of napping infants. Her studio near the Piazza Barberini became a popular stop for art-minded visitors to Rome, where the curious could watch her at work and purchase her works to take home. Visitors found her friendly and earnest, with wavy hair, "large, black, sympathetic eyes," and tiny hands with which she confidently handled her hammer and chisel. She was, wrote an American visitor, Henry Tuckerman, "unquestionably the most interesting representative of our country in Europe."

Like virtually all her contemporaries, Lewis worked in the neoclassical style that harked back to Roman and Greek models. Her preferred material was white Carrara marble, which generations of sculptors had been taught to regard as the most perfect material to express the eternal truths and elevated sentiments that connoisseurs sought. (In France, an emerging appreciation for transient effects in art—Impressionism—was just beginning to foreshadow a more subjective aesthetic.) Lewis specialized in portrait busts of John Brown and other abolitionists, and notables such as Abraham Lincoln, Horace Greeley, and Franz Liszt, whom she met in Rome. When the revered Henry Wadsworth Longfellow turned up in town she dogged his footsteps in order to capture his profile in her sketchbook. Sometimes she undertook explicitly classical subjects on commission—a bust of the Roman emperor-to-be Octavian, a statue of Clio the Greek muse of history—but her more ambitious efforts tended to represent abolitionist themes and evocations of her native heritage. In *Forever Free,* she presented a bare-chested freedman with a burst shackle on his wrist and his wife or daughter kneeling at his feet, with uplifted eyes and clasped hands. In her much-praised *Hagar,* she offered the cast-out slave of the biblical Sarah as a stand-in for the pathos of the American enslaved.

Her most popular sculptures of all drew on characters from Longfellow's much-loved poem *The Song of Hiawatha,* an epic celebration of the "Noble Savage" loosely based on Chippewa tradition, incorporating a chaste romance between the eponymous hero and his love Minnehaha. Critics often noted that Lewis's "native" women tended to resemble Greek goddesses draped in Indian costume, but praised their "authenticity" nonetheless; they had, after all, been chiseled by an "Indian girl." Asked by a white reporter why she had come all the way to California—she was the first sculptor to show on the West Coast—instead of staying in sophisticated New York, she blithely replied, "I have Indian blood in me, you know," and so was naturally drawn to the wilderness. She sometimes referred to herself as "Wildfire," a retooling of her "Chippewa" name Suhkhegarequa, which translates less colorfully as "fire-making girl." At a Catholic fair in San Jose, she welcomed no fewer than 1,600 visitors at fifty cents a head to her "wigwam," as she called her exhibit space. However, she expressed no opinions on Indian issues, and never actually affiliated herself with the Chippewas or any other Native community.

Exoticism was an essential part of her public identity, of her "brand," to use a later coinage. Even friends didn't quite know what to make of her. A fellow artist, Charlotte Cholmley, sculpted a weird bust of her, showing her with woolly hair on one side of her head and the soft hair of an Indian on the other, while one intrigued interviewer wrote that she "has something of the habitual quietude and stoicism of the Indian race . . . and has a trace of the sadness of both races in her manner, notwithstanding her assured artistic success." Rare, if not unique, among "colored" Americans of her time, she managed to turn race into money. "In Italy, Miss Lewis has enjoyed some advantages on account of the accident of complexion," wrote Frederick Douglass, a supporter. "[She] has met encouragement where she would not had she been white. We know that this was the case in Boston." At the same time, she disliked being judged by race alone. "Some people praise me because I am a colored girl, and I don't want that kind of praise," she told Lydia Maria Child. "I had rather you would point out my defects, for that will teach me something."

At least in the United States, where she traveled annually, race was inescapably a burden. After Italy the pervasive racism she undoubtedly encountered must have grated painfully. In Cleveland, Ohio, a hotel asked her to eat in her room to avoid the sight of her offending white guests in the restaurant, and in Syracuse, New York, a prewar abolitionist bastion, she trudged half the night before she found a minister willing to offer her shelter. Countless insults that she must have suffered in trains, steamships, and shops have been lost to the historical record. But she persisted. Armored with her seemingly unbreachable self-confidence, she trained herself to be affable and polite. "They treat me very kindly [in the United States]," she told *The New York Times,* "but it is with a kind of reservation. I don't like to be pointed out as a negress." She avoided controversy, maintained her dignity, and kept on working.

She proved a skillful businesswoman. She managed relations with a large clientele in Europe and North America, selling marble groups and busts for thousands of dollars, plaster copies for a few hundred, and miniatures for even less, both by mail and from her studio. Sometimes, she raffled off sculptures, or offered a free sketch or engraving along with a statue. When she traveled, she alerted local newspapers and organized interviews, and charged admission to view her work, usually twenty-five or fifty cents, sometimes earning thousands of dollars in such fees alone. She was also skilled at self-promotion. In *How Edmonia Lewis Became an Artist,* she unblushingly declared, "God's gift to Edmonia Lewis is unconquerable energy, as well as genius; and these two combined enable her to rise above all prejudices of race or color, and command the respect and honor of all true lovers of art."

LEWIS ARRIVED in New York on May 2, 1876, and headed directly for Philadelphia. Along with *Cleopatra,* she also brought a diverse selection of her other works: *Asleep,* a sentimental rendering of two sleeping infants; *The Old Arrow Maker* and *The Marriage of Hiawatha,* which were among her most popular interpretations of Longfellow's poem; busts of John Brown and Charles Sumner, and more.

Several other artists suffered dreadful mishaps. Some works were damaged en route. Harriet Hosmer's main submission proved too big to fit in the ship's hold, and another wound up exiled to the Centennial's Italian section. Margaret Foley, another Rome-based sculptor, had crafted a huge fountain adorned with frolicking children and was heartbroken to find it consigned to a remote garden where no critics noticed it. Not only women artists suffered such indignities. *The Gross Clinic,* by Thomas Eakins, now recognized as one of the greatest of all nineteenth-century American paintings, which showed a dissection in progress, was deemed so shocking that it was shunted off to the section on medicine.

When Lewis arrived in Philadelphia, she didn't even know if *The Death of Cleopatra* would be accepted for public display. With remarkable frankness, she described to a reporter her tumultuous feelings as she waited for the judges' verdict. She was lingering about within earshot of the committee room when the statue was brought in and opened. "She had seen with trembling for the fate of [her own submission], work after work rejected by the committee," the reporter wrote. At length, the box containing *Cleopatra* was brought in and opened. Said Lewis, "I scarcely breathed. I felt as though I was nothing. They opened the box, looked at the work, talked together a moment, and then I heard the order given to place it in such and such a position." It meant that she would be ensconced among the world's greats: Thomas Gainsborough, Sir Joshua Reynolds, Gilbert Stuart, and the up-and-coming Augustus Saint-Gaudens and Daniel Chester French. Wrote the reporter, "The Indian stoicism gave way. Miss Lewis swallowed her sobs for the moment, and went home and had a good cry by herself."

CHAPTER 4

GLADIATORS

★ ★ ★ ★ ★

But what is emancipation?

—FREDERICK DOUGLASS

Rutherford B. Hayes concealed the driving ambition that fueled his rise through Ohio state politics to Congress, to the governor's office, to become by the spring of 1876 a dark horse prospect for the presidency. Publicly, he spurned efforts to propose him as a candidate. He never said that he would refuse the nomination if it was offered, but he made clear that he would not seek it. "If other fools rush in, I shall not," he told a friend. Even as the "buzz" circulated among his political friends, he maintained an appearance of disinterest, and claimed that his well-known aversion to backroom deals would disqualify him anyway. As Ohio's governor, he had felt pressured to travel to Philadelphia for the Centennial's opening, but he begged off, surmising that it would be assumed that he was implicitly presenting himself as a presidential contender. He would only consider a trip to the Exhibition, he dryly remarked, after the Republican National Convention, in mid-June, "emancipates me from the bondage of candidacy."

In the Gilded Age, political conventions were a combination of dramatic theater, gladiatorial arena, and papal conclave, all taking place simultaneously. As the Republican delegates gathered in Cincinnati, the city's streets boiled with excitement. Brass bands led torchlight parades. Orators bellowed speeches in front of downtown hotels. Politicos bargained for alliances in smoky parlors. At noon on June 14, just over a month after the Exposition's opening, former Connecticut Governor Joseph R. Hawley, on leave from his duties as the president of the Centennial, called the convention to order at Exposition Hall, on Elm Street. Red-white-and-blue muslin banners festooned the walls, and in the center of the stage stood an immense gilded eagle flanked by American flags. Among the delegates were many of the nation's most powerful men, but none of the candidates, who in keeping with the custom of the time remained at their homes. Significantly, the delegates included a large contingent of Black Republicans from the Southern states, among them the former slave and war hero from South Carolina Robert Smalls; P. B. S. Pinchback, the first Black governor of a state, Louisiana; the influential Georgian Henry McNeal Turner, who was also an AME bishop; the fiery New York abolitionist Henry Highland Garnet; U.S. Senator Blanche Bruce of Mississippi; and Frederick Douglass, who was scheduled to address the convention, a first for any Black orator. Visitors' tickets were in such demand that they were being scalped outside the hall for $20 and more—roughly $600 in present-day dollars.

News from the convention competed with the daily barrage of reports from the Centennial, in which readers learned that one J. C. Temple had turned up at the Missouri state building with a fifty-pound barrowload of local minerals that he had wheeled 1,200 miles from his home in Joplin; that the Arkansas pavilion had recently put on display a piece of dried beef that had been exposed to the air for seven years, along with a piece of George Washington's coffin; that no fewer than 4,000 workers from the Singer Sewing Machine plant in Elizabeth, New Jersey, were touring the fair en masse; and that crewmen from the Brazilian warship *Nichteroy* were happily "regaling" themselves on "Yankee pies and milk." They were also informed to their amusement that the

Philadelphia police had raided an "immoral coffee house," where for twenty-five cents patrons could enjoy an "immodest" dance by a woman dressed in Turkish costume.

REPUBLICANS WERE NERVOUS. After sixteen years of their being in power, voters were turning against them. Oregon had just gone Democratic in state elections. Indiana, New Jersey, New York, and Connecticut all had Democratic governors. In the Reconstructed South, Republican administrations were steadily falling. Americans were fed up with what seemed to be pervasive self-dealing in Washington and wanted change. Meanwhile, the postwar expansion of the federal bureaucracy had turned government into "a massive job-creating and wealth-harvesting machine" that sucked revenue from the sale of offices and kickbacks from placeholders and investors seeking federal charters and lands. No one suggested that plain-living President Grant was personally dishonest, but many of his once-trusted underlings had been proven so. His first vice president, Schuyler Colfax, was tainted by a scheme to skim funds from the Union Pacific Railroad, while Grant's brother was implicated in an unsavory attempt to corner the gold market. Freewheeling corruption in the states was, if anything, even worse. In Illinois, every public job had a price tag set by Senator John Logan's machine; in New York, Senator Roscoe Conkling's organization controlled federal patronage, including the New York Custom House, the source of the bulk of the nation's revenue from commercial tariffs. Under Conkling's regime, judgeships reportedly sold for $15,000 apiece, a seat in Congress for $4,000, and one in the state legislature, a relative bargain, for $1,500. "Not more truly was slavery the mortal peril of this country twenty years ago than political corruption and demoralization in every form are its peril now," declared the reformer George William Curtis.

In both parties, the slogan of "reform" had become an all-purpose rhetorical sledgehammer to batter documented venality, featherbedding, and ordinary political horse-trading. As early as 1871, Senator Carl Schurz, a leader of the Republicans' reform wing, had urged his allies to "break up" the party because it had lost its ethical ballast. It was only with difficulty that in 1872 Grant had beaten back insurgent, self-described Liberal Republican reformers led by Schurz, who threatened to derail his reelection. In the end, the Democrats then sabotaged their chance of victory by nominating the eccentric and unpopular newspaper editor Horace Greeley as their candidate. Since then, Democratic calls for reform had only grown louder and all the more effective as scandals continued to unfold in Washington.

With Grant having declined to run for a third term, the Republicans faced their first open convention since 1860. Apart from the three "favorite sons" being promoted by their state delegations—Hayes, Governor John Hartranft of Pennsylvania, and Marshall Jewell of Connecticut, the U.S. postmaster general—there were four serious contenders, all of them party heavyweights who believed that they were destined to prevail.

Many influential reformers favored Treasury Secretary Benjamin Bristow. A Kentuckian, a wartime Unionist and former U.S. attorney in a state that had been rife with proslavery sentiment, he had won praise for aggressively prosecuting Ku Klux Klan terrorists and for investigating government fraud. He was well liked by clean-government men such as Curtis and Hayes, but he was detested by party regulars.

The party's shrinking Radical wing—those least willing to compromise on Black civil rights and Reconstruction—favored Senator Oliver P. Morton of Indiana, who as his state's wartime governor had held it firm for the Union against a Copperhead insurgency that threatened to subvert the war effort. Regarded as a demagogue by some, and harshly partisan in spirit, he was famous for describing the Democratic Party as "a common sewer and loathsome receptacle, into which is emptied every element of treason North and South, and every element of inhumanity and barbarism which has dishonored the age." Having suffered a stroke in 1865, Morton remained paralyzed from the waist down. If he were to win the nomination, he would be the first disabled candidate in American history.

Senator Roscoe Conkling was regarded by many as a veritable prince of machine politics. He often served as a de facto spokesman for the Grant administration in the Senate and was probably closer to the president than any of the other candidates. Nurtured by prewar abolitionist politics, he was more consistently outspoken on civil rights than most of his rivals: It was Conkling who had forced the police to admit Frederick Douglass to the presidential platform on the Centennial's opening day. By 1876, however, Conkling was better known for his pompous swagger than for his ideals. His mortal rival, James G. Blaine of Maine, sneered openly at his "turkey gobbler strut." At six feet three inches, Conkling was a commanding figure—"a Hercules in frock coat," in the words of one admirer—with wavy auburn hair that fell in curls over his brow, a golden beard, and a dandy's taste for cream-colored trousers and vibrant silk scarves. Although he didn't drink, he trailed a reputation for womanizing, most persistently with the wife of a Rhode Island senator, Kate Sprague, one of the capital's great beauties. The mean-spirited said that many of the Conkling delegates had been let out of jail on bail supplied by the grafters of the New York Custom House Ring, which he controlled.

Most observers felt that the man to beat was Blaine, until recently the Speaker of the House of Representatives, and the most powerful politician in the Republican cosmos. Of him, his colleague George Hoar wrote, "There has never been a man in our history whom so few people looked on with indifference. He was born to be loved or hated." Although conservative by instinct, he aligned himself with the Radicals during the war, and helped to draft the Fourteenth Amendment. In January 1876, he almost single-handedly defeated a bill proposed by the Democratic-controlled House that would have extended a pardon to Jefferson Davis and hundreds of other high-ranking Confederate leaders. He declared bitingly that the former Confederate president was not just a traitor but "the author, knowingly, deliberately, guiltily and willfully of the gigantic crimes and murders at Andersonville," the notorious Georgia prison camp where federal prisoners had died in squalor during the war. Although Democrats excoriated Blaine as a "ghoul" for evoking wartime atrocities, his Republican friends crowed that his eloquence had won the presidential nomination on the spot. At the very least, the speech had demonstrated that wartime feelings still had potency, and that the scandal-scarred Republicans were more likely to prevail in November if voters could be distracted from the party's problems—and Blaine's own—by shackling the Democrats to Confederate treason.

Blaine was burdened with very heavy baggage, however, having acquired a reputation for coziness with monied interests that had made him a very rich man. His relationship with the financiers Jay Cooke and his brother Henry was particularly close. He pointedly reminded them on one occasion, "I may say without Egotism that my position will enable me to render you services of vital importance & value. I am ready to do all for you in my power at any time you may desire." When he needed money, he felt free to invite them to purchase stocks that he wanted to unload. To refuse would be a mistake, since both brothers well knew that Blaine was a formidable power for good or evil.

Blaine was also known to have exploited his position as Speaker to favor certain railroad magnates, particularly Tom Scott of the Pennsylvania Railroad, epitomizing the quid pro quo synergy between politicians and big business that was eating away at the reputation of the Republican Party. Scott, like other railroad barons, wanted subsidies and concessions that would shut out his rivals and facilitate his railroad's expansion through the South, and ultimately to the West Coast. Blaine was perfectly positioned to shape legislation that Scott wanted, and he was very obliging. In return, Scott ensured that Blaine was able to enrich himself by personally selling securities in branch lines that would be absorbed by the Pennsylvania Railroad. In April, it was revealed that Blaine had facilitated a land grant bill for a failing Arkansas railroad, the Little Rock & Fort Smith, and then profited by selling the road's nearly worthless bonds to friends. When what was, in essence, a swindle was revealed, the Union Pacific "loaned" Blaine $64,000 and took $75,000 of the tainted bonds as collateral. The order to pay Blaine had come through Scott—who was also the president of the Union Pacific. Blaine denied that any such transaction had taken place, supported by a deposition from Scott. Then, in May, incriminating letters were leaked to the press by a whistleblower, making it clear that Blaine had lied. With astonishing bravado, Blaine showed up at the Washington hotel where the whistleblower was staying, asked to look at the letters, and when they were handed to him, pocketed them and left. On the floor of Congress, he then read aloud expurgated selections from the letters to, seemingly, exonerate himself, and excoriated the House's Democrats for hounding him. It was a bravura performance, and should have been the end of it. On May 31, however, a director of the Union Pacific testified that what the letters said was true, and that Blaine had received the $64,000 directly from Tom Scott himself.

Blaine, in short, represented everything that honest voters were repelled by in the Republican Party. Despite it all, most handicappers felt that Blaine was so far ahead in the delegate count that his nomination was virtually assured. Reflecting on the scandal, Hayes, who knew Blaine well and admired his political skill if not his ethics, surmised that if he stood any chance himself at this point, it could only come as the result of an alliance between those "who look for availability in the candidate, and those who are for purity and reform." However, that was a possibility so remote that he hardly considered it. Blaine might be vulnerable, he thought. But if he were to fail, Hayes told his diary, "My independent position, aloof from bargaining, puts me outside the list from whom the managers will select."

On June 11, three days before the convention was to begin, Blaine's campaign had been struck by a figurative bolt of lightning. While leaving the First Congregational Church in Washington with his family, Blaine suddenly collapsed paralyzed and unconscious on the street and was thought to be on the brink of death. Hayes wrote to Blaine upon hearing the news, "My eyes are almost blinded with tears. This affects me as did the death of Lincoln." Blaine remained unconscious for two days while rumors ran rampant: that he had suffered a heart attack or a stroke, or that he was already dead. (He had most likely been stricken by sunstroke.) When by the next morning he recovered, to the relief of his friends, his enemies sourly scoffed that he had faked the whole episode in order to win sympathy. At least some supporters wondered if he was healthy enough to carry on a campaign, much less shoulder the weight of the presidency.

* * *

AS THE CONVENTION got underway, rumors swirled everywhere: that Blaine was cutting a deal with Bristow; that Conkling was already out of the running; that Morton was on the upswing; that Blaine men were defecting en masse in Michigan and Maryland; that Louisiana would go for Hartranft; that Morton intended to block Blaine at any cost; that Blaine was virtually beaten, or he would win on the first ballot; that Bristow was already assured of two hundred votes; that if Bristow failed, the Democrats would make him their candidate. Embarrassing news reports rattled everyone. New York papers were reprinting the letters that incriminated Blaine. In Washington, Secretary of War Belknap's impeachment was moving forward: His lawyers were preparing to call the commander of the army, William Tecumseh Sherman, to testify on his behalf, while the prosecutors were summoning George Armstrong Custer from the faraway Dakota Territory, where he was preparing to lead the Seventh Cavalry against the Lakota Sioux.

Everyone knew that Blaine had the most disciplined organization and the largest number of pledged delegates. But many of them were committed only for the first or second ballot. After that, the real contest would begin, ballot after ballot, until one candidate or another won a majority. Blaine's opponents predicted that he would reach his high-water mark by the third ballot, and that his bloc would then disintegrate. The divisions among reformers, machine men, and favorite sons seemed unbridgeable.

The hall was a cauldron of steamy heat, brass bands, and "machine shouting" from battalions of partisan campaigners paid by the competing campaigns. Delegates stripped off their heavy broadcloth coats and fanned themselves as the first speakers got underway. With all well aware that the party's survival depended on it presenting a plausible path to reform, the first slot was allotted to New York author George W. Curtis, who was trusted to set the necessary tone of high moral purpose. He didn't disappoint. Too many officeholders, he declared, treated their jobs as their personal property, banding themselves "into an odious and intolerable oligarchy which menaces the very system of our government."

The Republicans had no hope of winning in November, he said, unless they regained the battered trust of the public. After this genuflection toward reform, the convention's next speaker was a full-throated incarnation of the machine politics that reformers hated, the generously mustached Senator John Logan of Illinois. He warned ominously of a Confederate counterrevolution in the making. A Democratic victory, he thundered would turn the nation over to the plunderers and murderers of the Ku Klux Klan. "Would four million unoffending freed people be allowed to become their prey? It is our duty to say that this shall not be done!"

Next, Frederick Douglass issued a stentorian challenge to Republicans to recommit themselves to the freedoms for which they had fought the war. It was clear to most of his listeners, in that era when students were taught to memorize Shakespeare's most famous speeches, that he was evoking Mark Antony's words over the murdered Caesar. "You say you have emancipated us. You have; and I thank you for it. You say you have enfranchised us. You have; and I thank you for it. But what is your emancipation?—what is your enfranchisement? What does it all amount to, if the black man, after having been made free by the letter of your law, is unable to exercise that freedom, and having been freed from the slaveholder's lash, he is to be subject to the slaveholder's shot-gun? Oh! you freed us! You emancipated us! I thank you for it. But under what circumstances did you emancipate us?" He begged, indeed demanded, that a candidate be nominated who would assure that "the black man shall walk to the ballot box in safety, even if we have to bring a bayonet behind us."

Like all party platforms, the one the convention adopted was an aspirational road map, a product of compromise, conviction, and evasion that tried to balance the growing power of conservative business interests with promises of reform and concern about the white terrorism in the South. In particular, the party committed itself to sustaining hard-money legislation to benefit investors who had bought federal bonds at low rates during the war and stood to reap enormous profits when they were redeemed in full. In a nod to the Radicals, it pledged to secure "complete liberty and exact equality" for the freed people. Reformers were meant to be reassured by planks calling for an overhaul in the appointment of public officials, and an end to the wholesale granting of public lands to monopolies and railroads. Veterans were wooed with language opposing the elevation of former Confederates to office, and decrying Democrats as heirs to treason. A plank asking for a constitutional amendment to forbid the use of public funds to support any sectarian schools was a sop to Protestant nativists agitated by supposed efforts by Catholic immigrants to establish parochial schools at taxpayers' expense.

And then there was the women's plank. Although no one could upstage the charismatic Douglass, Sara J. Spencer, "a slight and delicate person, but full of nerve and courage," came close, delivering the first ever speech by a woman to a national political convention. A seasoned activist with the National Woman Suffrage Association, in 1871 she and seventy other women had boldly, if unsuccessfully, sued the District of Columbia under the Fourteenth Amendment, demanding the right to vote. "In this bright new century, let me ask you to win to your side the women of the United States—the wives, daughters, and sisters of this republic," she ringingly declaimed. "We want the proposition established for women that a woman's head is her head, her body is her body, her feet are her feet, her hands are her hands, and that she should hold in them the ballot for self-protection." Like the British crown, which had claimed the right to govern the inhabitants of the colonies, she continued, men now as unjustly claimed the right to legislate for women. "If you would have the party of the future be the Republican party, you must now take the broad, noble ground of citizens' suffrage . . . and establish a genuine republic that shall know no class, caste, race, or sex." Although support for enfranchisement was growing within the party, the delegates expected women to be content with an anodyne plank stating that "the honest demands of this class of citizens for additional rights, privileges, and immunities should be treated with respectful consideration."

Most of the platform was hammered out behind closed doors. But one issue burst out in rancorous debate, casting a shadow on the convention's high-minded calls for freedom and justice. For years, hostility to Chinese immigrants had seethed on the West Coast, escalating to mobbing and murderous violence perpetrated by white working men whose votes in November might tip the balance in several states. Catering to the unrest, the platform committee had proposed a plank calling on Congress to investigate the effect of Chinese immigration "on the moral and material interests of the country." Venomous racism saturated the debate. John P. Jones of Nevada asserted that whites were suffering an "invasion there worse than the grasshopper plague, worse than the plague of the locusts. They have found a people who bring with them no respect for our government, no knowledge of our language; a brutalized people; a people that recognize neither honesty among their men, nor virtue among their women," who "have planted themselves like a leprous sore in our midst." To this, George Curtis retorted, "Now, as we begin a new century, is it for us to declare that the principles of the Declaration of Independence shall now be virtually revoked? If you mean to draw a cordon along the coast of this country—if you mean to say that any man of any race shall be excluded—then you have revoked the original principle of your party." Despite Curtis's appeal, the plank passed by a two-thirds majority, a sign that a party that six years earlier had celebrated the Fifteenth Amendment was, along with the rest of white America, undergoing what would become a seismic shift in its sentiments about race.

TENSION MOUNTED as the time for nominations finally arrived. R. W. Thompson of Indiana deftly made light of Morton's infirmity as he officially threw the senator's hat into the ring, saying, "True, he has been afflicted in his legs, but it does not require legs to make a statesman! His head is clear. His heart is sound." Bristow was nominated by his fellow Kentuckian future Supreme Court Justice John M. Harlan: "Let us understand that this government must be purified if the party is to be saved, and that Benjamin H. Bristow is the one man who stands before the country as the embodiment of the spirit of governmental purification." Stewart Woodford, a well-wired federal attorney, extolled his ally Conkling as "broad in culture, eloquent in debate, wise in council, fearless in leadership," unbendingly loyal to President Grant, and the only Republican who could carry New York in November.

When the famous orator Robert Ingersoll stepped to the stage and took his place between the great gilded eagles, the entire hall erupted with a volcanic roar that went on for ten minutes. A former Illinois attorney general and brilliant courtroom lawyer, later widely known as "the Great Agnostic," the portly and clean-shaven Ingersoll delivered with his characteristic prodigious force the most famous speech of the convention. In Blaine, Ingersoll declared, the Republican Party possessed a candidate who embodied "the grandest combination of heart, conscience, and brain the world ever saw." (More than a few delegates doubtless gagged when Ingersoll went on to proclaim that Blaine's "reputation is as spotless as a star.") In this the Centennial year, he continued, a year filled with proud and tender memories of the sacred past, the nation demanded a man who "like an intellectual athlete" had stood firm in defense of the victory that the Union's soldiers had won upon the battlefield. "Like an armed warrior, like a plumed knight, James G. Blaine marched down the halls of American Congress and threw his shining lance full and fair against the brazen forehead of every traitor to his country and every maligner of his fair reputation. For the Republican party to desert that gallant man is now as though an army should desert their general on the field of battle." Ingersoll was rewarded with a bedlam of cheering, foot-stomping, and waving hats and handkerchiefs. Many felt that had the vote been taken immediately, Blaine would have swept the nomination on the spot.

After Ingersoll, the nominations of the several favorite sons—Hartranft, Jewell, and Hayes—felt anticlimactic and perfunctory. Former Ohio Governor Edward Noyes unsurprisingly stressed Hayes's personal probity: "His private life is so pure that no man has ever dared to assault it." Hayes, who was monitoring the convention by telegraph at his home in Columbus, admitted feeling overwhelmed by the reality of his nomination. "It sobers me," he wrote. "I have kept cool and unconcerned to a degree that surprises me. I feel that defeat will be a great relief."

Although Hayes was born in Ohio, in 1822, his forebears hailed from Puritan New England stock. The ubiquitous William Dean Howells, his first biographer, rather romantically described his lineage as "a strong, brave, simple race, following the plow, wielding the hammer, and hewing out their way as plain men must in a new land." He was hardly a frontiersman: He held degrees from Kenyon College and Harvard Law School, and was widely read in both the classics and modern literature. In middle age, he was still physically striking, with penetrating blue eyes and a well-muscled physique, although his chiseled features were mostly obscured by a sandy, gray-tinged beard. Unusual for his time, he relied for his moral compass on freethinking, liberal ethics rather than conventional religion, in which he had little interest. He opposed plutocratic privilege, public dishonesty, and slavery; before the war, he defended fugitive slaves pro bono. He left his lucrative law career to enlist in the army soon after the firing on Fort Sumter, and was wounded four times, once leading his regiment in a near-suicidal bayonet charge during the Antietam campaign. In 1864, he was elected to Congress while still under arms, but refused to take his seat until after the war ended. "An officer fit for duty, who at this crisis would abandon his post to electioneer for Congress, ought to be scalped," he wrote at the time.

In Congress, Hayes spoke rarely, but when he did he could rise to Lincolnesque eloquence. In 1867, he attacked not just the rampant violence against freed people in the South but the racism that lay beneath it. Black Americans, he declared, "are not aliens or strangers. They are here not by the choice of themselves or of their ancestors. They are here by the misfortune of their fathers and the crime of ours. Their toil has added to the resources and wealth of the nation untold millions. Whether we prefer it or not, they are our countrymen, and will remain so forever. They are more than countrymen—they are citizens. Our government has been called the white man's government. Not so. It is not the government of any class, or sect, or nationality, or race. It is not the government of the native born, or of the foreign born, of the rich man, or of the poor man—it is the government of the freeman."

Elected governor that same year, he won praise even from Democrats for his independence as he pursued a bold, forward-looking agenda: reducing both taxes and the state debt, building public asylums for the mentally ill and modern "reform" schools for the young, instituting humane management of the state prison, founding a home for the orphans of soldiers and sailors. Against pressure from his own party, he retained capable Democratic appointees in his administration.

His style was sober, his personal life irreproachable. He was devoted to his wife, Lucy, an ardent temperance advocate, to whom he had been married for twenty-three years, and to his five children. What some saw as a lack of color was more accurately a distaste for drama wedded to strategic realism. Although his contempt for "corruptionists" was genuine, he was also a pragmatist who maintained the respect of the party's more cynical political operators, and "often masked his calculated political moves with a cloak of principle," in the words of his biographer Ari Hoogenboom. After his state's party convention unanimously declared support for him as a "favorite son," he expressed only exasperation, writing to a friend, "I now would be glad to be satisfactorily out of it." But in the privacy of his diary he confided that if he did become president, "I do not feel the least fear that I should fail!"

THREE HUNDRED and seventy-nine votes were needed to earn the nomination. Blaine's win still seemed assured. Balloting began a little before 11 a.m. on June 16. As expected, Blaine ran far ahead of his rivals, with 285 to Morton's 124, Bristow's 113, Conkling's 99, Hayes's 61, Hartranft's 58, and a sprinkling of votes for the others. On the second ballot, Blaine rose to 296. On the third, Bristow advanced to 121, and Morton dropped to 113. On the fourth, Bristow, Hartranft, and Hayes all advanced, while Conkling dropped to 84, and Morton continued to hemorrhage. On the fifth, Blaine slipped back to 286, Bristow and Conkling ebbed, and Hayes rallied to 104, his best showing so far. On the sixth ballot, Blaine leaped upward to 308, but Michigan's delegation broke for Hayes. It was a straw in the wind.

Delegates swarmed around the hall in hectic confabulations. When they returned to their seats, the chairman of the Indiana delegation dramatically withdrew Morton's name from contention and cast 25 of its votes for Hayes and five for Bristow. At this, the first significant break in the deadlock, men leaped onto their chairs, yelling and shouting, and waving their arms and hats. Moments later, Harlan withdrew Bristow's name and cast Kentucky's 24 votes for Hayes. Indiana thereupon threw its five Bristow votes to Hayes as well. The Hayes trend became an avalanche. Conkling was now clearly out of the running. In a Parthian shot at his hated rival, he directed New York to throw the 61 votes he controlled to Hayes; the nine he didn't were left to Blaine. Pennsylvania then withdrew Hartranft's name and cast 28 votes for Hayes and 30 for Blaine. When the air cleared, Blaine had reached 351, but been defeated by Hayes, who totaled 384. When Blaine's home state of Maine handed its votes over to Hayes, the Ohio governor was declared the party's nominee by unanimous consent. He was acceptable to everyone: He had no enemies, he was free of scandal, and he seemed to be the perfect antidote to the party's damaged reputation. Hayes confided to his diary, "It for a few moments quite unmanned me." Editorialized *The New York Times,* his nomination "was not the pluckiest thing to have done, but doubtless the wisest."

The choice of Hayes's vice presidential running mate was perfunctory. His men wanted someone from the pivotal state of New York, but preferably not the popular Woodford, who was perceived to be one of Conkling's creatures. (Hayes was grateful for the spoilsman's support, grudging though it may have been, but he wasn't prepared to taint his campaign by close association with him.) As a ticket-balancer, the convention then selected the obscure but respected William A. Wheeler, a five-term congressman, chairman of the House Appropriations Committee, and former banker from the northern reaches of the state, about as far from Conkling's downstate bastion as possible.

After his victory, Hayes soberly shook hands with his aides. Soon hundreds of his supporters were heard cheering in the streets of Columbus, and flags suddenly unfurled from countless windows. By evening, bonfires lit the avenues and spontaneous parades wound their way to the Hayes home. Similar scenes played out around the country. At the Centennial, in Philadelphia, well-wishers cheerfully swarmed the Ohio pavilion, and Emperor Dom Pedro's personal band serenaded the celebratory Republicans. Reformers, in particular, heaved a vast, collective sigh of relief. George Curtis wired Hayes, "I cannot help thinking that your nomination at this juncture is as fortunate for the country as that of Mr. Lincoln in 1860."

In his letter of acceptance, Hayes denounced the spoils system and pledged to retain capable officials regardless of partisan influence; promised to stabilize the currency and pay the government's debts; and swore to root out corruption. To underscore his independence from all special interests, he asserted that it was his "inflexible purpose" not to seek a second term. With respect to the South, he also spoke ambiguously. The South deserved peace, he said, but "there can be no enduring peace if the constitutional rights of any portion of the people are habitually disregarded." Was he speaking of Black voters—or to the embittered whites? Or both?

Those who were already familiar with Hayes thought him a superb candidate, a reformer to his bones, yet still a loyal party man who understood how to work with the satraps who wielded so much power at its core. But he remained a cipher to many. A reporter wondered, "Is he a figurehead or a man of force? Has he the intellectual breadth requisite for grasping the great features of the political situation? Has he the self-absorbent independence of a statesman, or is he a man of putty and a tame repeater of party shibboleths? Is he less than his party or greater? Can he mold it, or will he be molded by it?"

ALEXANDER GRAHAM BELL was locked in a tense contest of his own as he rode through Boston with his fiancée, Mabel Hubbard, on the morning of June 15. Until they arrived at the railroad station he didn't grasp that he was being shanghaied. For weeks, Mabel's father, Bell's main financial backer, had pressured him to hurry to the Centennial, where expert judges were to examine the latest electrical inventions. Without Bell there in person to explain his work, Hubbard feared, the telegraphy awards would all go to Elisha Gray, who was already in Philadelphia. There was Thomas

Edison, too, of course. Edison did not yet think of telephony as a transmission of pure sound, as did Bell and Gray, but rather as a system of signals to be decoded and then printed, but he could hardly be ignored. Several of his latest inventions were already on display, including an "electric pen," essentially an early version of a copier, which could produce several duplicate documents at the same time; a "quadruplex telegraph," which could transmit four messages along the same line simultaneously; the high-speed "automatic telegraph"; and, just possibly, his "harmonic telegraph," a precursor to the telephone.

Time was short, but Bell resisted the pressure to leave Boston. His telephone, he felt, was insufficiently perfected to be shown. Mabel then intervened, telling him disingenuously that he needed to get out of his lab for some fresh air. When they arrived at the station, Mabel pressed on him a ticket to Philadelphia along with his suitcase, which she had secretly packed. Bell protested that he had exam papers to write, lectures to prepare, exams to correct, speeches to write. Mabel burst into tears and refused to marry him unless he got on the train. Between changing trains in New York, he wrote to his mother, "When I saw how pale and anxious she was about it I couldn't resist her," adding forlornly, "What I am going to do in Philadelphia I cannot tell." To Mabel herself—he wrote to her almost every day—he promised to try to be patient in Philadelphia, for her sake, though he didn't see what good he could accomplish: "I shall feel far happier and more honoured if I can send out a band of competent teachers of the deaf and dumb who will accomplish a good work—than I should be to receive all the telegraphic honours in the world."

His most important equipment—packed and sent on by his assistant—had been damaged in transit: Seven glass cells were smashed, parts of the telephone flattened, and the organ he would play for the judges as a demonstration of electrical communication had completely disappeared in transit. Writing to Mabel from Philadelphia, he groaned that he was sorry he'd come and threatened to return to Boston on the evening train. He had been told by the Centennial authorities, or so he thought, that his apparatus had "no right" to be included at such a late date. "If I can't get them in openly, I won't put them in at all," Bell sulked. "I do not care who gets the glory of the telegraphic inventions."

Despite his grumbling, and probably with Gardiner Hubbard's assistance, Bell's apparatus was assigned a place in the Main Building. The damaged parts were repaired or replaced, and the organ miraculously turned up unharmed at his hotel. Space was made for drawings of Bell's inventions in the Massachusetts state exhibit, along with a display of his Visible Speech books and charts. And Willie Hubbard, Mabel's brother, hurried from Boston to help. Bell somehow found time to play the tourist and was particularly amazed by the 4,000-pound lump of silver from Mexico, the handiwork of the Chinese, a display of American-made clocks and watches, and a "splendid" exhibit of tuning forks. Nevertheless, he remained intensely nervous, worrying that the judges would find his apparatus embarrassingly "feebler" than Gray's.

Sunday, June 25, had been chosen for the demonstration of audio devices because the exhibition buildings were otherwise empty (and quiet), in submission to the religious prerogatives of Philadelphia's churchmen, who opposed opening on the sabbath. With relief, Bell found the chief judge, Sir William Thomson, who had helped design the first transatlantic cable, to be friendly and "very plebian" in demeanor, and endowed with a "good, broad, Scotch accent." Edison hadn't shown up to demonstrate any of his devices in person. Moreover, his submissions were subsumed in the sprawling Western Union exhibit and drew less attention than they might have, although Sir William did praise the quadruplex telegraph for its "exquisite ingenuity." Edison's "harmonic telegraph"—his proto-telephone—could be seen only in the form of sketches and diagrams. There was no model to show whether it would work. Gray's display, however, generously funded by Western Union, gave cause for worry. Bell surmised that Gray's design would be extremely expensive to operate compared to his own, a significant concern for consumers, if either system was to be commercially viable. Nonetheless, the sight of the Ohioan's "complicated and beautifully made apparatus" left Bell feeling underprepared and "heartbroken," and wishing the whole ordeal were over.

Bell joined a party of fifty or so who had gathered to watch Gray's demonstration, including the judges—a Canadian geologist, a pair of astronomers, a "geodesist" from the U.S. Coast Survey, all suffocating in formal black broadcloth—along with their wives, a bevy of journalists, and the inquisitive Dom Pedro and his empress, with her Brazilian ladies-in-waiting. When Gray electrically transmitted the strains of "Home Sweet Home" three hundred feet across the hall, it caused a sensation. Bell noted, however, that Gray, brilliant technician that he was, was "not a scientific man" and had had to recruit a professor from the University of Pennsylvania to explain the theoretical aspect of his system to observers. By the time Gray had finished, the judges and their entourage were withering from the heat, made all the more intense by the glass shell of the hall. They were on the brink of quitting from exhaustion when Dom Pedro happened to notice Bell in the crowd and greeted him, elatedly remembering their meeting in Boston a month earlier, and thanking him again for the books on Visible Speech that Bell had given him. Dom Pedro's enthusiasm spurred the flagging judges to continue on to Bell's exhibit, at the far end of the immense hall.

Bell had placed chairs around a small table that held a set of two current interrupters, with tuned receivers, each equipped with a vibratory circuit-breaker—to demonstrate harmonic multiple-telegraphy. There was also an "iron-box receiver": a hollow iron cylinder three inches long and closed at one end, with an iron rod inside and wrapped in a coil of insulated copper wire. A current sent through the wire would turn the device into an electromagnet. An iron lid fastened to the open end would function as a diaphragm that responded to the undulatory current. Wires ran along the railing of the gallery to Bell's transmitters, about a hundred yards away. These consisted of a variable resistance transmitter with a slender rod projecting from a membrane into a small cup of conductive liquid and two electromagnetic transmitters.

Bell offered to transmit a human voice, apologetically telling the judges that his device was but "an invention in embryo." He then went into a distant room and sang into the telephone, while Willie Hubbard monitored the receiver. In a letter to his father two days later, Bell described the moment: "Sir William listened and heard my voice distinctly. I then articulated the sentence 'Do you understand what I say?' Sir William started up exclaiming, 'Do you understand what I say?' He listened and said 'Yes—do you—understand—what I say?' He then exclaimed excitedly, 'Where is Mr. Bell—I must see Mr. Bell.'" Willie Hubbard began to lead him, but Thomson quickly outran him and suddenly came upon Bell shouting into the mouthpiece. He begged Bell to sing and then recite something. He listened and then started up with the exclamation "To be or not to be." Dom Pedro then pressed his imperial ear to the receiver and exclaimed in surprise, "I have heard!—I have heard!"

The rest of the entourage crowded around the table for a chance to hear Hamlet's famous soliloquy. One of them was Elisha Gray, who later testified that he heard a faint, ghostly ringing and the words "Aye, there's the rub." He turned to the audience and repeated the words, and they cheered. For an hour or more, oblivious now to the heat, men and women alike took turns talking and listening. When Dom Pedro asked if the machine could also speak Portuguese, he was thrilled to hear his native tongue, presumably from one of his aides stationed at the other end of the line. That night Bell raced home to Boston in order to administer the final exam to his students the next morning. His anxieties at last erased, he wrote excitedly to his father, "I have made a glorious success."

The Centennial's official report of the judges, penned by the eminent president of the Smithsonian Institution, Joseph Henry, declared Bell's invention "the greatest marvel hitherto achieved by the telegraph." One of the scientists who had accompanied Sir William Thomson wrote Bell a personal note predicting that "before long friends will whisper their secrets over the electric wire."

CHAPTER 5

THE DEMOCRATS RESURGENT

★ ★ ★ ★ ★

Reform! Reform! Reform!

—REPRESENTATIVE JOHN McCLERNAND

Compared to the free-for-all in Cincinnati, the Democratic National Convention two weeks later resembled a coronation. Betting was running five-to-one in favor of New York's governor, Samuel A. Tilden. The delegates who assembled in St. Louis were a mélange of disparate interests: states rights zealots, big-money men from the Northeast, Midwestern farmers demanding low tariffs and soft money, machine politicians who represented immigrants and workers, and white supremacists bent on regaining control of the Southern states. They fairly throbbed with anticipation at their return to power after long years in the wilderness. The convention was the first to be held beyond the Mississippi River, a symbolic punctuation of the nation's westward-shifting center of gravity. Bands thumped and blared, fireworks lit the night sky over the Mississippi, impromptu parades swarmed the streets in heat so sapping that marchers dropped in their tracks.

On June 27, the delegates crowded into the handsome new Merchants' Exchange building on Third Street, an Italianate showpiece adorned with mahogany paneling in the main hall, frescoed ceilings, and the seals of the states encircled by laurel wreaths. Augustus Schell, the chairman of the Democratic National Committee, reminded the delegates that exactly a century earlier, the continent's first popular assembly had met in Philadelphia to lay the foundation for American liberty. "In this Centennial year, the Democratic party has assembled to do that which our fathers did," but now to remedy the "sorrow and shame" that the Republicans had brought upon the nation.

The platform the delegates adopted—penned by the arch-Copperhead Manton Marble, a New York journalist—condemned the "rapacity of carpet-bag tyrannies in the South," and called for "rigorous frugality" in government, an end to the squandering of public lands for the benefit of railroads, an overhaul of the tariff system, and a total ban on immigration of "the Mongolian race." Speaker after speaker pictured the nation as failed state, a dystopian landscape filled with dying farms, shuttered factories, distraught workers, and withered commerce suffocated by the "tyrannical, corrupt, unscrupulous, and oppressive" rule of a Republican Party that had turned "organized charlatanism into a sort of public policy." Declared the convention's chairman, John McClernand, a congressman and former Union general, "The land is infected and blighted by spreading and cankering misrule," the Constitution trampled underfoot, and the civil service reeking with rottenness. "Is this the final outcome of essential republican self-government?" he cried. "Gracious God, forbid it! Reform! Reform! Reform! is the supreme commanding issue of the day. All else is trivial to it."

The lantern-jawed McClernand gestured repeatedly toward the white South. He condemned the Republicans' "centralization of power, political and monetary," and called for a revival of states' rights ideology. There were, he said pointedly, no longer any enemies to the nation except "the authors and abettors of administrative centralism." Among the nine hundred delegates, there was not a single African American. Instead, the convention was stuffed with wartime Copperheads and Confederates, including former

Confederate General Wade Hampton of South Carolina, who was soon to be tapped as the Democrats' champion for governor; William Breckinridge of Kentucky, a former bodyguard to Jefferson Davis; Edmund Pettus, a Ku Klux Klan leader from Alabama; and Fitzhugh Lee of Virginia, a nephew of Robert E. Lee. Senator Francis Kernan of New York flatteringly addressed the "warm-hearted men of the South" who, he astonishingly claimed, "have been trampled down, and have been wronged as no people ever have." The convention's only speech by a woman cast even feminism in a racist mold. "Are the rights of women in all the southern states, whose slaves are now their rulers, less sacred than those of the men of Louisiana?" demanded Phoebe Couzins of St. Louis.

During breaks between the speeches, delegates listened to Postlethwaite's band playing "Yankee Doodle," "Dixie," and other rousing tunes, chuckled to themselves over the steady drip of news stories about the sleaze in Washington, perused ads for thirst-quenching Anheuser's lager beer and for discounts on gents' gauze undershirts and side-laced shoes. They learned from the day's papers about Emperor Don Pedro's incognito ramblings through the Centennial in a democratically torn jacket and slouch hat, rumblings of war between Serbia and Turkey over an obscure region of the Balkans called "Bosnia-Herzegovina," the bill pending in Congress that would ban voting by Mormon polygamists in the Utah Territory, and the war brewing on the Western plains, where it was reported that Custer's force was approaching an immense Indian camp in the valley of the Rosebud River. "It is against this camp that Custer will soon move," the *New York Tribune* predicted. "The net is gradually being thrown around the swarthy Sitting Bull."

Exciting as such news was, it paled as the process of nominations unfolded. Tilden was not the only prospective candidate. There was Governor Thomas Hendricks of Indiana, a soft-money man and a wartime Copperhead who had opposed the Thirteenth, Fourteenth, and Fifteenth Amendments; the war hero Winfield Scott Hancock, of Pennsylvania, who had stood firm against Pickett's Charge at Gettysburg; and a handful of favorite sons. Few if any doubted that Tilden would win the prize, apart perhaps from a contingent of scowling Tammany Hall operatives from New York

City, who resented the governor for weakening their control of the state party. There was also a portion of the party, mainly Westerners, who disliked Tilden's Wall Street roots and hard-money views. But Tilden had laid the strategic groundwork for victory in what was the first truly modern political campaign in American history, dispatching an army of agents as far as California to scout the country for support; creating a "Literary Bureau" to manufacture colorful and easy-to-read handouts and brochures, along with a team that produced cartoons for distribution to newspapers; cultivating dissident Republicans such as Carl Schurz and Henry Cabot Lodge; and even gathering reports from college commencements in order to learn what young men were thinking. Now he had virtually colonized the convention, and indeed St. Louis itself. His supporters were posted in the lobbies of every hotel to buttonhole delegates. Rented shop windows showcased his portrait. His banners hung across the avenues. And in the convention hall, *The New York Times* reported, Tilden's paid "shouters" drowned out everyone else at every opportunity. As a New Jersey delegate was heard to say, "Sammy has all the politicians with him, all the money, all the brass bands, and all the gas."

Tilden's political ascent seemed meteoric for a man with a stiff, introverted personality and only modest officeholding experience, having served two terms in the New York State Assembly, and a year and a half as governor. Apart from his penetrating blue eyes, he was physically unimpressive: short and slight, nervous in his movements, with a round, bland face, and clean-shaven in an era of stylishly hirsute public men. A lifelong bachelor, he was born in 1814 in a small town south of Albany, to a father who turned a local trade in herbs into a lucrative patent medicine business. As a boy, he read prodigiously, devouring tomes like Adam Smith's *Wealth of Nations,* and immersing himself in the play of politics, with the encouragement of his family's friend and neighbor President Martin Van Buren. He began penning campaign materials for Van Buren before he was out of his teens. Trained in the law, he climbed steadily within the Democratic Party, while amassing a fortune as a corporate litigator specializing in the reorganization of failing railroads, earning the double-edged sobriquet "the Great

Forecloser." Senator John Sherman, a close observer, if a Republican, described him acutely as "a man of singular political sagacity, of great shrewdness, a money-making man."

In every era, there are politicians who excite the public with their gift for the theatrical and others whose field of action lies in the back room and the boardroom, and whose strategic gifts outrange those of their more charismatic rivals and allies. Tilden was one of the latter. Outside New York, few knew much about him except as the dragon-slayer who had brought down Boss Tweed and crippled the Tammany Hall machine. He possessed a masterly ability to straddle issues. Before the Civil War, he nominally opposed the extension of slavery, but in 1860 defended it as constitutionally protected, and denounced Lincoln for using force against the seceding South, excusing his early opposition to slavery as "youthful indiscretion." *The New York Times* labeled him "one of the most pliant tools of the slave power."

Tilden had nothing in common with the Democratic Party's working-class, immigrant rank and file, beyond the desire to maximize their vote at election time. Although dishonesty offended him and his wealth insulated him from personal corruption, he never emerged as a reformer until it became politically expedient in the late 1860s, when Tweed's shameless thievery had reached such gargantuan proportions that it could no longer be ignored. (Tweed boasted that during just one election he had shelled out the incredible sum of $600,000 to one man to buy votes wholesale, and bought off opposition Republican state senators for $40,000 a head.) Facing a political debacle, Tilden masterminded the prosecution of the worst offenders. Tweed and his closest henchmen went to jail. Tammany gained cleaner leadership, and Tilden emerged as the most powerful Democrat in New York. When Senator Kernan placed Tilden's name in nomination at the 1876 Democratic convention, he declared that Tilden would do for all Americans what he had done for New York.

Tilden won 417 votes on the first ballot, less than the two-thirds necessary, but far ahead of Hendricks's 149 and Hancock's 75, with an additional hundred votes scattered among the favorite sons. On the second ballot, Tilden swept the field, winning well over

500 votes outright, and was quickly declared the victor by unanimous consent. Even the Tammany men grudgingly accepted the inevitable. With no opposition, Hendricks was nominated as Tilden's running mate, uniting East and West, urban and rural Democrats, hard- and soft-money advocates in what the euphoric mass of delegates thought was certain to be a winning ticket.

Sure of the outcome, Tilden spent the day in Albany, talking tariffs and tax policy with a lawyer friend. At one point, he took out a carriage and raced it through the streets, terrifying his companion, then returned quietly to his home, where messenger boys from the nearest telegraph office brought him dispatches from the convention. When informed that he had prevailed, he remarked simply, "Is that so?" After a prolonged silence, he told journalists and friends who had gathered around him that the American people had asked for reform. "They have wanted it a long time, and in looking about they have become convinced that it is to be found here." He raised his hand and pointed at himself.

That evening, Tilden appeared in front of the illuminated statehouse atop the hill that overlooked the Hudson River as it flowed south toward New York City and the sea. Bonfires sprang up everywhere while a band serenaded the taciturn governor until he agreed to speak. Everywhere, he told a crowd of well-wishers, "abuses, peculations, frauds and corruption" had made Americans ashamed of their country. "Our centennial products are the evils to escape which our ancestors abandoned their homes in the Old World and planted themselves in the Wilderness." So predatory had the officeholding class now become that "the government no longer exists for the people" but the people for the government. "What is the remedy?" Roared thousands of voices, "The election of Tilden!"

In his letter of acceptance, which he issued in July, Tilden as expected promised to shrink government, cut taxes, and clean up chronic abuse in the civil service. Notably, he did not call for the enforcement of the postwar constitutional amendments, protection for Black voters, or for action against white terrorists in the South. Instead, he promised to bring an end to the "systematic and insupportable misgovernment imposed on the states" by "ignorant and dishonest administration," a formulation that echoed the disingenuous battle cry of the apologists for the former Confederacy.

SINCE THE END OF THE WAR, at least two thousand freed people had been murdered in an epidemic of persecution by the Ku Klux Klan. Thousands more had been beaten, shot, tortured, and driven from their homes and jobs. Backed by Congress, President Grant had dispatched federal troops into the worst nests of Klan activity, and by 1873 had broken it as a fighting force. Thousands of Klansmen were arrested, hundreds prosecuted, and some sent to federal prison. But Grant's success was his policy's undoing. As the Klan collapsed, Northern support for coercive measures faded. The new Democratic majority in the House of Representatives choked off funding for both the military in the South and the prosecution of terrorists. Although reactionary whites habitually denounced the so-called military occupation of the South, by 1876 there were just 3,300 federal troops stationed across the former Confederate states, apart from those on the Texas frontier.

Among unreconstructed whites, revanchism burgeoned. Deadly attacks on freed people resumed, without the Klan's spooky trappings: Perpetrators knew they were unlikely to ever be punished. In April 1873, between sixty and seventy Blacks were massacred by white vigilantes after a disputed election in Colfax, Louisiana, the vast majority after they had surrendered and been disarmed. In November 1874, at Eufala, Alabama, white gunmen murdered seven Black voters in broad daylight on Election Day, and swore to kill any Republicans who dared to take office. In December 1874, whites belonging to what they euphemistically called the "Tax-Payer's League" seized control of Vicksburg, Mississippi, and killed between fifty and a hundred people, the beginning of a slow-motion coup that in 1875 overthrew the legally elected Republican governor of the state. Isaac Bourne, a Mississippi freedman, one of many desperate Southern Blacks, wrote personally to Grant: "The White Peapel in Laurence County and in linclon County thae take up the Corldid Peapelan Haung thim. We are so Prass so We Cant Stand it."

In May 1876, two weeks after the opening of the Centennial, the *Chicago Inter-Ocean,* with little exaggeration, declared Southern Blacks defenseless against "negro-killing that goes on from day to day and week to week." Wherever freedmen lacked protection, the once-robust Black vote plummeted. All the former Confederate states except South Carolina, Louisiana, and Florida had already fallen to Democratic "Redeemers," who were busy looking for ways to permanently disenfranchise Black voters. In many localities, white Republicans began to shun Black candidates in a desperate effort to survive politically. The day the Centennial opened in Philadelphia, a prominent North Carolina churchman, S. Taylor Martin, declared to a gathering of Confederate veterans, "Slavery was a divine institution, and we must have that institution or the South will ever be bankrupt." He prayed that soon the Confederate flag would be "floating proudly over our sunny South."

At the same time, the increasingly conservative U.S. Supreme Court steadily weakened the ability of the government to enforce the equal rights provisions of the Fourteenth Amendment. In March 1876, in *United States v. Cruikshank,* the capstone of a series of decisions that essentially turned the Fourteenth Amendment inside out, the Court voided the indictments of the men—a token few, in any case—who had been convicted of murdering the Black Republicans in Colfax, Louisiana, ruling that the federal government lacked the authority to enforce the Bill of Rights within the states. "The people, for their protection in the enjoyment of [their rights] must therefore look to the states," Chief Justice Morrison R. Waite wrote. For Blacks and vulnerable white Republicans in Southern states that were determined to strip them of their rights, it was a devastating formulation. But the broader public was satisfied. *The New York Times,* a voice of the Republican leadership, praised Waite's "admirable clearness," while the Democratic *New York World* lavishly compared him to the luminaries of the early Court, John Jay and John Marshall.

Even the *New York Tribune,* once a clarion voice of abolitionism, now advocated a white supremacist line, telling its readers that outrages against Black Americans were mostly "myths." Advocates for civil rights were an increasingly rare species in Washington. Thaddeus Stevens, the most effective abolitionist in Congress, had died in 1868, and the silver-tongued Charles Sumner in 1874. Ben Wade was ousted from the Senate when the Democrats captured Ohio's state legislature, in 1874. Lyman Trumbull, the primary author of the Thirteenth Amendment, was about to abandon the Republican Party. Others had been swept out in the electoral debacle of 1874. Although Rutherford Hayes, James G. Blaine, and Roscoe Conkling had all pledged to defend Black Americans' rights, their political attention, along with the public's, was shifting elsewhere.

AMID THE ROILING uncertainties of 1876, Americans looked simultaneously to their future and their past for encouragement. History was treated as a gilded chamber of mirrors that flattered and reassured, reflecting back to Americans what they most wished to be true about themselves, assuring them that they lived in an ever-triumphant nation, not a deeply fissured one. At the Centennial, images and symbols of the American Revolution abounded. On one day in June, 150 spirited men from Hartford, Connecticut, calling themselves the "Putnam Phalanx" showed up wearing Continental Army uniforms. And just as the great Corliss Engine pointed the way to new national power, behemoth statues of Washington and Franklin that stood alongside those of Charlemagne, Shakespeare, and Confucius placed the United States at the culmination of civilization as heir to the culture of all the ages. In Memorial Hall, artworks by the sanctified American masters of the founding era, John Trumbull and Gilbert Stuart, were on prominent display. A spirited *Minute Man of 1776* by the young sculptor Daniel Chester French, representing a powerful young New England farmer who has dropped his plow and grasped his gun, was much praised. In the United States Government Building, like pilgrims in the presence of the sacred, visitors paid solemn homage to relics of the Puritans, and admired George Washington's buckskin breeches, his camp bed and table, sword and flintlock pistols, and surveyor's compass. There was more: the naval hero John Paul Jones's sword, a battery of bronze cannon presented to the United States by the Marquis de Lafayette, and a peculiarly inspiring confection that combined modern iron technology, epic sculpture, and national aspiration in a single luminous icon: a dazzling display of newly invented electric lights that illuminated the giant arm and torch of the as-yet-incomplete Statue of Liberty.

Marietta Holley's fictional "Samantha" captured the spirit that many Americans brought to the contemplation of patriotic artifacts. "Oh! What feelins' I did feel as I see that coat and vest that George had buttoned up so many times over true patriotism, truthfulness, and honor. The bed he had slept on, the little round table he had to eat on, the wooden bottomed chair he had sot down on, the belluses he had blowed the fire with in cold storms and discouragements . . . the bed quilts worked by his own mother . . . and then to see—a layin' on the bed—the cane that Benjamin give to George, and to see George's glasses and candle sticks, and trunk, and etcetery." Of her encounter with the Liberty Bell, Samantha exclaimed, "My emotions tuckered me out so that when I got to sleep that night, I was dreamin' that I was upon the top of that bell a swingin' over the land, soarin' right back and forth; a swingin' back into them times that tried men's and wimmin's souls, and then forth again into the glorious nineteenth century."

For countless visitors, such inspiring exhibits seemed to hold up the unity of the patriots of 1776 as a model for reconciliation between the North and South—at least among whites. The Centennial's commission hoped and expected that the Exhibition would do more to reunite the nation than any other event of the century. They were extremely sensitive to sectional wounds. They tried to avoid irritating white Southerners by discouraging exhibitors from calling too much attention to the Union victory or emancipation, in part by severely limiting the inclusion of African Americans. On Opening Day, when a company of Black soldiers—a most modest token of the 180,000 Black servicemen who helped the Union win the war—entered the exhibition grounds along with other military groups, the commissioners called it an accident. Whether by design or deliberate omission it is not clear, products and cultural artifacts from Africa were almost completely absent from the Centennial's exhibition halls, apart from the small display from the independent republic of Liberia and a few random items from European colonies.

No one worried about offending the sensibilities of Black Americans. Relatively few were to be seen among the hundreds of thousands of visitors, and those who did come were subject to the same thoughtless—or quite intentional—rudeness they experienced outside the Centennial's gates. A Black reporter dryly commented, "They say that if this is to be a white man's Centennial it is no concern of theirs." By contrast, white Southerners were warmly welcomed. *Scribner's Monthly* effused that Southerners were "the guests without whom we cannot get along—without whom there would be bitterness in our bread, sourness in our wine, and insignificance in our rejoicings." As noted, the Centennial's most popular eatery, the "Restaurant of the South," cheerily advertised "a band of old-time plantation 'darkies' who will sing their quaint melodies and strum the banjo" while patrons were served by Black waiters standing in for slaves. And one of the Centennial's most heavily attended single days was "Southern Day," dedicated to honoring and romanticizing the South, when as many as 170,000 visitors watched "gentlemen knights" garbed in "velvet, plumed hats, sashes, and colorful scarves" stage a tilting competition for the right to crown a "beauty queen," who was serenaded by another ensemble of "darkie" musicians.

Nevertheless, many Southerners were only too eager to find cause for offense. All but three former Confederate states—Tennessee, Mississippi, and Arkansas—spurned the official invitation to attend. Southern newspapers dismissed the entire Centennial as a "Yankee humbug" and "swindle," and a "bigoted sectarian show for the humiliation of the conquered South." They professed particular disgust at anything that reminded them of slavery. They erupted at the presence of a triptych by Thomas Waterman Wood that showed a freedom-seeking slave's transformation from fugitive, to Union soldier, to proud veteran; denounced a bronze statue of a Black man struggling with a bloodhound who had him by the throat as "a brazen slander on the Southern people"; assailed the statue of a muscled Negro bursting his chains; and proclaimed as a mere "dirty daub" a painting that portrayed Abraham Lincoln breaking the fetters of shackled slaves beneath the smiling eyes of angels. One Virginian was allegedly so revolted by the same painting that he turned on his heel, fled the Centennial, and caught the next train home. Others raged that a portrait of Robert E. Lee hadn't received prominent enough display and was too far from the center of the gallery.

Southerners also resented anything that even remotely seemed to celebrate the Union's victory, from the fairly numerous portraits of Lincoln, Grant, Seward, Stanton, and other wartime leaders, to the brooding larger-than-life statue known simply as *The American Soldier,* dressed in greatcoat and kepi, which stood between the Main Building and Memorial Hall. They complained most loudly about *The Battle of Gettysburg,* an epic canvas by Peter Rothermel, which at sixteen by thirty-two feet was the largest of all the 750 paintings in the American gallery. It was a dark, even hellish, but very powerful composition in shades of brown, gray, and blue beneath a brooding, smoke-filled sky, showing a compacted mass of federal soldiers repelling Pickett's Charge with a bristling wall of bayonets, the climactic moment of the battle that Americans considered the turning point of the war. Southerners claimed that simply hanging *Gettysburg* at all demonstrated a disgraceful lack of "common decency and taste," complaining that it spurred offensive memories that ought to remain buried.

Ironically, the painting was anything but triumphal in the way that Southerners alleged. Rather, it was a ruthless portrayal of the horrors of war, filled with bloody hand-to-hand combat, maddened faces, and the dead and dying trampled underfoot. Indeed, the two armies are barely distinguishable as they shoot, slug, stab, and hack at each other. Far more than a piece of Yankee propaganda, it was a realistic riposte to the romanticized and self-serving accounts of the war that were beginning to emerge in print, virtually all of them penned by generals for whom battles unfolded according to strategic logic, where heroism was de rigueur and carnage rarely acknowledged. Conciliation apart, papering over the war's horrors with platitudes doubtless also reflected a reluctance to evoke too bluntly the loss of hundreds of thousands of sons and brothers, an unhealed trauma that countless American families still found too painful to relive. It would be another generation before honest accounts by veterans like Ambrose Bierce and Frank Wilkeson punctured the sanitized misremembering of the war.

BLACK TOURISTS were disappointed to discover an artistic exclusion almost as thorough as the racial segregation of the Centennial's workforce. True, a painting by the Black landscape artist Edward Bannister was on display, and would win an award; ironically, his race would only be revealed in a scene of demeaning awkwardness later in the summer when the prizes were handed out. However, they could scarcely miss Edmonia Lewis, the single—and cockily assertive—exception to the racial erasure. She stood for hours at a stretch alongside her sculpture of Cleopatra's death, well aware that her very presence would attract attention amid the teeming maelstrom of the vast hall. A Black Washington lawyer and sometime writer, John Patterson Sampson, was admiring the statue where it sat beneath a colorful "Oriental" canopy—a characteristically flamboyant touch—when "a very ordinary looking colored girl (as I thought) offered very kindly to show me other statues carved by the same lady," and took him to see several representations of infants and of abolitionist luminaries. "I was more surprised when I found my guide, a plain and unassuming young woman, was the veritable sculptress herself."

Not everyone was as charmed as Sampson. The diminutive sculptor was insulted, spat at, and at least once struck by whites who were irate at the very sight of her, and doubly offended that she dared to advertise herself, so boldly inverting the docile self-effacement that Black Americans were expected to demonstrate. A reporter from Ohio seemed shocked that she was asking an astonishing $30,000 for her sculpture, and stuffily remarked that she seemed "very independent and somewhat insolent." How Lewis felt about such treatment isn't known since only fleeting traces of her feelings can be gleaned from her interviews. But she remained at her post until the close of the Centennial, a measure, perhaps, of both the emotional armor she had acquired and of her uncompromising commitment to her art.

Despite the abuse directed at Lewis personally, *The Death of Cleopatra* captivated visitors. One of the leading guides to the Centennial deemed it "the most remarkable piece of sculpture in the American section." *Cleopatra* was by far the largest sculpture that Lewis had ever undertaken: more than five feet in height and weighing more than 4,000 pounds. Thematically, it represented an ambitious break from the abolitionists' busts and sentimentalizing portrayals of Longfellow's Indians that had made her reputation in Rome. Cleopatra's story, at least the version presented by Shakespeare and known to readers of the Roman classics, was familiar to nineteenth-century audiences. As tradition had it, Cleopatra had loved both Julius Caesar and his younger protégé Mark Antony, and committed suicide by snakebite when she learned of the latter's death. To mid-Victorians, her death served as the very embodiment of thwarted love and woman martyred by fate, as well as a titillating evocation of female sexuality that was only partially sanctified by its classical cachet. Lewis's stated intent was to show the effect of death on beauty. The dying queen lay slumped on her lion-footed throne, in the throes of death, lips slightly parted, eyes sightless, her head flung back, one breast bared, the deadly asp still clasped in her hand. "The face wears a wearied, desperate expression," wrote a visitor from Chicago. Her "disgust and weariness of life is so intense, that she is indifferent to its poison and fangs. Her face represents a cruel, sensuous, and restless nature, without any satisfaction in the past, or hope for the future." It was a strange image, natural and at the same time ethereal, graceful and pain-filled, noble and voluptuous, poetically tendering the Victorian romance of death as an eternal, gentle sleep.

For Lewis, *Cleopatra* captured both a new depth of feeling and a technical delicacy that lifted her to the ranks of the most admired American artists of her time. In a sense, it seemed an unusual subject for a sculptor so rooted in the American experience. Like Lewis herself, however, Cleopatra was racially ambiguous. White artists typically presented her as Caucasian when stressing her nobility and beauty, but as "Oriental" when presenting her as a creature of pure passion, sometimes with "full Nubian lips, and other characteristics of the Egyptian physiognomy," as Nathaniel Hawthorne (admittedly, no anthropologist) put it. For abolitionists, there was yet another dimension. Cleopatra was commonly made to stand as a symbol of Africa and, by extension, "Blackness," proof of Africa's ancient greatness and the illustrious heritage of the contemporary Black diaspora. (This of course ignored the historical fact that ancient Egyptians were a people distinct from Black Africans, and that Cleopatra was of Greek lineage.) Lewis, interestingly enough, chose to portray her Cleopatra with classically European features and with no obvious reference to her "African" aspect. Her Cleopatra was neither Black nor white (one critic thought she looked Jewish), neither African nor European, but rather a tragic image of human mortality.

Lewis told John Patterson Sampson that when the Centennial was over, she was "going back to Italy to do something for the race—something that will excite the admiration of the other races of the earth." Whatever she might have meant by that, she would do it in her own way. She hadn't hesitated to exploit the public appetite for works that traded on her exotic background. But she also declined to be confined to the public's racial expectations. In Europe, she lived as an artist and as a free woman, who happened incidentally to be Black, or Indian when called for. She was never explicitly political; as a Black woman, politics as such was never open to her. She's not known to have ever given a political speech, or to have advocated publicly for civil rights. She was not confrontational by nature, although she showed that she was willing to stand up for herself during her crisis at Oberlin College, then among the upper-class abolitionists of Boston, and later among the art connoisseurs of Rome. She wanted her art to speak for itself. At the same time, she of course knew that she was not just Edmonia Lewis, a colorful young New Yorker. She knew that her success was on some plane also that of both her peoples, in a society that still largely denied the basic humanity of women like her.

A Black journalist visiting the Centennial observed sadly as he wandered through the Main Building that "you are surrounded with the productions and representations of every nation, save that of Africa; and anyone who is interested in any way in that race of people feels that there is something wrong somewhere; somebody has been left out, or to say the least have been overlooked." Of Edmonia Lewis, he then went on to write, *The Death of Cleopatra* was not only the artist's singular achievement, "but it wipes out the burning stigma that has been for centuries fastened upon this would-be prosperous people. It brands the nation with shame before God and, in the eyes of man, and renders Miss Lewis's name conspicuous among the most eminent and skillful artists of ancient or modern times." With *Cleopatra*, Lewis was negotiating a path between the abolitionist past and the post-Reconstruction future. Had she read about the nomination of Samuel Tilden and the Democratic platform, about the convention stocked with so many former Confederates and their plans to overthrow biracial government in the South? It's unknowable. Lewis wanted to succeed on talent alone, to be judged by her works, a perhaps impossible ambition in the America of the late 1870s. But she could hardly fail to be aware that there were forces at work that wanted to erase her future.

CHAPTER 6

INDEFATIGABLE WOMEN

★ ★ ★ ★ ★

> The aristocracies of the old world are based upon birth, wealth, refinement, education, nobility, brave deeds of chivalry; in this nation, on sex alone.
>
> —SUSAN B. ANTHONY

On the night of July 3, Philadelphia exploded as music, bell-ringing, the firing of cannon, and spectacular fireworks split the darkness in an extravaganza of sound and light. Uproarious crowds flooded into town to celebrate the Fourth of July, the patriotic linchpin of the entire Centennial. Elaborate pyrotechnic "conjurations" allegorized the birth of the republic in fiery images representing the thirteen original states, an immense temple symbolizing the rise and progress of America, and the conjoining of the North Star and the Southern Cross alongside the motto "Let Brotherly Love Continue." At sunrise, more artillery boomed, horns blared, church bells clanged, whistles hooted from steamboats and locomotives, and guns thundered from warships moored in the Delaware, in a deafening national salute that rolled from one end of the city to the other. Trumpeted a correspondent for *The New York Herald,* "The Fourth of July was to the third like Pelion piled on Ossa, a sky-aspiring peak of the Himalayas, with a range of the Colorado Rocky Mountains for its pedestal."

At 10 a.m., the greatest military parade the city had seen since the end of the Civil War set off down Chestnut Street, regiments fast-marching, their multihued uniforms aglow and bayonets gleaming in the sun, to the beating of drums and the peal of a 13,000-pound replica of the Liberty Bell cast from melted-down weapons from America's wars. (The original bell was not rung because of its crack.) Some 50,000 men, women, and children filled the area in front of Independence Hall, with many thousands more packed into the adjoining streets, filling every window, and clinging precariously to trees, at least some of which were old enough to have witnessed the stirring events of a century before. Facing the sweltering multitude, dignitaries sat in dense rows on an immense wooden platform festooned with the national colors, prominent among them Senate President Pro Tem Thomas Ferry of Michigan, Generals William Tecumseh Sherman and Philip Sheridan, members of the president's cabinet, Republican presidential candidate Rutherford B. Hayes, Pennsylvania Governor Hartranft, the Emperor Dom Pedro (of course), Prince Oscar of Sweden, General Saigo, the commander of the Japanese army, a French marquis, an abundance of politicians and foreign envoys of every category, and, more significantly than anyone yet realized, five radical women with a plan.

After making a few remarks, Joseph Hawley turned the program over to the amiable Senator Ferry, who since the death of Henry Wilson in November had been serving as Grant's de facto vice president, and was standing in for him this day. (Grant, after being obliged to shake hands with between five and six hundred "Centennial pilgrims" *per day,* who stopped in Washington to visit him en route to Philadelphia, simply couldn't face the July 4 crowd, and had gone to the beach at Long Branch, New Jersey, to recuperate.) Ferry then introduced Richard Henry Lee, Robert E. Lee's cousin, to "thunders of applause from the multitude." As Lee, a spare man with a modest demeanor, stepped to the rostrum, Mayor William Stokely of Philadelphia brandished aloft "the immortal document" encased in a mahogany frame to a "general delirium."

Even Dom Pedro tossed his imperial hat in the air. "The voice of the multitude was like a mighty cataract," gushed *The New York Times*'s reporter. Cheer upon cheer rose, with a clamor that the document should be turned around so that all "however distant, might catch at least glimpse of the sacred charter of our freedom . . . I was reminded of Moses when he came down from the fiery heights of Sinai, and held out to the kneeling children of heaven the stony tables on which were graven the commandments of God."

As Lee finished reading, the five women rose from their seats on the platform, in the lead Susan B. Anthony, her thick brown hair pulled tight as a helmet over her ears, followed by the veteran abolitionist Matilda Joslyn Gage, the novelist Lillie Devereux Blake, and Sara Spencer and Phoebe Couzins, who respectively had spoken a few weeks earlier on behalf of women's rights at the Republican and Democratic National Conventions. They advanced toward Thomas Ferry, barely noticed in the bustling prelude to the performance of the Brazilian national anthem, offered as a courtesy to Dom Pedro. Addressing Ferry politely as "Mr. President," Anthony handed him a scroll fat with signatures. It was titled "Declaration of Rights of the Women of the United States, July 4, 1876." The encounter took less than a minute, but symbolically it was one of the most fateful events of the Centennial year. Ferry, who probably knew who Anthony was, went pale as he took the scroll, too polite to refuse it in front of the assembled multitude, but too nonplussed to speak. The women turned, scattering printed copies of the Declaration among the dignitaries as they made their way off the stage.

No woman more fully represented the steely edge of the suffrage movement than Anthony, not even her more ebullient but equally radical political partner, Elizabeth Cady Stanton. They were a dynamic pair, whose friendship lasted more than fifty years: the matronly and charming Stanton, and the often spiky Anthony. As indefatigable as ever at fifty-six, Anthony had spent her entire life steeped in aspirational reform. Raised in a Quaker home that was in equal parts egalitarian and puritanical, she was forbidden "distractions" such as music and games, but taught that women and men alike shared equally in the Inner Light of godliness. Although most suffragists were married, contrary to popular stereotypes that portrayed them as cranky old maids, Anthony remained defiantly single, telling her diary at the age of nineteen that she did not want to be a man's "political slave," and an interviewer many years later, "I never felt I could give up my life of freedom to become a man's housekeeper." Before the war, she tirelessly organized antislavery and temperance societies across the Northeast, repeatedly facing verbal abuse, mobs, rotten eggs, threats of violence, and on at least one occasion the sight of herself being burned in effigy. Since the war, she had thrown her energy into the cause of women's suffrage with single-minded intensity. In one recent year, she and Stanton had traveled together more than 13,000 miles, as far west as Oregon and California, and delivered at least 170 lectures, probably many more.

They and Matilda Gage, the president of the National Woman Suffrage Association, led the more radical wing of the women's movement, which sought to pressure the federal government to recognize suffrage as a constitutional right. The less confrontational American Woman Suffrage Association, led by Lucy Stone, pursued an alternative strategy toward the same long-term goal, lobbying state legislatures to achieve suffrage piecemeal, a politically riskier approach since state laws could always be repealed. The two groups had split in 1868 in the struggle over the Fifteenth Amendment. Stone's faction supported it while the NWSA, despite its leaders' abolitionist roots, denounced it, in Anthony's cruel words, as an insult to white women, having elevated two million Black men to the dignity of citizenship and "dethroned fifteen million white women and cast them under the heel of the lowest orders of manhood." Both organizations, however, were committed to the enlargement of women's freedom in the workplace and the home, where under the laws of most states men still exerted virtually feudal power within the family.

By 1876, Anthony and Stanton were feeling desperate. They had lobbied aggressively but vainly for Congress to declare that the Fourteenth and Fifteenth Amendments implicitly incorporated women's suffrage. Thwarted by Congress's inaction, they then appealed to the U.S. Supreme Court, which ruled in 1875 that nothing in the Fourteenth Amendment guaranteed women—or anyone else—a right to vote, asserting that it fell under the purview of state rather than federal law, an outcome so devastating to suffragists that Anthony likened it to the *Dred Scott* decision. (It was one of a series of brutal decisions by the increasingly conservative Court, which gutted the civil rights guarantees of the postwar amendments and made it possible for Southern states to craft Jim Crow laws that stripped the hard-won franchise from Black Americans through a battery of discriminatory measures.) Defeated again, the radicals turned their rhetorical guns on Philadelphia, determined to expose the hypocrisy of the Centennial's celebration of democracy while the nation denied just that to half its population. They established a command center on Chestnut Street, filling its parlors with feminist books, tracts, speeches, and the texts of laws that repressed woman. Stanton, Anthony, and Gage worked sixteen hours a day with "many twists from our analytical tweezers," in Stanton's words, crafting one of the most powerful pieces of rhetoric ever deployed on behalf of an American cause.

AFTER THEIR STARTLING APPEARANCE on the main stage, Anthony and her friends marched to the far side of Independence Square where another group of women, including Stanton and the seventy-eight-year-old Quaker activist Lucretia Mott, had commandeered a bandstand. Gage popped open an umbrella to shelter Anthony from the sun—the temperature was by now in the nineties—and in her decisive Yankee voice Anthony began to read the Declaration. It eloquently seized the language of antislavery idealism and the American Revolution to equate women with the patriots who overthrew British repression. It also, provocatively indeed, suggested that the nation's history was less one that called for an unquestioning celebration of its values than it was a century-long failure of American democracy to live up to its aspirations. Among the many scores of speeches that were delivered at the Centennial, only Anthony's seriously came to grips with the contradiction that lay embedded in the Revolution's still unfulfilled promise of freedom and equality for all. Words that she applied persuasively to the millions of women excluded from the most basic rights of citizenship could also be applied to Black Americans who were being terrorized for attempting to exercise their right to vote, as well as to Native Americans, and embattled Chinese immigrants, who almost no one considered fit for citizenship, or even to consort on an even plane with white Americans. Was America really what it claimed to be, Anthony seemed to ask.

"While the nation is buoyant with patriotism, and all hearts are attuned to praise, it is with sorrow we come to strike one discordant note," Anthony declared. "The history of our country the past hundred years has been a series of assumptions and usurpations of power over woman. For the violation of these fundamental principles of our government, we arraign our rulers on this Fourth day of July, 1876." She charged that unconstitutional "bills of attainder" had been passed by the introduction of the word "male" into all the state constitutions, effectively denying to women the right of suffrage, "and thereby making sex a crime." The writ of habeas corpus, the most basic protection against unjust imprisonment, she continued, had been effectively nullified for married women by treating the marital rights of the husband as always primary. For women, she said, the right to trial by a jury of one's peers had also been negated, since women could not serve on juries but instead were "tried in all cases by men, native and foreign, educated and ignorant, virtuous and vicious." During the last presidential campaign, Anthony said, a woman had even been arrested for voting and was denied the protection of a jury, and tried, convicted, and fined.

Anthony was here alluding to her own experience. In 1872, she and fourteen other women had been arrested in Rochester for voting for President Grant. She had read the Fourteenth Amendment aloud to the male election inspectors, pointing out that it made no discrimination based on sex, and threatened to sue them in criminal court if they refused to permit her to cast her ballot. They reluctantly agreed to let her vote, at which point she was arrested on the spot, hauled into court, and fined $100, which on principle she refused to pay, telling the judge that she had no assets but only debt, incurred in publishing the suffragist journal *The Revolution*—"the sole object of which was to educate all women to do precisely as I have done, rebel against your man-made, unjust, unconstitutional forms of law." The government wisely dropped its case.

The Declaration further pointed out that women were taxed without political representation to support standing armies and "a dangerous army of civilians, buying and selling the offices of government and sacrificing the best interests of the people. And, moreover, we are taxed to support the very legislators and judges who make laws and render decisions adverse to woman." Fundamental human rights had thus been made "the football of legislative caprice." In most states, women were legally treated as perpetual minors; in some, a married woman was allowed to hold property and transact business, but in others her earnings belonged to her husband. Women commonly had no redress in case of damage to their person, property, or character, and in case of divorce, even on account of a husband's adultery, they had no right to their own children or property, unless by a special court decree. "By establishing an aristocracy of sex," Anthony asserted, the restriction of suffrage to men alone "imposes upon the women of this nation a more absolute and cruel despotism than monarchy; in that, woman finds a political master in her father, husband, brother, son. The aristocracies of the old world are based upon birth, wealth, refinement, education, nobility, brave deeds of chivalry; in this nation, on sex alone; exalting brute force above moral power, vice above virtue, ignorance above education, and the son above the mother who bore him."

In conclusion, she ringingly declared, "Now, at the close of a hundred years, as the hour-hand of the great clock that marks the centuries points at 1876, we declare our faith in the principles of self-government; our full equality with man in natural rights; that woman was first made for her own happiness, with the absolute right to herself—to all the opportunities and advantages life affords for her complete development; and we deny that dogma of the centuries, incorporated in the code of all nations—that woman was made for man—her best interests, in all cases to be sacrificed to his will. We ask of our rulers, at this hour, no special favors, no special privileges, no special legislation. We ask justice, we ask equality, we ask that all the civil and political rights that belong to citizens of the United States, be guaranteed to us and our daughters forever."

Probably only a few hundred women and men heard Anthony's words. No technology yet existed to amplify sound. Thousands, however, read the Declaration in the broadsides that the women distributed. Many were dismissive. One male journalist mocked the "indefatigable ladies" who advocated for women's rights, predicting that "this movement, all this efflux of female eloquence will soon vanish like smoke [since] the principal agitators have not the sympathy of the mass of women." Yet, if only symbolically, the women's Declaration was one of the most significant events of the Centennial year. Anthony was speaking as forcefully as the Corliss Engine and the Gatling gun to the future, although the manifold transformations in American life that she demanded still lay beyond the ken of the vast majority of women. But there were men who could see it, too. "The day is coming when the deep questions of woman's entrance amid the arenas of practical life, politics, trades, &c., will not only be argued all around us, but may be put to decision and real experiment," Walt Whitman wrote, a day when women would finally be "extricated from this daze, this fossil and unhealthy air which hangs about the word Lady," and raised "to become the robust equals, workers and, it may be, even practical and political deciders with the men . . . and launch forth, as men do, amid real, independent, stormy life."

Meanwhile, back on the main stage across the square, the noted poet Bayard Taylor—filling the official slot that Whitman had hoped to win for himself—was delivering his "National Ode," a seemingly interminable poem that was reassuringly flattering to the national self-image. Hearts thrilled to his invocation of the feminized spirit of Manifest Destiny, soaring with its racial throb:

She planted homes on the savage sod—
Into the wilderness lone
She walked with fearless feet,
In her hand the divining rod,
Till the veins of the mountains beat
With fire of metal and force of stone.

She set the speed of the river-head
To turn the mills of her bread;
She drove her plowshare deep
Through the prairie's thousand centuries' sleep.
. . .
The race, in conquering,
Some fierce Titanic joy of conquest knows
Our ancient blood beats restless in repose.

Although few visitors to the Centennial heard Anthony's Declaration, they did, in enormous numbers, encounter an alternative, quasi-feminist world at the handsome pale gray 30,000-square-foot building behind the Main Building, dubbed the Women's Pavilion. Beneath its elegantly arched ceiling, they could explore more than eighty exhibits arrayed in vitrines around a burbling fountain surrounded by a ferny rockery. The suffragists had no part in creating the pavilion. It was the singular achievement of Benjamin Franklin's great-granddaughter, the Philadelphia socialite Elizabeth Duane Gillespie. A year younger than Anthony, she had been steeped from birth in patriotism, having been raised among family mementos of the Revolutionary era and fellow descendants of the Founders, who taught her to regard the nation's traditions almost as family property. Unusual for her class and time, she was a single mother, having raised her daughter, Ellen, alone, apparently walking out on her husband after a very brief marriage, about which she left not even a wisp of information in her 1901 autobiography. She was long-faced and formidable, and often for official events in the Centennial year costumed like Martha Washington, in a mob cap and homespun dress with a white collar. Patrician though she might be, she nonetheless had a gift for making things happen. She founded the local chapter of the Colonial Dames, lobbied for the establishment of Flag Day as a national holiday, and pioneered the restoration of historic homes. When the Centennial's organizers sought to raise funds from American women, she was the natural choice to lead the campaign.

Gillespie first recruited a committee of women from among Philadelphia's moneyed elite and initiated an effort that would eventually net close to $1 million, including a $200,000 donation from the Pennsylvania Railroad, authorized by its then-president, J. Edgar Thomson, whose wife served as one of Gillespie's key lieutenants. They quickly established branches in twenty-four states and several of the Western territories. Their stagy fund-raisers were widely imitated across the country. A spectacular "Centennial Tea Party" featured five hundred women all dressed as Martha Washington, sipping tea at tables decorated with scraps of old flags, cannonballs, portraits of the Founders' wives, and flowers arranged in the shape of the Liberty Bell, the Battle of Bunker Hill, and Indians throwing tea from a British ship. To raise money, the committee sold thousands of teacups endorsed with John Hancock's famous signature, and patriotic swag such as silver medallions and linen napkins sporting Martha Washington's image. The committee also sponsored a bestselling all-American cookbook packed with sometimes surprising recipes: "General Washington's Breakfast Cake," "Lafayette Ginger Bread," Ben Franklin's favorite pickles, "Baked Matzoh Pudding," "Idaho Method of Roasting a Deer's Head," and "Seven Recipes from an Oneida Squaw," which included preparations for woodchuck, muskrat, and mud turtle. Gillespie's approach reached its zenith in the insistent sanctification of Martha Washington, who was portrayed as a model of staunch republican selflessness, a simple farmer's wife who wore homespun, rose with the sun, and gave her all along with her husband to the Revolution. This idealized image completely erased slavery from the Washingtons' lives. George, who was deeply ambivalent about slavery, in his will freed every slave he held in his own name; Martha freed none. The radical feminists, as an alternative to the aristocratic Martha, celebrated Abigail Adams, often citing her warning that women were not bound to obey laws in which they had no voice.

In return for her herculean fund-raising efforts, Gillespie expected that her organization would be assigned space for women's exhibits in a prominent location in the Main Hall. Then, in June 1875, ten months before the opening, the Centennial's director-general, Alfred T. Goshorn, abruptly informed that there would be no room for the women, and that their space would be allotted to foreign exhibitors. Gillespie immediately fell into a funk of "utter misery," feeling that her years of labor had gone to waste. On reflection, however, she told herself, "Unless we acted wisely, the womankind in America would be filled with righteous indignation and their work be nowhere." Women would have to erect their own building. "Up went my courage like a thermometer on a warm day." Reinvigorated, she and the committee managed to raise tens of thousands of dollars for what became the Women's Pavilion. Although Gillespie and her social register friends shunned radical rhetoric, they sought exhibits that would showcase a wide range of women's achievements. Wrote Gillespie, "We desired to give to the mass of women, who were laboring with the needle and obtaining only a scanty subsistence, the opportunity to see what women were capable of attaining unto in other and higher branches of industry. We did not shrink from competition with the works of men, but we sought to show our more timid sisters that some women had outstripped them in the race for useful and remunerative employment, and to encourage them."

The pavilion's exhibits looked simultaneously to the past and the future. Gillespie herself provided a letter from George Washington to her grandmother, along with Benjamin Franklin's table and chess set. There were vaguely historical odds and ends, such as a pair of red-white-and-blue mittens contributed by the daughter of a Revolutionary War veteran, jewelry made from fish scales by Thomas Jefferson's granddaughters, and a handwoven woolen tapestry of Washington's triumphal entrance into Trenton during the Revolutionary War. Other exhibits highlighted traditional domestic arts: needlework (including examples sent by Queen Victoria), weaving, waxed fruit, embroidery, pressed flowers, and—a favorite of visitors—an astonishingly lifelike sculpture of *Dreaming Iolanthe* made of butter by a woman in Arkansas. There were much-praised headboards, cabinets, and other home furnishings hand-carved by women from the Cincinnati School of Design, woman-designed fabrics and wallpaper, exquisitely engraved illustrations for a medical text on the microchemistry of poisons, an entire section devoted to photographs by women, and more than eighty patented women's inventions: an improved sewing machine, a device to speed dishwashing, a griddle greaser, a self-heating iron, a frame for stretching lace curtains, a glove-darner, an innovative mattress that had been acquired by the navy, a system of flares that had been adopted in five countries. Anthony's suffragists of the NWSA supplied a vitrine illustrating women's protests against taxation without representation, but Gillespie's controversy-averse minions put it almost out of sight in a dim corner of the pavilion.

Although the pavilion eschewed the political rhetoric of the Women's Declaration, it too pointed the way toward the future with its vision of ever more varied roles for American women, demonstrating how deeply feminist assumptions had already percolated into the aspirations of even more conservative women. Educational exhibits provided information about women's charitable organizations and colleges, including two medical institutions—the Female Medical College of Pennsylvania and the New York Infirmary and Medical College for Women—which promoted careers for women in medicine and pharmacy. Visitors could peruse the work of female botanists and zoologists, and an entire library of books by women writers from popular novels to a translation of the Bible by a woman from Connecticut. As wide-ranging as the pavilion's exhibits were, they paid little attention to the female working class; while they encouraged educated women to pursue professional careers, they scorned factories as hotbeds of vice that spoiled women for marriage and motherhood.

A popular annex to the pavilion enclosed an entire working kindergarten—a recent German innovation until now barely known to Americans—replete with orphaned girls and boys recruited from a local orphanage managed by one of Gillespie's friends, Louise Claghorn. As if at a theatrical performance, visitors sitting in a gallery observed the children, who sat at a long table where they were taught their lessons without the harsh discipline typical of American schools, on the principle that gentle nurturing would elicit their natural talents by inculcating harmony, cooperation, and civic virtue. Although it was not the first kindergarten in America, it was widely publicized and would help shape a changing perception of childhood for generations to come.

All in all, female visitors found the pavilion thrilling and revelatory. For Marietta Holley's fictional "Samantha," the countrified tourist from upstate New York, it was an epiphany.

> I can truly say without lyin' that my emotions as I went through that buildin' was larger in size and heftier in weight than any emotions I had enjoyed sense I had been to the Sentinel. Oh! Such proud and lofty feelins as I did enjoy a seein' the work of my sect from all over the length and breadth of the world. The wonderful, useful inventions of the sect, showin' the power and solid heft of her brains; the beautiful works of art showin' her creative artist soul, and provin' plain the healthy and vigorous state of her imagination. Oh! I can truly say that I felt perfectly beautiful, a goin' through them noble halls.

The pavilion's most popular exhibit by far was not in a vitrine. It was Miss Emma Allison of Ontario, an "educated and accomplished lady," who operated the six-horsepower engine that generated energy for all the looms and spinning frames and other machinery in the hall. Sitting in her small control room, she chatted amiably to curious visitors astonished at the seemingly impossible sight of a female engineer, brightly explaining to them that her work was no harder than overseeing a cookstove, and considerably less than minding a small child. Miss Allison was more than a curiosity. Her presence was both a revelation and a revolution, proof that women deserved a place in the new world of evolving technology, and that they could do so with undiminished femininity.

Allison's engine also powered a cylinder press that printed the weekly *New Century for Women,* an eight-page newspaper entirely written and edited by women, and was, in the prissily reassuring words of Elizabeth Duane Gillespie, "a sheet that could be read by any young person without detriment," since it contained no accounts of prizefights, "ghastly" deaths, or excessive French fashions. What the *New Century* did publish, until it closed with the Centennial in November, was a steady diet of serious articles on women's domestic and professional work, educational opportunity, clothing reform, property and inheritance laws, critiques of male authority in the home, women's financial autonomy, and such public issues as the "Chinese question." Declared one editorial, "The modern woman must not be confined 'within four walls' but be able to move outward withersoever her own purpose or the needs of others call her to go."

NEITHER VISITORS to the pavilion nor readers of the *New Century* would find any mention of—much less any work by—Edmonia Lewis, who was the living embodiment of precisely the values of ambition, autonomy, and professional success that Gillespie celebrated, but studiously ignored when it came to African Americans, no matter how talented. The Black women who had offered to collaborate with Gillespie's committee were told to work by themselves and informed that if they didn't approve they were welcome to emigrate to Africa. Snidely reported a New Jersey newspaper, "Silk refused to herd with calico—cologne couldn't stand musk." In the sixty pages of her memoir that Gillespie devoted to the Centennial, she said nothing about the Black women's thwarted efforts; and although she had much to say about her ancestor Benjamin Franklin, she didn't mention that he had been president of the Pennsylvania Emancipation Society and the city's most prominent enemy of slavery.

THE OFFICIAL Fourth of July program was also segregated. The day's main orator, the former U.S. Attorney General and well-known Republican reformer William M. Evarts, did refer passingly to slavery, perhaps the only such mention that anyone made from the main stage that day. After at great length enumerating the contributions of various European peoples to the nation's growth, he alluded to "that ingredient in the population of this country which came, not from the culminated pride of Europe, but from the abject despondency of Africa. A race discriminated from all the other converging streams of immigration by ineffaceable distinctions of nature," which though unrepresented among the nation's founders, had now been "raised by the power of the great truths then declared, as it were from the dead." Evarts meant well, but rather than acknowledge the horrific Ku Klux Klan assaults on the freed people in the South, and the mounting campaign there to drive Black voters from the ballot box, a stark challenge to his triumphal march from colonial subjection to present-day glory, his comments were a self-congratulatory asterisk, not an invitation to Black Americans to join in building the American future but an envoi to a people who were slipping from the Northern mind.

There had been talk of asking Frederick Douglass to read the Emancipation Proclamation from the main stage, but nothing came of it, presumably to avoid offending Robert E. Lee's cousin and all the Southern militiamen who had been welcomed so warmly to Independence Square. Instead, a scholarly but little-known Black minister from Arkansas, J. W. Jenifer, was invited to deliver an address at the site for a bust of Richard Allen, who had founded the African Methodist Episcopal Church in Philadelphia in 1816, which was to be installed in September. It would be the first monument ever commissioned by Black Americans.

The Centennial's commissioners had agreed to provide space for the bust in Fairmount Park, a seemingly significant concession given their chilliness toward virtually every other Black appeal for acknowledgment. But their agreement came with a catch: They required that the bust be removed from the park within sixty days after the Centennial's close. By contrast, other independently financed statues—of the scientist Alexander von Humboldt, Christopher Columbus, and the Presbyterian leader John Witherspoon—were intended to be permanent. The Black Philadelphians who gathered to hear Reverend Jenifer nevertheless rejoiced that Allen would, however temporarily, stand among the ranks of the nation's white Founders. "How becoming it is for us," Jenifer intoned, that "the children of ancestors who were the founders of the earliest civilization, the establishers of great cities and vast empires, the patrons of arts and sciences," to be able "to show that the spirit of our fathers has not expired; but with a purpose grander than that which built the Pyramids or founded Carthage, we come to make our contributions to the New World's fair, which shall stand forever as the first national scientific effort of a race heroically struggling to shake off the degradation of centuries."

Meanwhile, in Independence Square, William Evarts stem-windingly summarized the past century of American history in his famously supple baritone. Evarts was a master of plummy speech who would rarely spare a word when he could use three instead, but he was speaking to a deep anxiety that infected the nation. Yes, Americans justly exulted in the nation's material progress, of which the Centennial was a triumphant example, he said. But too many feared that the nation had lost the moral qualities that made a people truly great. Although he made no direct mention of the election campaign that was now fully underway, few could fail to realize that he was alluding to the rancorous political climate, and too many Americans' belief that the nation's political culture had become irredeemably corrupt. "How shall we answer the questioning of this day?" he asked. Had the American project in fact failed? But he meant these as merely rhetorical questions, he reassured. Americans had nothing to fear.

Naturally, the country faced challenges, Evarts admitted. Crimes and frauds continued to be practiced. Greed had not disappeared. Good laws went unenforced, power sometimes outgrew responsibility, temporary expedients were rashly embraced, parties devolved into battling factions, and there was a disheartening tendency toward finding conspiracies where they did not exist. But such "mischiefs" beset every generation. The founding principles of popular government still thrived in the habits of the American people. Doubtless, he grandly concluded, in 1976, "A hundred years hence, the piety of that generation will recall the ancestral glory which we celebrate today. What shall they say of us? How shall they estimate the part we bear in the unbroken line of the nation's progress? Under this double trust then, from the past and for the future, let us take heed to our ways, and resolve that the great heritage we have received shall be handed down through the long line of the advancing generations, the home of liberty, the abode of justice, the stronghold of faith among men."

When Evarts had finished, the orchestra struck up the "Hallelujah Chorus" from Handel's *Messiah.* White Americans could feel assured that they were indeed the most favored children of history.

AMID THE DAY'S CELEBRATIONS, Americans were further heartened by the latest report from the frontier—a falsehood, they would soon learn—that the army had scored a victory over the Sioux somewhere in the Powder River country of the Montana Territory, where three columns of troops were believed to be converging on the last desperate holdouts under Sitting Bull. Better still, the victory had most likely been won by the country's most famous Indian fighter, the glamorous blue-eyed Civil War hero with the golden hair, George Armstrong Custer. The decisive fight might still be a long way off, growled *The New York Herald,* but the expected victory to come would surely provide yet more evidence that the United States was rising toward the apogee of greatness, proof that American civilization was continuing to roll unstoppably across the continent, sweeping aside the last vestiges of primitive savagery as it careened toward its Manifest Destiny.

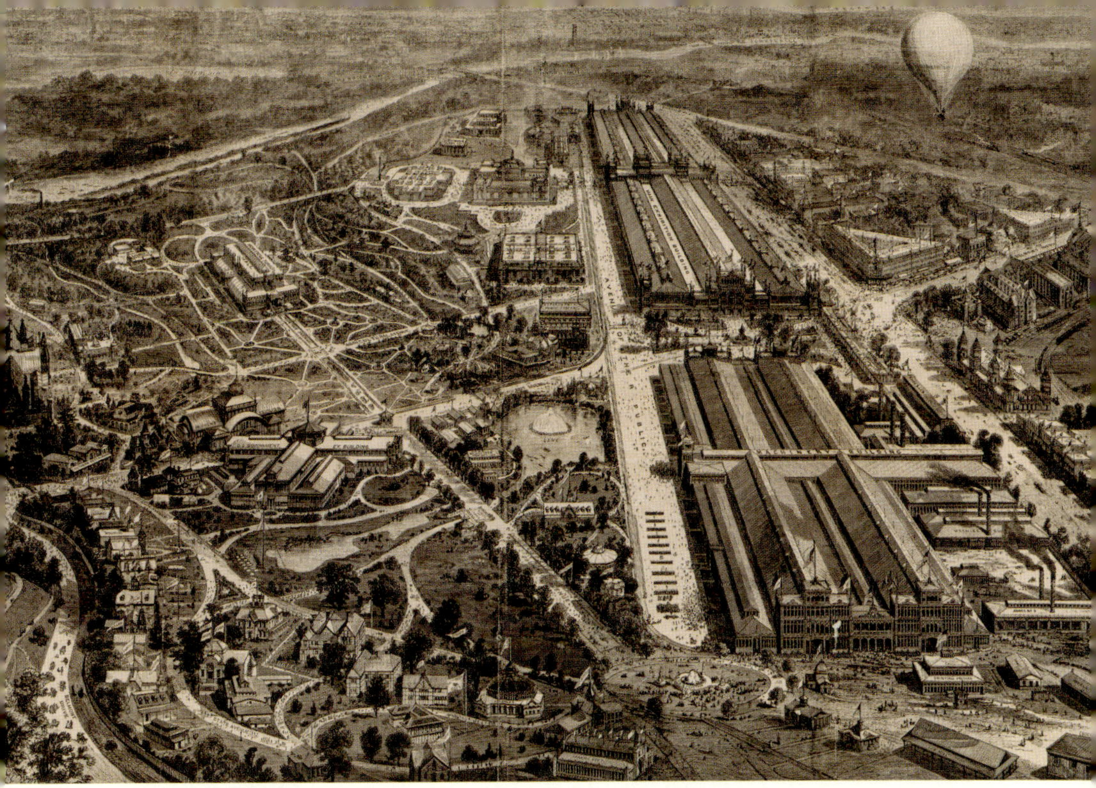

The Centennial Exhibition transformed Philadelphia's Fairmount Park into a vast universe of pavilions and halls that displayed America's and the world's industrial, commercial, and artistic achievements.

A youthful Uncle Sam bestrides the continent as a swaggering symbol of rising American power.

For twenty-five cents, visitors could climb the colossal arm of the future Statue of Liberty for a panoramic view of the Centennial and, at least symbolically, the American future.

Immensely popular Machinery Hall showcased the might of American industry with a cacophony of mostly steam-driven engines.

President Ulysses S. Grant and Emperor Dom Pedro II of Brazil opened the Centennial by setting in motion the titanic Corliss Engine, one of the largest machines of the day, which powered everything in Machinery Hall.

Among the hundreds of inventions exhibited at the Centennial, none would have more impact than Alexander Graham Bell's telephone. Bell's primitive transmitter, demonstrated publicly for the first time, astonished fair-goers. In less than a year it would be in commercial production.

The flamboyant sculptor Edmonia Lewis was a living contradiction of white America's racial assumptions. Her *Death of Cleopatra* was regarded by many visitors as the finest sculpture at the Centennial.

Exhibits that touched on slavery and the Civil War were often controversial. *The Freed Slave* was mocked by white tourists from the South, but it was admired by Blacks, who found little at the Centennial to represent them.

The handsome Women's Pavilion, financed, developed, and run by women, shunned political feminism, but it highlighted women's activities and encouraged their entry into the professions.

Interior of the Women's Pavilion.

On the Fourth of July, radical suffragists led by Susan B. Anthony (standing) seized the speakers' platform at the Centennial to draw attention to the "Declaration of Rights of the Women of the United States," which she had co-written with her friend Elizabeth Cady Stanton (sitting) and other allies.

Although he was a war hero, a former member of Congress, and a successful Ohio governor, Rutherford B. Hayes entered the 1876 presidential contest as a dark horse. Many Republicans expected him to lose.

Hayes rarely appeared in public as a candidate, in keeping with the custom of the time. But political campaigns were the most popular form of national entertainment in the era before mass media and professional sports, and Americans expected plenty of hoopla. Punning on Hayes's name—"A GOOD HONEST LOAD OF HAYes"—the image portrayed his campaign rolling toward Washington past cheering African Americans.

Democrats strove, not always successfully, to liven up the campaign of their semi-reclusive candidate, New York Governor Samuel J. Tilden, with songs, rallies, and partisan propaganda.

Tilden's surrogates campaigned tirelessly against "carpetbag rule" and "military occupation" of the former Confederate states under outgoing President Grant. "Carpet-bagging" was a smear against Northerners who came south after the war, alleging that they were all corrupt outsiders who looted Southern treasuries and stirred up the freed people. Many were in fact idealistic Union veterans, churchmen, and teachers helping to rebuild the postwar South.

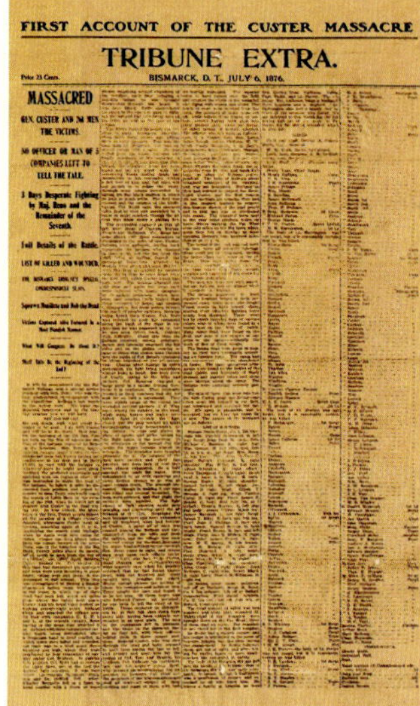

FIRST ACCOUNT OF THE CUSTER MASSACRE

TRIBUNE EXTRA.

BISMARCK, D. T., JULY 6, 1876.

MASSACRED

Full Details of the Battle.

Above: In July, Americans were stunned to learn that General George Armstrong Custer and hundreds of his men had been wiped out by Sioux and Cheyenne fighters led by Sitting Bull. Retribution would come swiftly, opening the prairie West to white settlement and the new agricultural machinery that fair-goers saw at the Centennial.

Below: An artist's rendering of a supposed gathering of clandestine "Molly Maguires" in the Pennsylvania coalfields, where mine owners claimed that Irish American strikers were terrorists who threatened American prosperity and the foundations of capitalism itself.

John Kehoe, a former miner and a rising political leader in the coal region, was charged with masterminding the "Molly Maguires." Framed by the mine owners, he and other Irish American labor leaders were tried during the summer of 1876, and later hanged.

FRANK LESLIE'S ILLUSTRATED NEWSPAPER

NEW YORK, MARCH 3, 1877.

Top Left: During the long-drawn-out counting of ballots in the 1876 presidential election, extremist Democrats threatened rebellion if Tilden was not confirmed, while fearful Republicans warned of a possible bloodbath in the South.

Top Right: Southern racial violence also exploded during the Centennial year, most notoriously in Hamburg, South Carolina, where local Black militiamen were massacred by white paramilitaries. Republicans blamed Samuel Tilden, who welcomed support from former Confederates.

Left: Senators delivered the electoral certificates in early February, but the controversial vote count continued until the eve of the inauguration.

With the election's outcome in doubt, the Electoral Commission met secretly at the Capitol, desperately struggling to resolve conflicting returns. Many Americans feared that violence was imminent, or even renewed Civil War.

Thomas A. Scott, president of the Pennsylvania Railroad, one of the most powerful magnates in Gilded Age America, and a leading sponsor of the Centennial Exhibition. His harsh labor policies helped to bring on the Great Railroad Strike of 1877.

The strike brought a halt to railway service from the Atlantic coast to the Mississippi River and beyond. Strikers battled the federalized National Guard in scores of cities. Newspaper reports featured shocking images of mobbing, looting, and arson. In Pittsburgh, nearly one hundred strikers and ordinary citizens were killed, thousands of railway cars destroyed, and much of the Pennsylvania Railroad's property burned to the ground.

Walt Whitman foresaw that the United States would someday dominate the world. However, he cautioned, "The problem of the future of America is as dark as it is vast." Whitman had hoped for a prominent role at the Centennial, but he was ignored by its organizers. He visited it, unnoticed, only as a tourist.

CHAPTER 7

THE LAW OF PROGRESS

★ ★ ★ ★ ★

It seems almost too terrible to be entirely true.

—WILLIAM TECUMSEH SHERMAN

On July 5, as Americans across the country sobered from their exuberant celebration of Independence Day, an army scout named Muggins Taylor emerged from the high desert and rode into Salt Lake City with news that shocked the country. Ten days earlier, he said, on June 25, General Custer had been killed with nearly three hundred of his men in the Montana Territory. Taylor's news reached the East Coast two days later. *The New York Times* announced in numbed staccato, "Nothing is known of the operations of this detachment, except their course as traced by the dead." When fresh troops arrived, dead horses and mutilated bodies lay piled in every direction. "The battlefield looked like a slaughter pen."

Reporters tracked down the commander of the army, William Tecumseh Sherman, at the Transcontinental Hotel in Philadelphia, where he had been visiting the Centennial, with his coat and boots thrown off, sweating in an easy chair by the window. "It seems almost too terrible to be entirely true," he exclaimed. "It must be exaggerated. I don't think there were enough Indians there to do it like that." Many at first discredited the news as a mere rumor, but it was soon confirmed. One of the most famous Americans of his time was dead, and the entire Seventh Cavalry, it was feared, virtually wiped out. At the army's western headquarters in Chicago, all was confusion. Waves of horror rolled through official Washington, followed by a backwash of intense sadness. Members of Congress talked of nothing else. The families of Custer's men flooded the War Department, begging for information. Fears spread that the entire northern frontier would be "depopulated by massacre." There was panic-stricken talk of calling up volunteers to whip the Sioux into submission.

For Americans of the Centennial year, Custer's annihilation felt utterly unprecedented. It marked the worst defeat of an American army by Native Americans since 1792, when nearly six hundred soldiers and militia were slaughtered in western Ohio, a catastrophic event in its time, but one that by 1876 had virtually disappeared from the nation's memory. The battle was also a family disaster: The dead included two of Custer's brothers, a nephew, a brother-in-law, and a childhood friend.

IN THE WEEKS BEFORE his death, Custer had caromed around the East Coast, testifying in Congress about corruption in the War Department, hobnobbing with Democratic politicos in New York, hastening west to join his troops, being abruptly stripped of his command, grudgingly reinstated by Grant, and then hurrying west again. Somehow, amid all his frenetic bustle he found time to see the Centennial Exhibition. He didn't record his impressions, but he must undoubtedly have taken in the large collection of tribal artifacts and paraphernalia in the United States Government Building, which was essentially a museum of the "Vanishing American," a popular literary trope that Custer had for the past decade been instrumental in turning into seemingly inevitable reality.

The Smithsonian—founded in 1846 "for the increase and diffusion of knowledge"—had originally intended to bring several hundred people from diverse tribes to the Centennial as a living exhibit, with their horses, dogs, and accoutrements. Visitors would observe these vanishing Americans as they tended their families, crafted arrows, tanned hides, and wove baskets, but the Smithsonian eventually abandoned the idea given the worsening instability in the West, considering it no longer "prudent to bring these half-subdued savages to the Exposition." As cringe-inducing as this project may seem to present-day sensibilities, in its time, it had a certain laudable intent in a country that mostly considered Native cultures beneath contempt. The Smithsonian was at least encouraging white Americans to take them seriously, albeit as a spectacle.

In 1873, Joseph Henry, the Smithsonian's director, had dispatched expeditions to scour the West for material that would "present savage life and conditions in all grades and places," not omitting objects "because they are either rude or homely." Henry added, "The fact that the monuments of the past and the savage tribes of men are rapidly disappearing from our continent, and that, ere another century will renew an incentive so great and universal as the Exposition, they will have disappeared forever, should be all the stimulus required to give the enterprise the conscientious labor it demands." He also wrote to the army high command requesting that its troops in the field procure specimens of Indian dress, ornaments, and weapons from the battlefield, presumably by stripping the dead. (The ruthless looting of Indian graves and the collecting of Indian bones became a cottage industry: "It is most unpleasant work to steal bones from a grave, but what is the use, someone has to do it," the eminent anthropologist Franz Boas sighed some years later.) Despite the Centennial's proclaimed celebration of American history, the Smithsonian's exhibit took no note of the tribes that had allied themselves with the patriots in the Revolutionary War, in hope of preserving their autonomy within the new nation, much less of the land-hungry white frontiersmen who had used the war as a screen to surge westward over the Appalachian Mountains to seize Native territory. Rather, the exhibit was consciously designed to juxtapose "the extreme lowness of our remote ancestors" against the Exposition's spectacle of technology and engineering in order to illuminate "the great truth that *progress* is the law that governs the development of mankind." Finely crafted artifacts from ancient burial mounds—pottery, flints, pounders, pestles—fostered the theory that Indians were peoples of mysterious origin, and in the past far more "civilized" than their living descendants. Like many Americans, Custer entertained the idea that at least some were descended from the so-called Lost Tribes of Israel, and that others may have come from medieval Scandinavian settlers.

Custer would have seen tribal costumes, hatchets, spears and arrowheads, bone implements, basketry, cooking utensils, rattles, tools, gouges, harpoons, scrapers, zoomorphic tobacco pipes, war clubs, masks, totem poles, buffalo-skin tepees, models of Southwestern cliff dwellings, an immense dugout canoe from Vancouver Island, a Peruvian mummy, carved masks, and "fiendish-looking household gods," many of them confusingly combined in vitrines without regard to chronology or place of origin. Visitors were both fascinated and repelled by "case after case filled with the most grotesque idols—all with big, misshapen heads, and a severe burlesque on the human body," and by the life-size wax figures of famous Indian leaders, "with names indicating their bloodthirsty dispositions," covered in "paint without stint, war feathers, colored blankets, huge coils of beads," necklaces of bear claws and scalps dangling from their waists. William Dean Howells, for one, wrote with disgust in *The Atlantic,* "The red man, as he appears in effigy and photograph in this collection, is a hideous demon, whose malign traits can hardly inspire any emotion softer than abhorrence. In blaming our Indian agents for malfeasance in office, perhaps we do not sufficiently account for the demoralizing influence of merely beholding those false and pitiless savage faces; moldy flour and corrupt beef must seem altogether too good for them." Such thinking reduced Native peoples to a cartoon-like cliché of savagery which blinded white Americans to the aggression that was being perpetrated against tribes that were still struggling, and mostly failing, to somehow come to grips with the onrushing modern world of the nineteenth century.

Custer couldn't have failed to take in the stark counterpoint of the "primitive" Indian exhibits to the futuristic new machinery in Agricultural Hall. That cathedral-like confection in the "modern" neo-Gothic style displayed a panoply of steam-threshers, excavators, reapers, mowers, stump-pullers, rock-lifters, road-scrapers, plows, and balers, automatic binders, harvesters, and drills to speed the planting of crops, which were already, acre by acre, transforming the Great Plains into a vast cornucopia able to sustain millions of white settlers. This ongoing transformation was bringing to dramatic fruition a utopian vision of heroic yeoman farmers pushing the frontier ever onward, inspired by the widespread, if scientifically delusional, assumption that the very act of tilling the soil would generate rain upon even the dryest landscapes. "In the sweat of his face, toiling with his hands, man can persuade the heavens to yield their treasures of dew and rain upon the land," the agronomist Charles Dana Wilber assured Americans with evangelical fervor: "the polished raindrop never fails to fall in answer to the imploring power or prayer of labor."

Few Americans doubted that the seeming disappearance of the Indians was a natural process that was beyond human control. Physical genocide was promoted by some, and accepted by many, as a perfectly reasonable solution to what was often termed "the Indian problem." James Gordon Bennett, the publisher of *The New York Herald,* probably the most widely read national newspaper in the 1870s, called repeatedly for outright extermination, suggesting that it was less expensive to kill Indians than to feed them. Frederick Douglass, who called the tribes' destruction "the saddest chapter in our history," nonetheless believed that Indians who remained "uncivilized" must always retreat before the onrush of railways, steamships, and electricity. Even humanitarians hoped to see their erasure as distinct peoples by means of boarding school education, the promotion of property ownership and farming, Christianization, and the suppression of tribal customs. Horace Greeley, the nominally "enlightened" editor of the *New York Tribune,* had declared categorically, "These people must die out—there is no help for them. God has given the earth to those who will subdue and cultivate it, and it is vain to struggle against his righteous decree."

SUCH CONTRADICTIONS were embedded in the white man's psyche long before Custer's birth, posing a mythic idealization of "the Indian" as an innocent child of nature against a darkly emotive image of a monster beyond redemption, a savage terror in the eternal struggle between good and evil. It was among such half-submerged shoals that Edmonia Lewis strove to survive, one of the very few Americans claiming a Native identity who managed to craft a successful career in the public eye. Indeed, her success rested largely on her exploitation of romanticized imagery of the "noble savage" that appealed to the white middle class, which placed Hiawatha and Minnehaha in a timeless and soothing prehistory, even as bloody war festered on the frontier. Friendly art critics such as Henry Tuckerman found her renderings so enchanting that he extolled her as the paramount interpreter of "her race," and urged her to turn her genius toward the noble Native personages of the heroic past—Pontiac, Osceola, and Montezuma—whose tragic fates, he asserted, would elevate her art to new and transcendent heights. (Tuckerman did not recognize these as yet another set of stereotypes; nor did Lewis take his advice.)

Lewis's greatest work of art was, perhaps, the crafting of her public persona. Her "Indianness," as we've seen, was at least partly performance. She claimed to have been "born in a wigwam," unlikely as that was since she grew up near Albany, New York. She told interviewers that she sometimes thought of returning to "the wild life," but held off only because of her love of art, and asserted that she had gone to California to show her work not because it offered a good market but because travel was in her "Indian blood." She added that she almost envied the freedom of the Indians she saw along the way but was also repelled by them because they were "so dirty." In other words, she was a proud Indian when it suited her, but also a "civilized" one, who shared the biases of white prejudice.

Her early supporters in Boston found her "Indianness" more intriguing than her African American ancestry; not even abolitionists thought of Blacks as objects of romantic fancy. They could also blame her "aboriginal" nature for personal qualities in her that they found frustrating, particularly her resistance to their patronizing domination and her unreliability in practical matters, habits that, even if true, might in others be attributed simply to her creative temperament. Lydia Maria Child, her first patron, condescendingly remarked to a correspondent that "Edmonia is younger than young—brought up as she was among Chippewas and negroes, without any education," complaining that "she is in too much of a hurry to get up to a conspicuous place." In other words, she was ambitious, a quality they would likely have praised in a white man. (Lewis, it shouldn't be forgotten, had been educated at Oberlin College, knew at least some Latin and French, and had turned her talent into a profitable business, rare enough for an artist in any era.)

LEWIS WAS PRECISELY the kind of assimilated individual that "humane" federal policy hoped to create from the raw material of the unsettled tribes, a "post-savage" Indian, so to speak. Ulysses Grant had come into office promising leniency toward the tribes, which he hoped would lead to permanent peace on the frontier. He felt genuine personal concern for Native Americans, having served among them in the Pacific Northwest when he was a young officer in the early 1850s, writing in 1872, "I do not believe our Creator ever placed the different races of men on this earth with the view of having the stronger exert all its energies in exterminating the weaker." As president, he ordered a thorough reevaluation of Indian policy by a commission that included religious leaders as well as representatives from industry and education, and named the country's first-ever Native American commissioner of Indian Affairs, his wartime aide Ely Parker, a Seneca from upstate New York. The "Peace Policy," as it was known, was meant to convince Indians that it was in their own interest to adopt American habits and to abandon their traditional practices. Bands that refused to negotiate would still have to be dealt with severely. The Western tribes "have become falsely impressed with the notion of national independence," wrote Parker, who advocated assimilation. "It is time that this idea should be dispelled." In the meantime, Parker added, "the Indians should be made as comfortable as it was in the power of the government to make them."

Grant's plan meant well, but it took no account of what Native peoples—highly diverse among themselves—might want, much less the traumatic stresses of adopting radically different lifeways under federal pressure. In addition, entrenched interests resisted reform, as the impeachment of the corrupt secretary of war, William Belknap, illustrated only too well. The Peace Policy also suffered from fatal contradictions: It aspired at the same time to protect Indians' rights and to eliminate the tribes as independent powers; to protect Native land from white incursions but also to extinguish Native title to that territory; and to facilitate the building of railroads across Indian Country. Although most of the Sioux and allied Cheyenne bands agreed to yield their ancestral hunting lands and settle at government agencies, those led by the charismatic Sitting Bull and Crazy Horse resisted, ignoring the government's assurances, and continuing to raid white settlements and parties of railroad surveyors. It was clear to whites and Indians alike that the coming of the railroad would put them on a collision course.

The railroad was not the only source of imminent conflict. Rumors of gold were in the air when a thousand-man expedition led by Custer marched into the Black Hills, in the Sioux heartland, in 1874. The expedition heralded Custer's spectacular reentry onto the national stage after several years of unglamorous service in dusty frontier forts far from the national spotlight that he felt he deserved. At thirty-seven, he eagerly welcomed renewed war as a respite from the anonymity of garrison duty. He had emerged from the Civil War already famous as a brilliant cavalry officer daring in close combat, who reveled in his sobriquet "the boy general." A Democrat in politics, and an unapologetic racist in sentiment, he disdained postwar Reconstruction and admired the aristocratic veneer of Southern officers he had known since his days at West Point. Stationed for several months in Kentucky, he expressed more sympathy for former Confederates than for newly empowered Black citizens harried by the Ku Klux Klan.

CUSTER'S ATTITUDE TOWARD Indians was more complex. Even as he boasted of his skill as an Indian fighter, he expressed a degree of respect for his foes. In his 1874 memoir *My Life on the Plains,* he remarked—in terms that were taken to be empathetic for the time—that Indians were no crueler than whites would be if they had been raised the same way, writing, "If I were an Indian, I often think that I would greatly prefer to cast my lot among those of my people who adhered to the free open plains, rather than submit to the confined limits of a reservation, there to be the recipient of the blessed benefits of civilization, with its vices thrown in without stint or measure." He also believed, however, that "nature intended the Indian for a savage state," and that white civilization "like the car of Juggernaut, will roll mercilessly over him, destroying as it advances. Destiny seems to have willed it so."

Although Custer's primary task was to survey sites for future forts in the Black Hills, he also confirmed the existence of gold deposits. Once word got out, the press trumpeted his discoveries to a public still reeling from economic depression and unemployment, thrilling the desperate and the ambitious with the prospect of a gold rush that could spur settlement and make men rich overnight. Custer once again became an instant celebrity. The more popular he grew, the more warmly he was welcomed by Democratic power brokers such as August Belmont, the party's leading financier, and other East Coast moneymen, who lionized him on his periodic trips to New York.

As prospectors flooded into the Black Hills, throwing up overnight boomtowns like notorious Deadwood, the public clamored for the wholesale removal of the tribal holdouts, treaties be damned. The *New York World* argued that the country had never belonged to the Indians any more than it did to wolves and bears, "which white settlers shoot without mercy." Gold lured whites in a swelling stream, so many, President Grant confessed, that "an effort to remove the miners would only result in the desertion of the bulk of the troops that might be sent to remove them." By December 1875, there were over 4,000 miners scouring the Black Hills, with more arriving every day. As Indian raids picked off isolated travelers, news reports stridently exaggerated the death toll and demanded revenge. By mid-February, Sitting Bull and Crazy Horse were mustering their followers for war.

Custer was initially offered the command of one column in the three-pronged campaign to corner Sitting Bull's band in southern Montana, where they were known to be concentrating. Before the campaign got underway, however, Custer was called to Washington by congressional Democrats to testify against Secretary of War Belknap. The Democrats would gleefully exploit Custer's testimony to torment Republicans through the entire campaign season, as proof of the Grant administration's allegedly bottomless corruption. On Capitol Hill, Custer asserted that Belknap's wife had arranged for a sutler's post to be given to a friend who would in turn kick back half the "sale price" of the appointment to Belknap, and retailed familiar claims about crooked deals implicating the president's brother Orvil. Having recently suffered big losses in the stock market, Custer almost certainly had political ambitions for himself, most likely a high-level appointment in a Tilden administration, which he hoped would triumph in the November elections. Custer's attacks infuriated Grant, who considered him an insubordinate show pony, and abruptly removed him from the campaign against the Sioux. After personal pleas from Sherman and Sheridan, who considered Custer indispensable, however, he was allowed at the last minute to rejoin his troops but demoted to the command of just his own regiment.

Custer, back once again in the West, mounted up the Seventh Cavalry in mid-May, seething with resentment and impatient for a headline-making victory. "An impetuous man of quick and almost boiling sensibilities," *The New York Herald* later wrote, he had doubtless been "rendered desperate by ill-usage, and decided to either prevail in an act of daring or die trying." That he could fail was beyond imagining. The plan called for General George Crook to march north from Fort Laramie in Wyoming with 1,200 men; General John Gibbon east from Fort Ellis in Montana with 450; and General Alfred Terry—Custer's replacement—westward from Fort Abraham Lincoln, in the Dakota Territory, with 1,000 men, including Custer and 600 troopers of his Seventh Cavalry.

They were hampered from the start by poor intelligence and difficult topography. The army's high command underestimated the number of fighters the tribes could field, supposing that the army would face no more than 1,000 warriors, a number easily overcome by superior firepower. The true number was somewhere between 2,000 and 4,000, the largest combined force ever mustered by Indians on the Great Plains. Sitting Bull first defeated Crook's column in northern Wyoming with losses so steep that it was unable to proceed. The Sioux then turned to meet Custer, who had marched rapidly up the Big Horn River.

Custer felt supremely self-confident. He didn't bother to reconnoiter either the lay of the land or the size of the enemy. He then divided his vastly outnumbered force, probably hoping to trap the Sioux by a surprise attack on their camp, thinking that if he could capture the women and children Sitting Bull would quickly come to terms. Instead, his nearly 300 men were trapped and destroyed piecemeal, leaving only an isolated detachment of battered survivors to be rescued two days later by a relief column.

THE BATTLE OF the Little Big Horn almost instantly took on a mythic dimension. Within days of hearing the news, writers recalled the martyrdom of ancient Roman heroes, the last stand of the Jewish Maccabees, the doomed charge of the Light Brigade in the Crimean War. "Beside them in heroic remembrance must stand the name of Custer," intoned *The New York Herald* on July 7, conjuring an imaginary scene of a "mad charge up the narrow ravine, with rocks above raining down lead upon the fated three hundred, with fire spouting from every bush ahead, with the wild, swarming horsemen circling along the heights like shrieking vultures waiting for the moment to swoop down and finish the bloody tale." Every man, from private to general, "rises to heroic size; yes, they died as grandly as Homer's demigods."

In the *New York Tribune,* Walt Whitman published a passionate, racially tinged "Death-Sonnet for Custer":

The fall of Custer and all his men.
Continues yet the old, old legend of our race!
The loftiest of life upheld by death!

In the weeks that followed, false reports and contradictory rumors came in a tumbling avalanche. Custer was said to have been killed by a vengeful warrior named Rain-in-the-Face, who had cut out his heart, stuck it on a pole, and paraded it through the Indians' camp, where they used it as a centerpiece for war dances. Or Custer's body had been left completely unmolested out of respect for his bravery. Crook and his 1,500 men had been wiped out. Or "hostiles" were pouring into the Western forts to surrender. Rampaging tribesmen were pillaging ranches in Wyoming . . . an uprising of the long-friendly Nez Perce was imminent . . .

A century and a half later, Custer has largely become a historical cliché about clueless ineptitude. But in 1876 he was the very incarnation of the aggressive force that was thrusting the nation westward across the continent, a larger-than-life hero of the new America that was coming into being, a "superhero" before the term was coined. He had done as much as any man of his time to make possible the opening of the West to white settlement. The annihilation of his command was felt by countless Americans, who cared nothing for the fate of Native peoples, to be not just a military disaster but an insult to the America being celebrated at Philadelphia, an inexplicable triumph of the barbaric over industry, "civilization," Christian values, and the future itself.

Although Custer's superiors in the army blamed him for squandering the lives of his men, public calls for vengeance grew ever louder. Never since the end of the Civil War had Americans sounded more warlike. The Republican *Nation* loftily asserted that under the laws of "civilized jurisprudence" the Indians had no rights to the land they occupied. Democrats blamed Grant personally, claiming that he had humiliated Custer in a fit of personal spite that left the president's hands stained with a hero's blood. Declared *The New York Herald,* "The denunciations expressed on all sides against the [federal] policy which allowed life and liberty to savages no more amenable to our civilization than the buffaloes of the plains were loud and earnest." The paper called for "deadly aggression, looking to the total extermination of the treacherous Indians of the plains," with "war to the knife and the knife to the hilt." Warned the *Richmond Examiner,* "Either our people must kill the savages or else the savages will destroy our people."

In response to the public outcry, Congress appropriated $1.6 million to recruit 2,500 more men to serve in the cavalry. Reinforcements were dispatched from the Western forts while Congress considered calling up volunteers. Sherman announced that he was also prepared to dispatch more troops from the Atlantic and Pacific coast garrisons. But he cautioned Grant that he was afraid to remove any from the unstable South, where the enemies of Reconstruction were massing to seize the few remaining Reconstruction state governments from Republican control in the coming elections.

ALONG WITH CUSTER'S MEN, and an unknown number of Native warriors, the dead of the Little Big Horn included Grant's "Peace Policy," which was widely denounced with renewed vehemence as an exercise in wishful thinking by soft-headed do-gooders. Raged one Dakota paper in a boldfaced headline: "CUSTER AND HIS ENTIRE COMMAND SWEPT OUT OF EXISTENCE BY THE SPECIAL PETS OF EASTERN ORATORS." With similar contempt, *The New York Herald* sneered that Grant's "stupidity" had "nursed Indian strength" by placing it in the indulgent hands of "the praying brigade"—that is, missionaries—and then stoking the Indians' fury by allowing corrupt officials to cheat them and leave them to starve.

Defenders of the Indians were few and their voices faint. "The Indians were cheated and robbed without stint or mercy," and the money appropriated to save them from extinction had become a slush fund for politicians, a writer in *The New York Times* ventured to remind readers. "It may be hard to confess in the presence of the heroic dead, but because the nation, in its greed, had cheated these savage tribes"—seizing the Black Hills, plotting railroad lines, and destroying the buffalo herds—"the wild leaders, embittered by a sense of their wrongs, burst into war, or more correctly resisted invasion." Such plaints were met with scorn or silence. Humanitarians forfeited their political leverage, and even Native bands that had declined to go to war abruptly lost most of the sympathy they had once enjoyed, meager as that was to begin with.

Unsurprisingly, the impact of white rage even on bands that had shunned war often proved disastrous. For them, there would be no glamorous afterlife. In September, Sioux led by Red Cloud, a powerful chief whose followers numbered in the thousands, met with representatives of the army and the federal government at Fort Robinson, in far western Nebraska. Restive as his followers had been that spring, he had restrained the great mass of them from slipping away to join Sitting Bull. But the government agents now pressured Red Cloud to sign away his band's claims in the Black Hills and relocate east of the Missouri River, where they could more easily be monitored, or even to the Indian Territory, seven hundred miles to the south. If they didn't agree, they were warned, they would no longer receive the rations that they had been promised by treaty: They would starve. The bitterness of the helpless boiled up from virtually every Native delegate's words. Protested Red Cloud, "I am a friend of the president, so I should say yes to what he asks," but "I don't like it that we have a soldier here to give us food. It makes our children's hearts go back and forth." As for moving, he said, "I think if my people should move there to live they would all be destroyed." Young-Man-Afraid-of-His-Horses, an influential Lakota, said, "The Great Father has not lived up to his promises. I have been ashamed ever since soldiers came here." In the end, the Sioux had little choice but to agree to the government's terms. One at a time, Red Cloud and his allies reluctantly signed the new treaty that had been laid before them. One of them, Fire Thunder, came up holding his blanket before his eyes and signed blindfolded, then returned to his place refusing to see what he'd done.

CHAPTER 8

THE SHOTGUN PLAN

★ ★ ★ ★ ★

A dead Radical is very harmless.

—RED SHIRT MANIFESTO

As the contest gathered speed, neither presidential candidate wanted to say much about the South. Both preferred to talk about less emotive subjects like governmental efficiency, taxation, monetary policy, and civil service reform. And both left the close combat of the campaign to surrogates. In keeping with the posture of public modesty that was the custom of the time, Hayes, in particular, elevated silence to the level of policy, remarking, "On general principles, I think explanations and defenses are bad things." He told William Dean Howells, who was racing to produce his campaign biography, to "be careful not to commit me on religion, temperance, or free trade. Silence is the only safety."

The campaign was not going well for Hayes. The electoral math looked very discouraging. There was little hope of winning New York, Tilden's home and the largest state of all. The swing state of Indiana was also likely to go to Tilden, whose running mate, Thomas Hendricks, was the state's governor. "If we lose it, with the South gone (as it is all but one or two states), our chances are small," Hayes worried. Even normally safe Republican Maine was in play. With a touch of desperation, Hayes encouraged his allies to agitate against the spending of public money on "sectarian" schools—a coded appeal to the anti-Catholic and anti-Irish vote. At times, he almost seemed to welcome the prospect of defeat. He wrote to his wife, Lucy, "When I am alone I always wish I was a quiet private citizen again. But it will soon be [so] if we are beaten. I almost hope we shall be." Privately, he reassured himself that there would be no shame in losing as long as he retained his integrity and self-respect, which was unimpaired, he apparently felt, by his uneasy embrace of nativist demagoguery.

In the eyes of many ordinary voters, Hayes was tarnished by their fear that Grant-era hacks would control his administration. Carl Schurz glumly reported, "Your letter of acceptance is sneered at as a bundle of well-meaning promises which the opposition of the old party leaders will prevent you from carrying out." Hayes also alienated many spoilsmen by promising to appoint Democrats to senior offices as a gesture of sectional reconciliation. The unlikelihood of Republican victory undermined fund-raising, leaving the party so short of cash that its national committee temporarily suspended operations. Financial strains were further exacerbated by Hayes's principled resistance to soliciting kickbacks from appointed officeholders, which pleased reformers but made the campaign's organizers grind their teeth. "I hate assessments," Hayes wrote to a supporter. "They are all wrong. Office-holders should be free to contribute or not as they choose." Secretary of the Interior Zachariah Chandler, the campaign's chairman, ultimately ignored Hayes's high-mindedness and compelled his department's employees to turn over 2 percent of their annual income to the party. The campaign was further weakened by festering rivalries between pragmatists and idealists. Hayes had counted on the usually vigorous Roscoe Conkling to stump for him, but the New Yorker cold-shouldered him, sore at Hayes for winning the nomination and for espousing reforms that threatened to dry up Conkling's deep well of patronage. Conkling, who postured as a hypermasculine athlete, whined that his eyes were sore and that he needed to protect them by staying indefinitely in a dark room.

Tilden rarely left New York and made few public speeches, leaving the stump to a gamut of supporters ranging from Joseph Pulitzer, to P. T. Barnum, to the husband of Elizabeth Cady Stanton. Despite Tilden's decades as a wielder of power in the corridors of New York politics, he cast himself as an outsider devoted to selfless public service, in an early example of the professional image-crafting that is now known as "spin." His speakers' bureau dispatched orators across the country, and organized mass meetings, nurtured local Tilden clubs (six hundred in New York State alone), while his "Literary" office spewed out a steady stream of news releases, editorials, broadsides, and a massive 750-page reference tome for the field staff laying out Tilden's policies. (Since typewriters were still in their infancy, having been publicly exhibited for the first time at the Centennial, every campaign text initially had to be written out by hand.) In contrast to Hayes's cash-starved campaign, Democratic funds flowed in rivers, $100,000 of it from Tilden's copious private accounts. A Tammany operative canvassing Indiana on Tilden's behalf promised, "We'll sway the state with money."

It inexorably seemed, however, that the election was going to turn on the fate of the South. Hayes was confident of his ability to achieve a solution to the region's problems, if he was elected. He felt sure that the winning formula for peace lay in "intelligent and honest administration," the supremacy of law, and adherence to constitutional rights for Black citizens. But he feared that should he be defeated the fruits of the Union's victory could be undone by unrepentant former rebels. Many Democrats were openly denouncing the enfranchisement of Blacks as unconstitutional and declaring that every Black vote cast was therefore fraudulent. In many areas of the South, only the presence of federal troops, few as they were, ensured the safety of Black and white Republican voters. However, the Democratic-controlled House of Representatives was already holding federal policy hostage by refusing to appropriate any additional funds for the army beyond the end of the fiscal year in June

1877. Conservative Republicans urged Hayes to outflank the Democrats by reaching out to Southern whites. "The darkies you'll have anyhow; the white Whigs are what you want to capture," Charles Nordhoff of *The New York Herald* cynically urged.

FIVE WHITE-MAJORITY southern states were already governed or effectively dominated by Democrats: Alabama, Georgia, North Carolina, Tennessee, and Virginia. In Florida, Republicans shunned Black candidates in a hapless effort to win Democrats' support. Republican governors clung precariously to office in Arkansas and Texas, but their authority had completely evaporated. Louisiana hovered on the edge of anarchy. There, the White Leagues openly menaced Republican sheriffs, judges, tax collectors, and other officials, forcing many of them to abandon their posts, and in several parishes no Republicans at all were willing to risk voting. A year earlier, Mississippi's Republican government had fallen to a coup. First, white gunmen seized Vicksburg, killing between fifty and a hundred Republicans, and in another heinous incident attacked Black Republicans at a barbecue to which they had been invited as a gesture of reconciliation, killing seven or eight men on the spot, and an estimated fifty more in the aftermath. Scaring terrified Black voters into staying home, the Democrats swept Mississippi's state elections and proceeded to impeach its impeccably honest Republican governor, Adelbert Ames, a former Union general, on trumped-up charges of corruption and inciting a nonexistent Negro insurrection. Opined the bitter and dispirited Ames, "The state has gone beyond redemption."

Republicans had what seemed like an unassailable position in South Carolina. On paper, registered Black voters appeared to guarantee the party a 35,000-vote statewide majority. Two of the state's congressmen were Black, and Republicans held hundreds of state offices at all levels. But the state had become a national byword for misgovernment, an accusation rooted partly if not entirely in outright racism, since the large number of Black officeholders lent a veneer of plausibility to Democrats' fulminations about "Negro rule." Public opinion even in the North had been widely influenced by James S. Pike, a former abolitionist and a journalist for the *New York Tribune,* whose intensely racist, book-length report on South Carolina, *The Prostrate State,* deemed Reconstruction an abject failure for having placed "the dregs" of the population—that is, Black Americans—"in the robes of their intelligent predecessors," and left them to impose a regime, a "moral morass," of shocking ignorance and corruption. (Many Blacks in public life were in fact middle-class lawyers, clerics, and businessmen, and others talented autodidacts.) Claimed Rep. S. S. Cox of New York, one of the party's most popular orators, Republican-ruled South Carolina was "the worst-governed state in the Union; it is bad all around; bad at its borders; bad on the seacoast; everywhere rotten to the core." Black citizens didn't need, or perhaps, he implied, even deserve protection. Their fears came to bloody fruition just after Independence Day in the river port of Hamburg. In the run-up to the election, its name became a byword for unfolding terror.

THE SITE OF what was once Hamburg is today covered partly with scrubby forest, partly with a golf course and condominiums that obscure the last traces of what happened there on July 5. It was then a desultory town of about 1,200 residents, most of them former slaves, who worked at local brickworks and pottery kilns, or across the Savannah River in Augusta, Georgia. On July 4, forty members of the state militia, all of them Black, were staging their annual parade on Market Street, Hamburg's main thoroughfare, when two young white men in a carriage peremptorily ordered them to make way. The militia's captain pointed out that there was room to pass easily on either side. The whites demanded that the militiamen clear the road anyway. Words were exchanged, guns were brandished. Finally, the militia parted ranks to allow the men through.

Such ugly incidents were not unusual in the volatile, racially divided county of Edgefield. But the next day, scores of armed and belligerent whites poured into Hamburg, riding "in regular cavalry fashion" down Market Street. The two young whites, accompanied by their lawyer, former Confederate General Matthew Calbraith Butler, demanded that the town judge, a formerly enslaved coachman named Prince Rivers, issue a warrant for the arrest of the militia's officers for obstructing a public road. Butler further declared that the militia was a menace to public order and demanded that its weapons be confiscated and handed over to the white civilians. If they did not, he said, the whites would take them by force. The remaining militia—now about thirty in number—were uncowed but were increasingly outnumbered by the hour. They assembled at a brick warehouse where the company stored its guns and ammunition. They had only two rounds per man. At 5 p.m., the whites ordered them to yield up their weapons, shouting that they "had lost all patience."

At sunset, the whites spread out through the town and began shooting. More poured over the bridge from Augusta, by mid-evening growing to probably a thousand. When one fell dead, possibly shot accidentally by one of the arriving Georgians, their fury, it was reported, grew "ten-fold." The Georgians had brought a cannon, which they loaded with scrap iron and began firing at the militia. When the militiamen ran out of ammunition they ran for their lives. Allan Attaway, the militia's first lieutenant and an elected county commissioner, was caught, murdered, and mutilated. Jim Cook, the town marshal, "was almost shot to pieces." Fleeing men were shot in the back, dragged from their hiding places, and herded together near the railway bridge. Butler boasted during the fight that this was just the beginning; that they planned to fight through the election in November.

Benjamin Tillman, one of the gunmen, later a state governor and U.S. senator, recalled matter-of-factly what happened next: "Some [of the whites] asked the question as to whether it was not a dear piece of work for us to lose one of our best men and have only two negroes dead and another wounded. It was agreed that we could not have a story like that go out as a record of the night's work." A man who claimed to know all the Black residents of the town was asked to pick out "those of the meanest character and most worthy of death. As fast as he would select from among the prisoners those he thought ought to be killed they were taken off a little ways down the street and shot. After six had been thus dealt with, the little squad of white men who were still in town seemed satisfied and it was decided that the rest of the negroes some 25 or 30 in number were told to run for their lives." By the next morning, the "ghastly sight of seven [actually eight] dead negroes lying stark and stiff certainly had its effect. This had been a momentous and strenuous day's work. We were all tired but more than satisfied with the result." After the massacre, the killers stopped on the outskirts of town and feasted on watermelon.

News of the slaughter produced disgust far beyond the South. The *Times* of London declared of the murderous whites, "They have done a deed as detestable in its atrocity as many of the murders committed by the half-savage Turkish soldiery." On the floor of Congress, J. H. Rainey, a Republican from South Carolina and a former slave, protested, "What would be thought if here in Washington City, when a military company was parading on the Fourth of July, two men should come up in a buggy and demand of the officers that the company should get out of the way, and if they did not, should at once set to work and murder the men of that military company? Would you stand it? Do you, then, expect negroes to stand all this? Do you expect my race to submit meekly to continual persecution and massacre? Are you not going to allow us any right of self-defense?"

White Southerners quickly began weaving a defensive web of fiction. Augusta papers reported that Black "ringleaders" had been executed, as if the whites had been protecting themselves from attack. Some claimed that on July 4 the militiamen had charged the innocent young white men at bayonet-point, others that the events, while regrettable, were a "spontaneous combustion," a "riot by the negroes gone wild" against white people who "were forced to defend themselves and their families." It was even said that an "ex-Union soldier" had come up with the ungentlemanly idea of blasting the Blacks out of their armory with a cannon. Still others suggested that the whole affair had somehow been "got up" simply to serve Republican interests. When a Charleston paper ventured to deplore the killing of the Blacks as cold-blooded murder, Martin Gary, one of the instigators, challenged the editor to a duel for "insulting" the white men who had been on the scene.

* * *

IF EDMONIA LEWIS ever expressed her feelings about what was happening in the South that summer, they went unrecorded. Ignoring as best she could the ongoing harassment, she held tenaciously to her post at the great fair. Although she sold many copies of her smaller works—Hiawatha and Minnehaha, angels, and busts of famous men—*The Death of Cleopatra* remained stubbornly unsold, perhaps due to its $30,000 price. But she had acquired in the meantime a prestigious commission that was to be unveiled as the capstone of her contribution to the Centennial: the pedestal for the bust of the AME Church's founder, Richard Allen, a hero to African Americans. The bust itself was created by the Black sculptor Alfred White of Cincinnati, but Lewis's pedestal was a work of art in itself: twenty-two feet in height and incorporating Gothic columns with bas-reliefs illustrating aspects of African civilization surmounted by a small, open-sided structure that would shelter the bust.

Of all the ambitious projects that hopeful Blacks had initially proposed for the Centennial, only this remained. Congress had appropriated $3,000 toward the cost of the statue. The rest had been raised from individual Black citizens; the largest private contribution, of $100, came from William Montgomery of Mound Bayou, Mississippi, a former slave of Jefferson Davis. The monument's promoters celebrated it as a symbolic Black counterpart to the Liberty Bell and Independence Hall, a declaration of the promise of America anticipating the day when, in the words of Reverend J. W. Jenifer, on July 4, color and caste divisions would be erased and moral excellence be everywhere the measure of man. Also at the July dedication, added Reverend Andrew Chambers, one of the sponsors, "We intend to leave Philadelphia in 1876 as did the heroes in 1776, with a fixed resolve to achieve noble results; and in 1976 we expect our progeny to gather around the monument in question, shed tears of gratitude for the example we have left them, and call us blessed."

The erection of the Allen monument had been postponed, initially until September, because the sculptor had failed to finish the bust on time. But ill-fortune continued to dog it. The train carrying it from Cincinnati went off the rails in Pennsylvania, toppling Edmonia Lewis's exquisite pedestal into the Lehigh River and destroying it utterly. Although the bust survived without severe damage, its installation had to be postponed yet again. Only in November, a week before the Centennial closed, would it at last be unveiled before a modest gathering of mostly Black Philadelphians, on a new, plain granite pedestal shaped like a pyramid. In the joy of the moment, few dwelt on the monument's ironic fate as the fortunes of Black Americans were beginning their accelerating ebb into the darkness of Jim Crow. (The bust is now at Wilberforce University, a historically Black school affiliated with the AME Church, in Ohio.)

Tellingly, the few dozen well-wishers who gathered to celebrate the bust's installation were dwarfed to near insignificance by the tens of thousands who had flooded the Centennial grounds for "Southern Day," a few weeks earlier, in October. Gaily beribboned ladies and their escorts packed the low, rolling hills of Fairmount Park and the towers of the great halls to witness what was billed as "a genuine Southern tournament" staged by teams representing the thirteen original states. (Nearly all the riders were from the South, no matter their official designation.) To the clarion blast of trumpets, fifteen lance-wielding "knights," some of them wearing glittering armor, others decked out with crimson sashes and cocked hats, galloped the length of a three-hundred-yard course attempting to pierce, in sequence, three small red rings suspended from arches overhead. They were declared to be serving "the honor and glory of knighthood and chivalry," values that, it was supposed, the men of the South uniquely embodied. The winner, the champion from Delaware, was granted the privilege that evening of crowning the "Queen of Love and Beauty." The tournament was deemed one of the most successful events of the entire Centennial, notable not just for its entertainment value but even more as a demonstration of a supposedly new South in which "heroic" traditional values, however fictionalized, were fast obscuring the shame of secession and slavery, and the news from Hamburg and other terrorized Black communities.

* * *

THERE WAS NOTHING spontaneous about what had happened at Hamburg. The massacre was a calculated strategic step in the overthrow of the state's biracial government. Wrote Benjamin Tillman, "It had been the settled purpose of the leading white men to seize the first opportunity that the negroes might offer them to provoke a riot and teach the negroes a lesson, as it was generally believed that nothing but bloodshed and a good deal of it could so well answer the purpose of redeeming the state from negro and carpetbag rule." It was an opportunity "to set the ball rolling, and if one did not offer, we were to make one." The killers were following a systematic plan of action that had been developed mainly by former Confederate General Martin Gary, a fiery, famously profane lawyer and former slave owner with piercing eyes and an ingrained hostility to Blacks who, he maintained, understood only intimidation and violence. Reasoning with them, he once sneered, is like "singing Psalms to a dead mule." Many of the men he recruited likely had been members of the Ku Klux Klan whose cases had been dropped by the overloaded courts or had received government pardons. A frightened Republican official based at Columbia reported to President Grant that they "are more bitter today than they were then, simply because they think the government will not punish them now any more than it did then. The leniency and clemency of the national government have been mistaken for cowardice, and the longer they live, the bolder and more outspoken they grow."

Unlike the Klan, there was nothing secretive about Gary's organization, or the proliferation of similar "rifle clubs" that rapidly formed around the state. They met openly and were forthright about their determination to restore white rule. They wore no disguise, but as a sort of uniform they adopted red shirts, which served as an elaborate double metaphor that was meant both to imply the "suffering" of whites under "Negro rule" and to mock the clichéd rhetoric of Republican politicians who ginned up support for their candidates by, it was said, "waving the bloody shirt" of the Ku Klux Klan's victims.

Based on a similar strategy that had been employed in Mississippi, Gary's "Edgefield Plan," or "Shotgun Plan," as it was also called, was as detailed as a plan of battle. Its goal was the destruction of the Republican Party by driving Blacks out of public life. Its thirty-three provisions called upon every Democrat to be enrolled in a "club" divided into companies each commanded by a war veteran, who would ensure that every man was supplied weapons and ammunition, and prepared to act on a moment's notice. Democrats were further directed to engineer their appointment as election officials and poll monitors, and to personally control the vote of at least one Black voter by any means necessary. The plan's sixteenth article was especially memorable: "Never threaten a man individually; if he deserved to be threatened, the necessity of the times requires that he should die. A dead Radical is very harmless—a threatened Radical . . . is often very troublesome." South Carolina's Republican governor, Daniel H. Chamberlain, a Massachusetts-raised lawyer, warned, "Hamburg is only the beginning."

President Grant was sensitive to the danger faced by Republicans both Black and white. Desperate pleas flooded his mail. "Republicans cannot hold meetings nor make any effort to organize the party without the eminent [*sic*] danger of being massacred," William Simonton wrote to him from Mississippi. Jasper Starr, a Texas Republican from the town of Plenitude wrote, "Rebel grand juries find bills of indictment against loyal men without any foundation of fact, while murderers, robbers, and such as are guilty of arson and other great crimes are winked at." Grenville Peirce, a correspondent from Louisiana, reported to Grant that white night-riders were "riding roughshod" over the countryside near Baton Rouge, dragging Black men from their homes and murdering them. "In the name of common humanity, for myself and familly [*sic*], and more than thirty colored famillies, cannot some protection be given us?" Almost daily, national newspapers reported some assault on Republican officeholders or the symbols of the nation. In Carlisle, Kentucky, in just one of many such incidents, *The New York Times* reported, the U.S. flag had been taken down and replaced with a ten-foot-long rebel ensign to cheers for Samuel J. Tilden and the Confederacy.

Grant knew that military intervention was the only sure way to protect Black citizens and their new freedoms. But he had little room for maneuver, with his hands tied by the erosion of public support for Reconstruction. He was also tired of Washington, of politics, of unending upheavals in the South, of the relentless assaults on his integrity. He had only a few months left in his term. Surely, he hoped, some peaceful remedy for South Carolina's woes would be found. He promised Chamberlain what aid he could "for which I can find law or constitutional power." These were the words of a man who knew that he no longer had the political power to deliver. The Custer debacle was but the latest nail in the coffin of Reconstruction, arming congressional Democrats with yet another pretext to pull troops from the South and dispatch them to the frontier. The problem would be up to Grant's successor to solve. Chamberlain and South Carolina Republicans were on their own.

SOUTH CAROLINA DEMOCRATS had long been divided between violent hard-liners like Gary and Matthew Calbraith Butler, and conventional conservatives, who believed just as fervently in white supremacy but opposed the kind of terrorism that might provoke Grant into sending more federal troops to the state. Now, smelling electoral victory in November, the extremists became willing to accept a strategic compromise by supporting a gubernatorial candidate palatable to the less radical electorate. During a fox hunt soon after the Hamburg massacre, Gary and Butler found themselves talking about their former wartime commander, Wade Hampton, an Edgefield native who had taken up farming in Mississippi. Gary announced "with an emphatic expletive, that is the winning card."

Hampton looked the part they wanted him to play. He had the manners of a gentleman, a magnificent full beard and handlebar mustache, and unimpeachable Confederate credentials, the latter a sine qua non for any Democrat seeking advancement in public life. Though he was once one of the wealthiest men in the state and emblematic of the old slave-owning aristocrat, the war had nearly ruined him. In 1861, he had raised his own unit of cavalry, in which both Gary and Butler had served as officers, and had fought from Bull Run to the surrender. Although never directly implicated in the Ku Klux Klan's terrorism, he had contributed to the defense of arrested Klansmen. "His war record, principled stands, and magnanimous promises helped South Carolinians convince themselves that they were still a noble, heroic people even as they violated the rule of law, stuffed ballot boxes, and gave the lie to their claims of being paternalistic, charitable protectors of African Americans," wrote his biographer Rod Andrew Jr.

The state Democratic convention met in August, in the statehouse at Columbia, a city that was still scarred with scattered ruins left from its incineration in the last days of the war—galling reminders of Confederate defeat. Butler himself nominated Hampton, bestowing on him the imprimatur of the party's radical wing, and he was approved without dissent. He readily embraced the party's carefully calibrated platform, which condemned official "mismanagement" and emphasized reform, low taxes, good government, hard money, and home rule—the last a euphemism for states' rights and the expulsion of the few federal soldiers remaining in South Carolina. Significantly, at least as a matter of rhetoric, it also condemned "disturbances of the peace" and promised to protect the rights, safety, and property of all its people, a formulation intended to quell the fears of local Blacks and national Republicans.

In 1871, with no reason at that time to conceal his true sentiments, Hampton had told a congressional committee investigating Klan atrocities, "The negro has an exaggerated opinion of his own power. You gentlemen do not know the negro at all. You all think the negroes are actuated by the same feeling as the white men, but that is a mistake." He now told South Carolina Blacks, "I shall be the governor of all the people, knowing no party, making no vindictive discrimination . . . protecting all classes alike." He promised to obey the postwar amendments but warned Blacks that they would not be allowed to rule the state.

Perhaps sincerely, Hampton hoped that his moderate-sounding posture would win him enough Black votes in November to overcome the racial disparity in registration. It also benefited the national Democrats, who although they openly embraced the principle of white supremacy were nonetheless concerned that the presence of a Southern general at the top of any state ticket might stoke

Northern fears of a Confederate revival. Even the impetuous Gary announced that no matter what Republicans claimed, the "Edgefield Plan" never intended to spill even a drop of Black blood.

IN FACT, Gary's "Red Shirts" saw the election as nothing less than an apocalyptic struggle between "civilization" and "barbarism." They soon demonstrated what they intended. When Chamberlain arrived in Edgefield to deliver a campaign speech to local Republicans, red-shirted horsemen swarmed the town square by the hundreds, "eager for frolic or fight," as a laudatory writer later put it, shrieking the wartime rebel yell. They planted their banners on the rostrum that had been set up for Chamberlain, perched in trees like sharpshooters with their rifles across their knees, and when Chamberlain rose alongside local Black politicians, the Democrats roared "Gary! Gary!" and demanded to "share the meeting," warning that if any trouble resulted it would be the Republicans' fault. Chamberlain tried to leave the rally but was prevented by Gary, who loudly excoriated him—verbally "firing red hot shot," as a reporter approvingly put it—calling him and the Blacks crooks and liars. Chamberlain was swarmed again when he tried to speak at Newberry and again at Abbeville, where he was subjected to thinly veiled threats of lynching and drowned out by a brass band, and the Red Shirts' local leader, Colonel D. Wyatt Aiken, yelled "If you want war, you can have it—yes, war to the knife, and knife to the hilt!"

In neighboring Union County, reported the Red Shirt Robert Shand, "A small cannon was found and put in charge of some veteran artillerymen who carried it around the county accompanied by a brass band. The cannon would be fired off from the hilltops, often at night, along with skyrockets. We made dark mysterious hints and even threats of what would befall [Black voters] if Hampton was not elected. Was all this justifiable? Yes. We had to fight as we could. Our campaign was an evil, but its success overcame a greater evil." When Chamberlain ordered the gun clubs to disband, they simply ignored him, and weapons that he had ordered for Black militias were stolen by the hundreds. After Abbeville, he rarely ventured to speak anywhere outside the safety of the capital, while Hampton seemed to be everywhere, galloping into town after town with a phalanx of whooping Red Shirts. Following one such affair, a Black Republican wrote bleakly to President Grant that the Red Shirts "march up to the colored men and toll theme that they must give up [the national] flage and as the Colored Men would not give up the flage they thence commence firen they pistol and Near to Theme as to Shoot holes in they Clothing." The message to Black voters was stark: Another Hamburg could occur again anytime.

Similar scenes played out in other states. In Louisiana, which lacked a unifying conservative leader like Hampton, who imposed at least some restraint, a federal investigation detailed vicious attacks on Republican organizers, voters, and their families that ranged from flogging and pistol-whipping to sexual humiliation and cold-blooded murder. Reports to Congress were bloodcurdling: a former member of the state legislature murdered . . . a "colored boy" dragged to death at a horse's tail . . . court broken up and the judge driven from his home . . . a sheriff shot at and forced to resign . . . "woman, whipped" . . . houses broken into and burned, wives and daughters flogged . . . sixty Blacks fired from their jobs for voting the Republican ticket . . . Ferdinand Bynum, "colored found dead in Ouachita River. Democratic militias were heard to sing a piece of doggerel with the lines: "A charge to keep I have, a God to glorify / If a nigger don't vote with us he shall therefore die." Charged with reporting on conditions in Louisiana, Senator John Sherman later wrote, "It seems more like the history of hell than of civilized and Christian communities. The means adopted are almost incredible, but were fearfully effective."

ON AUGUST 19, the perpetrators of the Hamburg massacre appeared before a county judge in Aiken, South Carolina. Witnesses had identified ninety-four of them at a coroner's inquest overseen by the state. They were charged with varying degrees of involvement, including first-degree murder. Evidence of their guilt was abundant. Failure to convict them, everyone knew, would mean an admission that the state government was impotent to protect its citizens. On the appointed day, the accused accompanied by hundreds of their supporters galloped into Aiken and circled the town at breakneck speed, with rifles at the ready, as white residents waved them on with fluttering handkerchiefs. Aiken's white women had provided them with new red shirts for the occasion, many of them decorated with splotches made by pokeberry juice meant to symbolize bullet holes, as if it were they rather than the dead at Hamburg who were the real victims of the riot. The defendants were allowed to wear their sidearms into the courtroom, unchallenged by court officers. Six of the twelve jurors were also among those on trial. Insofar as they bothered to make any argument at all, the defense attorneys—Martin Gary among them—asserted falsely that the militiamen at Hamburg had no official status but had been organized specifically "for the purpose of killing whites." (The militia had in fact been raised by the state government to protect otherwise defenseless Black citizens.) Gary then submitted 130 fraudulent affidavits providing alibis for the defendants. They then signed bail bonds for each other and were sent home. Ben Tillman, one of the defendants, later admitted that the proceedings were a "laughable travesty," adding, "If they had attempted to put us in jail I am sure few or none of us would have acquiesced; and we would probably have killed every obnoxious radical in the courtroom and town, and gone to Texas or some other hiding place." No one would ever be punished for the Hamburg massacre.

CHAPTER 9

THE MOLLIES

★ ★ ★ ★ ★

Well, we've been beaten all to smash.
And now, sir, we've begun to feel the lash.

—MINERS' BALLAD

Strangely, given the Centennial's mesmerizing arrays of machinery, there was barely any mention of the men and women who comprised the nation's industrial workforce, much less their struggle to survive through the years of economic depression. There were, of course, docents who cheerfully explained new machines, and the capable Miss Allison who oversaw the printing press in the Women's Pavilion. But for the most part it seemed as if the dazzling technology that the fair celebrated existed in a human vacuum epitomized by the majestic Corliss Engine, whose lone operator was like a mere apostrophe, an incidental appendage, to its steel mechanism.

The great engine prompted William Dean Howells to a remarkable flight of poetry that subtly hinted at the still inchoate divide between technology and human well-being, which in the coming century would increasingly seem both ubiquitous and unbridgeable. "It rises loftily in the center of the huge structure, an athlete of steel and iron with not a superfluous ounce of metal on it," Howells wrote, awed by its "majesty" and its "vast and almost silent" grandeur.

> The mighty walking-beams plunge their pistons downward, the enormous flywheel revolves with a hoarded power that makes all tremble, the hundred life-like details do their office with unerring intelligence. In the midst of this ineffably strong mechanism is a chair where the engineer sits reading his newspaper, as in a peaceful bower. Now and then he lays down his paper and clambers up one of the stairways that cover the framework, and touches some irritated spot on the giant's body with a drop of oil, and goes down again and takes up his newspaper; he is like some potent enchanter there, and this prodigious Afreet is his slave who could crush him past all semblance of humanity with his lightest touch.

Apart from its hypnotic power, the engine symbolized a rapidly emerging industrial culture that prized efficiency over the already frayed dignity of human labor, and the advent of violent class conflict to challenge for decades to come Americans' wishful ideal of a unified nation striding confidently toward a harmonious future.

ALONGSIDE THE REPORTS from Hamburg and demoralizing news of Custer's defeat and its aftermath, horrified Americans were also reading about the unfolding exposure of a labor struggle in the coalfields of Pennsylvania. In a series of trials that summer, prosecutors presented the shocking portrait of an American hellscape held hostage by a "diabolical conspiracy" at war with American capitalism. At its core, prosecutors charged, lay a secret society of assassins, thugs, and incendiaries known as the "Molly Maguires," who sought to seize control of the collieries. Respectable society demanded their "extermination," roared a newspaper in nearby Lancaster County.

Just what the Mollie Maguires were—or even *if* they were—still remains controversial. What is certain, however, is that the *idea* of the "Mollies" terrified Americans, who feared them as a menace on the scale of the South's Ku Klux Klan and the "savages" of the frontier, perhaps even more so, embedded as they were like a deadly worm in the North's industrial vitals, just eighty miles from the Centennial, amid the corrugated, coal-rich hills of Schuylkill County and the surrounding area. The Mollies had become ideological shorthand for revolutionary forces that increasing numbers of Americans feared were poised to exploit the widening fissure between capital and labor. Deepening labor strife loomed over the states, Walt Whitman wrote in 1871, like "an ominous, limitless, murky cloud, perhaps before long to overshadow us all." In America's cities, Whitman saw a desperate proletariat who lived from hand to mouth, with nothing to look forward to, without property, as capital aggregated in the hands of a few, new machinery replaced handwork, and "countless squads of vagabond children [roamed] everywhere the streets and wharves" alongside "pompous, nauseous, outside shows of vulgar wealth."

LABOR CONFLICT had been rare in less-industrialized antebellum America. In response to the growth of postwar capitalism, workers' protests proliferated. Most were spontaneous and localized, and almost none succeeded. To Americans imbued with a near-religious faith in individualism, trade unions seemed suspiciously foreign, perhaps even unchristian. As a result, the country's first attempts at union-building soon withered, notable among them the short-lived Knights of Labor, organized in 1870, which espoused a universal alliance of skilled working men, but that hobbled its leverage by requiring its members to support laws which claimed to harmonize the interests of labor and capital, and accepted only men who avowed belief in God. The Panic of 1873 wrought havoc on the embryonic labor movement. As unemployment topped 15 percent nationally and 30 percent in some places, the number of trade unions plummeted from thirty in 1873 to fewer than ten by 1875. In the absence of unions, employers brazenly slashed wages, while cities saw marches of the desperate unemployed, and the authorities increasingly responded with violence.

Labor activism repelled even high-minded Republicans, who had long taken pride in their role as the nation's conscience, championing antislavery, temperance, and moral reform. But they had never found support among wage laborers. Workers—many of whom were immigrants—were alienated by both the Republicans' ingrained nativist tilt and their bias toward the interests of big business. A rare divergent voice was that of former Senator Ben Wade, an uncompromising Radical, who warned that the coming generation would face a war between labor and capital unless Congress addressed "the terrible distinction between the man that labors and the man that does not." But Wade's warning was drowned out amid Republicans' fears of outright revolution.

Marxist thinking was nearly unknown in America until 1871, when Victoria Woodhull, the flamboyant feminist—and protégée of the infatuated financier Cornelius Vanderbilt—published a translation of *The Communist Manifesto* in her weekly newspaper. The same year, the bloody rise and fall of the Paris Commune turned the still muddy notion of ideological communism into a battle cry that rattled capitalists and conservatives. In March, Parisians seized control of the city center in a quixotic effort to oust the country's incompetent royal government after its battlefield humiliation by Prussia. Led by self-proclaimed radicals, the Communards seized armories, looted the homes of the wealthy, and shot hundreds associated with the royal government, including the archbishop of Paris. When loyal troops retook the city two months later, they massacred more than 20,000 people in retribution, including women and children. France's trauma immediately became an international touchstone for mob rule and fostered a fear of "Communism" that would last for generations. In the years that followed, menacing new ideas began to circulate among American workers: "Let the factories with all their machines be ours!" declared a workingmen's paper, the *National Labor Tribune,* in 1875. "Down with work for wages! Arise and battle for possession of the materials!" No words could terrify the business class more.

Tourists in Philadelphia for the Centennial thronged to North & Co.'s Music Store on Chestnut Street, to visit a spectacular cyclorama of the siege of Paris, in which on 20,000 square feet of canvas they could see the harrowing of the French capital by the Commune, along with a sort of grisly bonus, a painting of the murder of the archbishop. Fear fueled resistance to labor demands of any sort, however reasonable. The ongoing economic crisis further hardened public opinion against "philanthropy" generally, whether on behalf of embattled Southern freed people, starving Native Americans, or the struggling unemployed. "Every man is capable to do something which the world wants enough to keep him alive while he is doing it," harshly editorialized the *New York World*. "If he will not do that something he ought to starve."

LIKE HIS RIVAL TOM SCOTT, Franklin B. Gowen, the thirty-nine-year-old president of the Reading Railroad, was already a prime architect of industrial capitalism in Pennsylvania and a star in the nation's corporate firmament. He was aggressive and supremely self-confident, a brilliant speaker whose "wit, eloquence and stage presence seemed to administer a local anesthetic to the seat of logic." It was said that he could hold a shareholders' meeting in thrall for hours, even when he was delivering bad news. Ironically, perhaps, Gowen was a stalwart Democrat. Although his party's rhetoric generally claimed to represent the interests of immigrants and working men, its leadership was not much less plutocratic than that of the Republicans. After serving as public prosecutor in Schuylkill County during the Civil War, he became the Reading's corporate counsel, and in 1870 its president. Gowen turned it into an omnivorous empire that consumed railroads, coal mines, canals, and deepwater shipping. To underwrite it all, Gowen jettisoned the Reading's reputation for probity and multiplied its corporate borrowing twelve times over until, by 1876, it was shouldering $7 million in debt, which his creative accountants shuttled back and forth between the railroad and its mining subsidiary, as it suited them.

In the process, Gowen created the country's first price-fixing cartel by organizing Northeastern industrialists to manipulate the coal market, and flouted the Reading's own state charter by forming a false-flag holding company to amass 100,000 acres of prime mining land, in turn enabling it to dominate production across the entire region. The Pennsylvania Railroad was furious at Gowen's ambitions, but could hardly take legal action since Scott had himself pioneered the invention of shell companies. Powerful as Scott was, Gowen repeatedly bested him, first thwarting the Pennsylvania's acquisition of a valuable line between the oilfields and New York City, and again when the Pennsylvania tried to invade the Reading's home territory by building its own competitive line up the Schuylkill Valley. In 1873, when Gowen engineered the creation of a coal owners' cartel, allotting shares of the anthracite trade to several smaller rail lines that served the mines, he pointedly excluded the Pennsy.

PENNSYLVANIA COAL was as essential to the American economy of the 1870s as Texas oil would be to a later age. The state's deep seams of anthracite powered the nation's railroads and factories and warmed its homes everywhere. Extracting it was brutal work. Miners toiled in a fog of coal dust, threatened by asphyxiation, poisoning, floods, and collapsing tunnels. "Breaker boys" as young as eight broke coal with hammers for up to ten hours a day, sometimes falling onto conveyor belts or chutes to be crushed by hurtling streams of coal. There was no safety net for the injured, no compensation for the dead. Similar conditions of course existed throughout American industry. One of Andrew Carnegie's plant managers in Pittsburgh reported to him matter-of-factly one day, "Had an unfortunate accident this morning. Rope on cupola hoist broke and cage fell catching the Hoist Boy in the act of crossing under, crushing him to a jelly. It was caused by the boy's carelessness, and disobedience of order and the poor fellow paid the penalty with his life. Delayed works slightly." Immigrant workers were also subject to a rigid ethnic caste system under which most of the skilled and better-paid work was done by Protestant English and Welsh, and the roughest by Irish Catholics who were rarely allowed to advance no matter how much experience they had.

The coal region had long been a national byword for instability. During the Civil War, Copperheads, then too labeled "Molly Maguires," agitated violently against the Union war effort, while strikes roiled the tunneled hills as coal prices rose and fell. Miners defied draft enrollment officers, halted trains carrying draftees, and overpowered militiamen dispatched to subdue them. Several mine bosses involved in labor disputes were killed. Federal officers in some townships were finally directed to fake the conscription returns to prevent even worse violence.

After the war, Pennsylvania miners established one of the first successful industrial unions in the United States, the Workingmen's Benevolent Association, which at its peak enrolled as much as 85 percent of the total workforce in the state. The union opposed violence and strikes as strategically counterproductive, and negotiated effectively for stable wages, safe working conditions, welfare for the injured, and an eight-hour workday. These were hardly threatening goals, but they were intolerable to Gowen and his fellow capitalists, who regarded them as a criminal restraint on corporate profit-making.

Gowen liked to portray himself as an honest broker willing to fairly balance the interests of management and labor, for instance proposing a sliding scale for wages based on the price of coal, a system that satisfied miners as long as the price remained high. When the national economy collapsed in 1873, however, the value of coal plummeted, and wages crashed along with it. Where miners experienced crisis, Gowen saw opportunity. He set out to force a strike, defeat it, and break the union. In late 1874, the mine owners demanded across-the-board pay cuts of 20 percent or more. Their cartel was well prepared for a strike, having stockpiled enough coal to meet orders for months to come, but the union dreaded its consequences at a time when miners' families were already at risk. Snubbed by Gowen and pressed by the desperate rank and file, however, the union's leaders felt they had little choice, and in January 1875, they struck. Contemptuously accusing the strikers of failing to understand the basic laws of supply and demand, Gowen ordered that all union men be suspended from employment unless they repudiated their membership. Pro-business newspapers chimed in with inflammatory stories alleging a (nonexistent) reign of terror in the coalfields, illustrating them with images of feral, drunken, ape-faced Irish miners hurling rocks and brandishing clubs.

Gowen fostered not just the idea that the union was controlled by the legendary Molly Maguires. He also argued that they were one and the same as the Ancient Order of Hibernians, a legal, state-chartered Catholic organization that resembled the Masons and promoted Irish nationalism and the welfare of Irish immigrants in America. At the time, there were believed to be about 500,000 Hibernians nationwide, some 60,000 of them in Pennsylvania. Gowen was tapping a deep reservoir of anti-Catholic and anti-Irish bigotry that had flourished since the Great Famine sent a tidal wave of starving refugees to America in the 1840s. References to "Molly Maguires" began appearing a few years later, with the nativist press wildly claiming that they were a secret order bent on murdering Protestants and taking over the United States. The name had originated in British-ruled Ireland as a catchall for impoverished farmers who resisted the collection of confiscatory land rents, sometimes with violence. It surfaced in the United States once again during the 1860s as an umbrella term for troublesome miners, especially those who threatened mine bosses who discriminated against the Irish-born. There is little evidence that they were an organized body, although at least some Irish mine workers may have referred to themselves that way. Hibernians certainly were numerous among the strikers and in the broader cause of labor reform, however. By tainting them as subversives, Gowen put both the union and the Hibernians on the defensive, forcing them to deny the reality of an organization that because it was supposedly secret couldn't be proven *not* to exist. It made effective propaganda by diverting public opinion away from the railroad's all too real harassment of the strikers.

Gowen launched a venomous campaign of character assassination against John Kehoe, the region's most prominent Irish American political figure and, claimed Gowen, the secret commander of the Molly Maguires. Photographs of Kehoe show a handsome man—like Gowen, he was thirty-nine years old in the Centennial year—with clear, almost delicate features, piercing eyes, dark hair, and chin whiskers. Born in County Wicklow in Ireland, according to his biographer Anne Flaherty, he was a natural leader with at least a fair education and must have been both a hard and reliable worker, having achieved the privilege of working his own coal face, unusual for an Irish Catholic. By 1870, he had left the mines and was operating a hotel and tavern, and beginning his ascent in local politics. In 1874, he was elected the Hibernians' county delegate, and in 1875 a local constable. Unusual in rock-ribbed Democratic Schuylkill County, he lent his support to progressive Republican politicians who embraced labor reform, including a demand for the cooperative ownership of railroads, a cause guaranteed to inflame Gowen and his fellow magnates. In 1875, Kehoe helped swing Schuylkill County for Republican Governor John Hartranft's reelection. It isn't clear if he played a central role during the strike, apart from efforts to keep the peace, but Gowen nevertheless painted him as the satanic genius at the heart of its chaotic aftermath.

By the late spring of 1875, the union's treasury was empty. The strikers were growing increasingly desperate as their families foraged for roots in the woods. Embittered miners seized trains and overturned tenders. Company buildings were burned down, rebuilt, and burned again. Switches were spiked, locomotives derailed. Threatening messages illustrated with hand-drawn coffins were sent to colliery bosses. Sometimes shots were fired. To restore order, Governor Hartranft dispatched 1,800 state militia to the region. The pro-management *Miners' Journal* declared that if the strikers "will learn tolerance only by being shot down, it is better to shoot them down than to let them shoot others." In June, after five grueling months on strike, the union conceded defeat. Miners returned to work with no contract at all to face near-starvation pay that was 25 percent below what they had earned a year earlier. An unknown miner penned a ballad that captured their despair:

Well, we've been beaten, beaten all to smash
And now, sir, we've begun to feel the lash,
As wielded by a gigantic corporation.
Which runs the commonwealth and ruins the nation.

In the vacuum that ensued, Schuylkill descended into near anarchy. The mayhem that Gowen had alleged during the strike now became a reality. Mobbing, shootouts, and melees spread. "The union is Broke up and we Have got nothing to defind ourselves with

But our Revolvers and if we don't use them we shal have to work for 50 cints a Day," warned an anonymous letter to the press purporting to be from a vengeful miner. Before the summer was out, six men were dead, most of them mine foremen and local officials. Although there is scant evidence that the murders were related to one another, Gowen portrayed them as a part of a diabolical campaign by the Mollies to take over the coalfields.

Determined to smash what remained of the labor movement and its modest but not insignificant influence in the state capital, Gowen hired more than twenty undercover Pinkerton detectives to penetrate the Hibernians and gather what he promised would be damning evidence. (Founded to spy for the Union during the Civil War, the Pinkerton Agency went on to specialize in pro-business espionage and union-busting.) The Pinkertons also fed information to Protestant vigilantes who attacked Irish miners and their families. In December 1875, more than thirty masked men invaded the home of a reputed Molly, Charles McAllister, in the hamlet of Wiggans Patch, pistol-whipped his mother-in-law, murdered his pregnant wife, and tortured two other residents of the home, then shot one of them fifteen times in the head. John Kehoe arrived in the aftermath to learn that two of his kin were among the dead. Influenced by Gowen, however, the national press attributed virtually all the mayhem to Irish Catholics: Typically, *The New York Herald* shrilled that "the Molly Maguire not only murders but he crucifies . . . as our Saviour's hands were nailed to the cross."

ON MAY 19, 1876, Gowen made a dramatic move: With a theatrical flourish, eleven alleged Mollies were marched chained into the county courthouse at Pottsville, on a hilltop overlooking the city and the snaking Schuylkill River. All the accused were family men and community leaders: union delegates, election officials, school directors, small business owners, local constables, and of course miners. Most had been labor activists during the strike of 1875. And all were principal figures in the Ancient Order of Hibernians: county delegates like Dennis Canning; Christopher Donnelly, the Hibernians' treasurer for Schuylkill County; and local Hibernian officials—known as "body masters"—like Michael O'Brien, James Roarity, and John Gibbons. The *New York Sun* proclaimed them "the most extensive and desperate body of organized incendiaries, thugs, and assassins ever known on this continent." Gowen's biggest prize of all was John Kehoe. Almost none of them would walk out of the court as free men.

The trials that followed were a travesty. Irish Catholics were excluded from the juries. Most of the prosecutors worked for the railroads or mining companies. Gowen, who had a vested interest in the outcome, took charge of the prosecution. Even the flimsiest prosecution testimony was treated as fact while defense witnesses were speedily convicted of perjury and sentenced to years in prison, frightening others from coming forward. The defendants were denied the right to testify on their own behalf. A defense attorney, Samuel Garrett, told a jury, "Their mouths are closed and we cannot detail before you one single thing that took place . . . No matter how innocent the prisoners may be, they can never prove it." No one at all was charged with the vigilante murders at Wiggan's Patch. Virtually every defense witness was tarred as a Molly Maguire. One judge explicitly instructed his jury to give less weight to the defense, since its witnesses' testimony was "negative" while the prosecution's was "positive," while another told the jury that "any agreement, combination or confederation to increase or depress the price of any vendible commodity, whether labor, merchandise, or anything else, is indictable as a conspiracy under the laws of Pennsylvania." Mere membership in the Hibernians was treated as a crime. Newspaper coverage was apocalyptic, speaking of "a harvest of death and rapine" that had left "the prostrate form of Justice blind and bleeding." Even *The New York Times* extravagantly damned the Mollies as social revolutionaries who sought "to control all matters in connection with the management of the mines." Fearmongers raved that an army of Mollies might march on the courts to seize the prisoners.

Throughout the summer and into the autumn, the alleged Mollies were paraded through courtrooms in Pottsville and nearby Mauch Chunk under the guns of Gowen's Coal and Iron Police. In all, more than fifty men would be indicted on charges ranging from assault to murder and conspiracy, or simply membership in the Hibernians. Gowen stage-managed the courtroom show for maximum dramatic effect. By turns charming and bullying, he declared that to "be known as a Mollie Maguire is the worst character mortal man can have under the broad canopy of God's heaven." He cast himself as simply an ordinary citizen devoted solely to the public good, terming his case a "glorious crusade" destined to be forever remembered by a grateful and "redeemed" people. Far from pursuing a self-interested vendetta, he said, he was helping to ensure "the onward progress of reform."

Gowen's attack on the Hibernians was relentless. "Almost within the shadow of Independence Hall," he thundered, "tens of thousands of citizens are subject to a tyranny and a despotism such as neither Khan nor Caliph ever exercised, and such as in the wildest dream of power was ne'er conceived by Sultan or by Czar." In one trial, of two probably innocent Hibernians charged with murdering two Protestant mine employees, Gowen made explicit his nativist bias, charging that the defendants were "wretches so diabolical in their natures that murder was to them a pastime, ruling by the sympathies of a race and religion over a majority of the population of the region. The Irish element ruled Schuylkill County, and the Molly Maguires ruled the Irish element."

He blamed the Hibernians for every murder that had occurred in the county within memory. The bones of "hundreds of unknown victims," he astonishingly declaimed, devoid of evidence, lay moldering everywhere "in hidden places, in the dark ravines," turning Schuylkill County into "almost one vast sepulcher." He went on to evoke a grotesque image of half-buried bodies, skeleton hands bleached by the sun stretching up from the earth, slaughtered infants. There was no room for "false sympathy," he told the jury. To acquit any of the Mollies would be to "place the dagger and the pistol in their grasp," and to send them out once again to murder. Such men, he said, posed a dire threat not just to the county and Pennsylvania but to the stability of the entire capitalist system. "Of what use would capital, or wealth, or industry, or enterprise, or protection amount to," he demanded, "if the administration of the resources of this county and the development of its wealth were intrusted to those who went to do their duty, dogged by the assassin and the murderer, unknowing whether, when they left their houses in the morning, they would not be carried back dead before the night?" Such assertions were baseless, but they both fit and fed the growing public fear of organized labor.

JOHN KEHOE took the old Republican war cry of "Free Labor" at face value. To him, it meant liberating workers from the grip of industrial magnates like Gowen. But the influence of reformers within the Republican Party, never as great as Kehoe thought, was fast waning in a world where politics was ultimately driven by the imperatives of big business. Republicans and Democrats both tended to see the assertiveness of wage laborers not as a justified reaction to intolerable conditions but as a disease as innate to the poor as supposed cruelty in Indians and the primordial bestiality of former slaves. Beneath the soaring patriotic rhetoric of the Centennial year, for many Americans, ingrained belief in the biological and moral superiority of the white race was fusing with a sense that class differences, too, were elemental, and that pity for the suffering poor, white or Black, was merely soft-minded. *The Nation,* a leading voice for the conservative wing of the Republican Party, denounced public charity of any kind as "thoroughly communistic," complaining that it sapped "the foundation of that independence of character, and that reliance on one's own resources." (During the harsh winter of 1875, *The Nation* had even condemned the dispensing of free soup because it would spoil the "character" of the poor.)

Gowen cast John Kehoe as a satanic incubus tied to every crime the Mollies had ever perpetrated. "The young Irishmen of this county are ruined by hundreds and by thousands" by Kehoe, he fulminated, the "lord of life and death," who thought that he was so immune from punishment "that he could go into the crowded streets of a populous town, with his minions at his back, and shoot down in cold blood any citizen who had opposed his designs." Unable to tie any recent deaths directly to Kehoe, he had him charged with a murder nearly fifteen years old. He alleged that on July 4, 1862, during the agitation against wartime conscription, Kehoe had spat on the American flag, and that a mine foreman named Frank Langdon had rebuked him, after which Kehoe joined a mob that beat him so badly that he died the next day. The prosecution produced no evidence that Kehoe actually hit Langdon or even confronted him, only that he had been seen in the same town that day, drinking in a tavern. It would send Kehoe to the gallows.

Although Kehoe may have known who some of the perpetrators were, there was no evidence that he plotted any murders, except in the tainted testimony of paid witnesses, mainly a professional Pinkerton spy named James McParlan and a dapper Hibernian turncoat, Jimmie "Powderkeg" Kerrigan. The colorful McParlan had worked as a teamster, a deckhand, a logger, and a bartender before joining the Pinkertons in 1871. Supposedly on the run from the law in New York, he infiltrated the Hibernians in 1873 and became privy to its inner councils in Schuylkill County, or so he claimed. He portrayed Hibernian meetings that John Kehoe had called to discuss labor reform issues as a cabal to plot murders. Edward Monaghan, a defense witness, however, testified that at Hibernian meetings McParlan was sometimes the *only* man to urge the beating or killing of enemies. Four days after his testimony, Gowen had Monaghan charged with murder; witnesses against McParlan abruptly stopped coming forward.

Kerrigan, a wholly unreliable character—denounced as a liar even by his own wife—was almost certainly guilty of one or more of the murders. He turned state's evidence to escape the gallows, throwing blame onto men who were most likely innocent of anything but being in the wrong place at the wrong time. But he consistently repeated what Gowen wanted said. Two other key prosecution witnesses, the Butler brothers, were provocateurs whom Kehoe had specifically ordered to avoid using violence during the 1875 strike. Yet another turncoat informer, Michael Lawler, invented a preposterous scheme, allegedly concocted by Kehoe, to set fire to an entire village, burn down the homes with the residents in them, and shoot them down as they fled.

Not allowed to put his own clients on the stand, the Hibernians' lead attorney, Martin L'Velle, argued that if there was any crime wave in Schuylkill County, it dated from the arrival of McParlan himself, who, he noted, though supposedly privy to the Mollies' plans, had failed to warn any of the victims beforehand. The Hibernians' only real "crime," L'Velle said, lay in helping to organize workers in the Schuylkill County mines. "There was not a transgression or serious crime of any character in our county for years, until wealth and capital made aggressions upon the rights of the private citizen. For God's sake," he pleaded, "give labor an equal chance. Do not crush it. Let it not perish under the imperial mandates of capital in a free country." He surely knew that his defense was futile in a court where the outcome was preordained.

John Kehoe's personal ordeal was only beginning. While he fought on and the shackled Hibernians shuffled in and out of the courtrooms, Gowen's Reading Railroad profitably shuttled tourists by the hundreds of thousands to the Centennial in Philadelphia. Among them were contingents of Pennsylvania miners traveling free of charge as guests of the Reading's subsidiary, the Iron & Coal Co. With their wives and children, they were shepherded through the Centennial's wonders by the company's guides and treated to lavish lunches that included ice cream—for most of them a rare delight—and then returned home the same day on the Reading. Some of the miners and their families may have seen Edmonia Lewis's *Death of Cleopatra* in Memorial Hall, which remained on display until the close of the Centennial in November, a popular attraction to the end beneath its exotic red canopy. Not surprisingly, however, the miners were most impressed with the wonders of Machinery Hall, where they were awed by the Corliss Engine and other marvels of modern of engineering. Although Alexander Graham Bell was no longer there to demonstrate his apparatus, it is quite possible that the miners did see displays describing the technology of the telephone. One miner, Thomas King, in a letter to the Pottsville *Daily Miner,* wrote that his favorite exhibit was the powerful new Allison and Brannan air compressor, which, he opined, "would be a splendid thing for pushing air up gangways." Philadelphia newspapers patronizingly praised the visiting miners for their "intelligent and respectable" look and their "orderly and decorous" demeanor. For workers, the Reading's message was that while insurgency would meet with a hard hand, obedience would be rewarded. In letters prominently published in the Schuylkill County newspapers, the miners unctuously thanked Gowen for his kindness and for the "baskets well-loaded with good and substantial lunch. [He] could not have provided for us better if we were his children." The miners' docile presence at the Centennial offered public evidence of Gowen's boast that he had finally brought an end to mayhem in the coal country. In Pottsville, he triumphantly declared, "Now all are safe in this county. Come here with your money; come here with your enterprise; come here with your families and make this county your residence. The foul stain that had rested upon us has been wiped out forever."

Organized labor was indeed finished for the foreseeable future in Schuylkill County. The miners were cowed and frightened. Families were shattered. The Hibernians were decimated. The strike had won them nothing and left them more dependent than ever on the will of Gowen and his fellow mine operators. But the legacy of bitterness and radicalism continued to radiate far beyond the coalfields. The mine owners' cartel, a pro-labor Scranton newspaper caustically had editorialized in 1875, "with one hand reaches for the pockets of the consumers, and with the other for the throats of the laborers, and while it sits serenely gathering in the profits, like Tweed, in his palmy days." It was an analysis that swelling numbers of workers were taking to heart. American labor was newly astir, gathering itself for a great spasm of confrontation, one that in less than a year would reveal the agonies of Schuylkill County as a mere prelude to the shape of industrial conflict for generations to come.

CHAPTER 10

THE CONSTITUTIONAL ABYSS

★ ★ ★ ★ ★

I know nothing grander, more positive proof of the past, the triumphant result of faith in humankind, than a well-contested American national election.

—WALT WHITMAN

On September 21, looking dour and impatient, Samuel J. Tilden made his second appearance at the Centennial to mark "New York Day," one of a series of state fetes that had been held at the great fair. *The New York Times,* which supported Hayes, described it as a "very tame affair," asserting a bit churlishly that Tilden received only a "faint" cheer when he showed up at the New York pavilion. (A friendlier Philadelphia paper reported that pushy Democrats crowded the stairs of the small building in such numbers that some were "lifted by the pressing multitude [and] rolled off like potatoes from a heaped half-peck.") Tilden was so small and inconspicuous, however, that some well-wishers passed him by to shake the hand of one or another of his more impressive-looking aides.

Introverted by nature, Tilden spoke barely a word to those who greeted him. After space was made for him to address an expectant crowd that had gathered to hear him, he climbed onto a chair, and after a band encouragingly played "Hail to the Chief" and partisans raised three cheers for "Uncle Sammy," he laconically offered them simply a "cordial salutation" and a greeting from "New York's 5 million citizens." As the cheers died disappointedly away, he replaced his stovepipe hat and then hurried off through the Main Building and the Arts Hall to review a delegation of six hundred visiting New York City policemen and their brass band, and went back to New York.

Tilden had some reason for brittleness. The presidential contest was growing increasingly nasty. Democrats accused the Republicans of protecting the Molly Maguires, who they alleged would undoubtedly assert a poisonous influence in a Hayes administration. Republicans attacked Tilden personally as a tax evader, a shyster, an ally of Boss Tweed, and a wartime defeatist. In *Harper's Weekly,* the Republican cartoonist Thomas Nast sketched a pile of dead freedmen at Tilden's feet amid the smoking ruins of their homes under a poster that read "Niggers Reformed at Hamburg: The Centennial of our republic." It was hard for the Tilden campaign to attack the upright Hayes in personal terms. Instead, it tirelessly vilified Ulysses Grant as an American Mephistopheles and shrilled that the Republicans had left the country morally and materially bankrupt. Some darkly hinted that the Hamburg massacre had been cynically staged by the Republicans themselves to foment racial hatred.

A month after Tilden, on October 26, Rutherford B. Hayes appeared with some reluctance at the Centennial as the guest of honor to mark "Ohio Day." Serenaded by a brass band and chiming bells, and accompanied by his wife, Lucy, two sons, and Pennsylvania Governor Hartranft, he strolled through cheering crowds to the Ohio building. There in the course of several hours he shook an estimated four thousand hands of well-wishers, sometimes reaching the rate of thirty-eight per minute, an impressed journalist reported, conceding that Hayes's arm periodically "demanded relaxation and cease its pump-handle vibrations." Never a tub-thumper, Hayes said nothing that could be construed as political. The Centennial, now near its close, would never be forgotten, he blandly prophesied, speaking from a platform on the building's roof. "We hope, nay we confidently believe, that the influence of this celebration will be to extend and to perpetuate the principles of our Revolutionary ancestors, and to give an increased insurance to all mankind that the new nation brought forth on this continent a hundred years ago is destined, under Providence, long to remain the home of freedom and the refuge of the oppressed." It was quintessential Hayes: warm, heartfelt, and cautious. In his diary, he mainly expressed relief that he had carried off his speech "without saying anything that I regret." Even so, by all accounts he had outshone Tilden.

Anxiety spiked in the last frenetic days before the election. It was reported that gangs of professional repeaters were being recruited in Philadelphia to cast illegal votes in the neighboring states. Black Republicans were mobbed in Cincinnati. Troops were put on alert against street riots in New York and Baltimore. President Grant was inundated with reports of abuses from across the South: Black voters driven away from the polls at gunpoint, their ballots seized by whites and torn up in front of their eyes, Republicans forced to take Democratic ballots, election monitors threatened, Blacks told they were not allowed to vote at all. In Louisiana, the state Democratic committee appointed White Leaguers to "keep order" at the polls, while gangs of white gunmen from Mississippi and Arkansas poured into the state to threaten Black voters, confiscating the registration papers from some and beating others. At Edgefield Courthouse, in South Carolina, the Democratic election manager sequestered the ballot box in a room crowded with armed white men who prevented Blacks from entering, while permitting whites to vote up to four or five times each. And in nearby Union County, remarked the Red Shirt Robert Shand, "We got the managers—for a consideration—to count the heavy negro boxes last, and leave them overnight under my guard, while a party had been chosen to raid the room and carry off those boxes."

That evening, in New York, crowds ignored the drizzling rain, rushing back and forth among the newspaper offices clustered in lower Manhattan, impatiently waiting for the latest results as they were posted in the glare of calcium lights, roaring every time new numbers appeared. Republican hopes for a decisive victory were soon dashed. Hayes was swamped in New York and beaten squarely in Connecticut, New Jersey, North Carolina, and Indiana. It appeared for a time that he might even have lost his home state of Ohio. By morning, it became clear that he had at least carried the Pacific coast states, most of New England, and some of the Midwest. In anarchic Louisiana, Republicans were claiming a majority of 8,000, and Democrats a margin of 20,000, and in South Carolina, Republicans were asserting that they held a majority of at least 15,000, while jubilant Democrats claimed one of 4,000. A reporter wrote, "It is impossible to describe the wild delirium of the people of Charleston at what they regard as their deliverance from long subjection to the rule of robbers and negroes." *The New York Herald*'s breathless headline that morning declared:

NECK AND NECK
Who is it?
The Continental Conundrum from Maine to Oregon.

Tilden would go on to win the popular vote by more than 250,000, and although the Republicans would retain their majority in the Senate, the Democrats again secured control of the House of Representatives. Betting on Wall Street was running ten-to-one that Tilden would finally prevail in the electoral count. His campaign, flush with optimism, immediately began handing out invitations to an inaugural party at the White House. The results seemed to confirm what Hayes had feared all along: "We must, I now think, prepare ourselves to accept the inevitable."

While Hayes was preparing to surrender, his campaign chairman, the blunt-spoken spoilsman from Michigan, Zachariah Chandler, was not. Ensconced at party headquarters in New York, surrounded by a miasma of defeatist gloom, he decided to fight. That meant that Hayes would have to win the electoral votes of every contested state. "In the heated state of political feeling in those states," Senator John Sherman wrote, "it was a matter of grave doubt whether the count of the vote might not result in violence, tumult or war." Indeed, as news filtered through the country that Tilden had not been declared the victor, Democrats erupted.

Even in relatively quiescent Virginia, a federal informant telegraphed the White House, "At no hour have we been secure from an outbreak."

AS POLITICAL UNCERTAINTY agitated the nation, the Centennial came at last to a spirited if soggy end on November 10. Beneath raw skies, the little train, packed with riders, putt-putted in its circuit around the grounds, past halls packed to the last minute with tourists, to the final ringing of chimes and bells. Many exhibitors had already packed up and left. The popular Japanese Bazaar was empty except for a pair of tall bronze cranes. Rain drove the closing ceremonies indoors, where in the cramped quarters of the Judges' Hall an orchestra played Wagner's march, the "Hallelujah Chorus" from Handel's *Messiah,* and a chorale by Bach for an audience that included President Grant, members of the Supreme Court and the cabinet, senators and representatives, foreign diplomats, and bevies of lesser officials.

Valedictory speeches attempted to capture what the Centennial had achieved. Said John Welsh, a Philadelphia merchant and the Centennial's chief financial officer, the Exhibition "has taught us in what others excel, and excited our ambition to strive to equal them. It has taught others that our first century has not been passed in idleness and that, in at least a few things, we are already in the advance." To this, Joseph Hawley, the Exposition's president, added that the Centennial had proclaimed to the world that the United States must henceforth be reckoned with as a global power. When Hawley finished, the orchestra struck up "America" and a Miss Stafford unfurled above the speakers' dais the American flag carried on board Commodore John Paul Jones's frigate *Bon Homme Richard* in the Revolutionary War. (She was the daughter of an officer aboard the ship.) Hawley turned to Grant and said, "Mr. President, we await your pleasure." Grant rose and said, "I now declare the International Exhibition of 1876 closed." He waved his hand to a nearby telegrapher, who tapped out an order to the operator of the Corliss Engine. Its immense piston rods began to make slower and slower strokes, and then, at 3:40 p.m., finally stood still. For the first time in six months, there was complete silence in the great hall.

Within days, workers began to pack up all the machinery, displays, paintings, and exotic handicrafts to ship back to their makers and owners. They then dismantled all but a handful of the buildings. Auctioneers sold off most of what remained: the contents of Agricultural Hall, the Women's Pavilion, the state pavilions, the restaurants, the celebrated Turkish café, the butter and cheese factory, the sawmill, organs, fire engines, pipes, brooms, vitrines, millions of feet of lumber, veritable mountains of wrought iron trusses, girders, columns, and beams. The Japanese pavilion was removed to the Philadelphia suburbs, where it became a commuter station on the Pennsylvania Railroad. In its promotional materials, the railroad touted the entire Centennial as a corporate triumph: "The Corliss engine did not perform its appointed work, hour by hour, revolution by revolution, from May till November more perfectly than this great corporation."

THE NATION TEETERED on the edge of a constitutional abyss. Unprecedented challenges faced the intensely polarized parties all across the electoral map. For days, weeks, and ultimately months, Republicans and Democrats bitterly fought over the disputed results as the presidency hung in the balance. Rival sets of electors had been submitted from Alabama; in Nebraska, Democrats were seeking an injunction to prevent Republican electors from casting their votes; and although Oregon had voted overwhelmingly for Hayes, the Democratic governor had arbitrarily invalidated one of the three Republican electors and named one of the losing Democrats in his place, apparently handing Tilden one more vote in the Electoral College. There was even a question about the outcome in usually reliably Republican Vermont. But the crisis focused mainly on three Southern states whose votes, nearly everyone agreed, would determine the outcome of the election: Florida, South Carolina, and Louisiana. Even the phlegmatic John Sherman was nervous when he contemplated the risky seas on which the nation was embarked. Although he felt reasonably sure that Hayes would eventually be seated, he saw grave danger in the contest's dependence on the doubtful votes of three unstable states where fraud, murder, and violence had prevailed for years.

Not for more than half a century had Americans questioned the legitimacy of a president's election. Under the Twelfth Amendment, ratified in 1804, each state's members of the Electoral College were to send their votes to the presiding officer of the U.S. Senate, normally the vice president, who in the presence of both houses of Congress was charged with counting the votes and certifying the election; if no candidate had a majority, the House of Representatives would then choose the president, voting by states, with each state having a single vote. Nothing in the amendment addressed the possibility that states might submit multiple or disputed slates of electors, thereby crippling the system. There was no obvious resolution. Republicans held that the Senate's presiding officer, Thomas Ferry, a staunch partisan Republican, had the unilateral authority to declare Hayes elected, Vice President Charles Wilson having died in office. The Democrats' strategy was to force the count into the House, where they expected to prevail. Fears of a new civil war spiked. Grant directed army commander William Tecumseh Sherman to personally take charge of defending Washington against Democratic paramilitaries if they attempted to seize power. Sherman immediately deployed soldiers to protect leading Republicans and public property, and ordered four thousand troops back from the frontier to defend the capital.

As indignation flooded the country on his behalf, Tilden remained strangely passive, "less confiding and more distrustful even than Grant," in the words of one friend. Others complained that he seemed sluggish and uncombative in the midst of the greatest challenge of his career, and that he was forever huddled in confabulations with a handful of his closest advisors. He said little in public beyond reiterating confidence that he had won the election and would be inaugurated in March. When he did speak, he was typically dry and elliptical, simply repeating his hope to improve the civil service by recruiting educated men of high ideals who disdained the scramble of competitive politics. Influential supporters pressed him to show some fire, without success.

The contested returns were eventually winnowed to four states. In Oregon, Governor LaFayette Grover claimed that as a federal official—an assistant postmaster—Republican J. W. Watts was ineligible to serve as an elector and replaced him with Democrat E. A. Cronin. When the remaining two Republican electors refused to cooperate, rejecting up to $10,000 in bribes, Grover highhandedly "disqualified" them, for which he had no authority, and named two more Democrats in their place, a sleight of hand so bold that even some national Democrats disapproved. Watts thereupon resigned his postmaster's job and with his fellow Republicans cast their votes for Hayes, leaving the two parties to submit warring certificates to Washington.

Florida appeared to have been won by Tilden, but it had submitted *three* separate sets of returns. The Republican-dominated canvassing board had systematically invalidated local returns favoring Tilden on technicalities, but declined to do the same in districts that had voted for Hayes. While the board's bias was obvious, it was equally clear that had Black voters not been scared from the polls Hayes would have won in a landslide. The state's Republican governor, Marcellus Stearns, whose election was also in doubt, quickly certified the results for Hayes. But the state supreme court overturned the board's certification of Stearns's election and declared his Democratic opponent, George Drew, the winner instead. Drew thereupon certified Tilden as the winner in the presidential race. Next, the new Democratic-controlled legislature ordered a recount of the presidential ballots by its own canvassing board, which also certified Tilden and submitted its own certificate—the third—to Congress. Reports reached Washington that gangs of rampaging Tildenites were derailing trains and tearing up telegraph wires.

In South Carolina, both parties had declared victory in the gubernatorial and legislative elections. Grant initially directed the army to "sustain" Daniel H. Chamberlain, the Republican candidate-elect, as governor. Democrats then threatened to "exterminate" the state's leading Republicans if they prevented Hampton from taking office. Thousands of Red Shirts invaded the statehouse, where the Republican-dominated legislature declared Chamberlain reelected by 3,044 votes. (Georgia railways offered discount fares for militant whites to travel to Columbia to join the mob.) Ignoring Chamberlain, Hampton asserted himself as de facto governor, calling on citizens to pay their taxes to his men rather than the state's, effectively crippling the state's finances. Democrats also formed their own self-declared legislature, which crowded into the statehouse, where the rival bodies held their sessions on the same floor and both parties' speakers occupied the same podium. Virtually everyone was armed. "One pistol shot would have been the occasion of a massacre," recalled Red Shirt Robert Shand. The Red Shirts eventually withdrew. But their point had been made: They had the power to sweep Chamberlain from office at gunpoint, if they chose to.

The situation was also volatile in Louisiana, where armed White Leaguers roamed the streets and threatened to unseat the state's precarious Republican administration. Grant appointed Senator John Sherman to join a committee of monitors to oversee the counting of votes, warning him on November 12, "Unless you reach there by Friday morning"—five days later—"it will be too late." Sherman stopped en route in Columbus to see Hayes, who told him "in the strongest possible language" that he opposed any effort by his supporters to influence the returning board in his favor: "We are not to allow our friends to defeat one outrage and fraud by another. Let Mr. Tilden have the place by violence, intimidation and fraud, rather than undertake to prevent it by means that will not bear the severest scrutiny." Hayes preserved his sense of integrity, but by all accounts great sums of money changed hands as agents of both parties attempted to buy electoral votes in what was essentially an open market. The canvassing board found plentiful evidence of widespread fraud, mainly against Black voters, and threw out ballot boxes in fifteen parishes, where "intimidation by murder, hanging, whipping, and other outrages" was so ubiquitous that every vote was disqualified. None of this had any effect on coup-minded White Leaguers, who declared their candidates elected anyway, and in January seized the city courts and police headquarters, threatening to shell the statehouse with the cannon they had captured from the state armory.

Grant, with just weeks left to his presidency, was increasingly exasperated. "They are always in trouble down there," he complained to his cabinet. Speaking to the Senate in January, he warned that the degree of agitation the country was suffering could not be tolerated any longer. "It needs and it desires peace and quiet and harmony between all parties and all sections; its industries are arrested, labor unemployed, capital idle, and enterprise paralyzed by reason of the doubt and anxiety attending the uncertainty of a double claim to the Chief Magistracy of the nation. It wants to be assured that the result of the election will be accepted without resistance from the supporters of the disappointed candidate, and that its highest officer shall not hold his place with a questioned title of right."

Hayes's reserve had faded and his will had stiffened. Although he still eschewed active involvement in the count, he now felt that he was fully entitled to the presidency. To his ally Representative Samuel Shellabarger he wrote, "We must rely on our own strength to secure our rights. With firmness it can be done." What would happen if no compromise could be reached, he worried, if both he and Tilden were sworn in by their partisans, like the rival governors in South Carolina. It would mean "a contest ruinous to the country, dangerous, perhaps fatal to free government." He struggled "to keep cool, master all tendencies that may lead me astray, and endeavor to act as Washington would have under similar circumstances." Despite his ethical disclaimers, he could hardly have been completely unaware of his agents' efforts to buy off Democratic electors, or that he could win over many Democrats if he promised to treat former Confederates with "consideration"—a euphemism for acquiescence in the restoration of white rule and access to federal patronage.

A subtle shift was becoming discernible in Hayes's thinking about "the unfortunate topic" of race. He had always professed sincere commitment to the rights of the freed people. As recently as November, he had reflected that if he lost the count the likely nullification of the postwar amendments by the Democrats would erase the promise of equality and safety for "the colored people." But he increasingly expressed a reluctance to confront the forces that threatened those rights. He had come to accept, like most Republicans, including Grant, that use of the military to protect Black Southerners was no longer politically possible. He told himself that in time the South's economy would expand, whites' bitterness would naturally soften, and the races would find a humane way to live together. "Too much politics, too little attention to business, is the bane of that part of the country," he wrote to a friend on Christmas Eve. Then, in February, he told the German American journalist Carl Schurz, who had for years promoted reconciliation with Southern whites, "My anxiety to do something to promote the pacification of the South is perhaps in danger of leading me too far. I do not reflect on the use of the military power in the past. But there is to be an end of all that. We must go cautiously and slowly. Perhaps we must be content not to obstruct time's healing processes by injudiciously meddling." And to John Sherman he wrote, "It has always seemed to me wise in case of decided antagonisms to heal by compromise, not to aggravate." He was seriously entertaining the idea of appointing Southern Democrats to his government—perhaps even a former rebel general such as Joseph E. Johnston.

WITH BOTH Hayes and Tilden remaining high-mindedly aloof from the political trench warfare of the count, the solution of the country's crisis was left to more pragmatic men. In this vacuum of leadership, Representative George McCrary, an Iowa Republican, proposed the creation of an entirely new, extraconstitutional body empowered to rule definitively on the disputed electoral votes. By January, McCrary's idea had evolved into an Electoral Commission composed of five senators, five members of the House, and five members of the Supreme Court who would elect one of their own number as chairman. It was an impressive panel, stuffed with constitutional lawyers, eminent statesmen, future Secretary of State Democratic Senator Thomas Bayard of Delaware, and a future president, James A. Garfield. Many Republicans initially resisted the scheme as a ploy that might be exploited by Hayes's rivals—

notably the disgruntled New Yorker Roscoe Conkling—to undermine their president-elect. Democrats liked it because they assumed that Supreme Court Justice David Davis, a political independent who leaned Democratic, would be named chairman, and that in the event of ties his deciding vote would most likely favor Tilden.

Neither Hayes nor Tilden—both sticklers for constitutional precedent—personally approved of the idea but, like the great Corliss Engine, the machinery of politics had begun to move, and it churned along largely without them. The scheme almost collapsed when Davis declined the appointment, having just been elected to the U.S. Senate from Illinois. The four remaining members of the Court then turned to Joseph Bradley as the least objectionable of the justices available. Bradley was a Republican but he was a moderate. An expert in commercial law, he was the author of the notorious *Slaughter-House* decision in 1873, which crippled federal enforcement of the Fourteenth Amendment. He was also an ally of Tom Scott, having served as chief counsel for two of the Pennsylvania Railroad's subsidiaries.

Conclusive evidence that Scott directly intervened in the crisis is lacking, but it was widely understood that a Hayes victory would benefit Scott's Texas & Pacific Railway. With most Southern Democrats claiming to scorn railroad subsidies as a hallmark of Republican corruption, Scott couched his appeals for federal support as a matter of "sectional justice" for the South and cynically asserted that his war against Collis Huntington for control of the southwestern route was a populist struggle against the Californian's monopolistic greed. Scott had achieved some success, for instance winning (or buying) the cooperation of L. Q. C. Lamar of Mississippi, a former Ku Klux Klan lawyer who was now the chairman of the House Pacific Railroad Committee. However, Scott's best hope for a decisive victory over Huntington depended on Republican control of the White House.

Beyond pure self-interest, Scott certainly was concerned that the continuing crisis threatened the nation's economic stability as well as the Pennsylvania Railroad's, given its far-flung holdings. One well-connected journalist argued that dozens of Democrats in Congress could be persuaded to abandon Tilden if "Scott with his whole force could come [to Washington], and get those votes in spite of all human power, and all the howlings which blusterers North and South could put up." Significantly, in January, it was reported that if Hayes was elected the government would guarantee the Texas & Pacific a payment of 5 percent interest on the company's bonds. (This would entail a liability of almost a quarter of a billion dollars, "more than double the total of all federal internal-improvement spending from 1789 to 1873," according to the leading historian of the Pennsylvania Railroad.) Just how much effort Scott put into this initiative may never be known, but he likely induced at least some Democrats to contemplate a compromise that otherwise repelled them.

The Electoral Commission was approved by Congress on January 29, and with barely a month to Inauguration Day, it pitched immediately into the wilderness of antagonistic claims and counterclaims. Its hearings spanned more than three tense weeks as, one by one, it dealt with the disputed states. Its findings were strictly legalistic, its mandate having allowed the commission no scope to further investigate the ample evidence of Democratic intimidation, and in some areas outright terrorism, that had clearly skewed the popular vote in all the Southern states. With Bradley's deciding vote favoring Republican arguments, infuriated Democrats watched one state after another slip from their grasp. The commission ruled that since Florida's Republican-dominated canvassing board had filed its admittedly flawed slate of electors by December 6, as legally required, the two belated Democratic slates had to be disqualified and the state assigned to Hayes. It nullified the Oregon governor's certification of the single Tilden elector because he had overreached his legal authority. It rejected as legally baseless the claim of Louisiana Democrats that their state's election board was unconstitutional. And it dismissed the Hamptonites' challenge in South Carolina by noting that the so-called Democratic electors were self-appointed and had no legal standing at all. The commission further noted that while the Democrats' charge that federal troops had been present in the vicinity of some polls on Election Day was accurate, they were there not to threaten but to protect voters.

The commission had accomplished what it was created to do, by hacking its way through the tangled maze that had paralyzed politics for months. However, the Constitution still required Congress to officially certify the results. Although some Democrats were grudgingly prepared to accept the commission's rulings, others remained determined to thwart the process at all costs, even if it led to bloodshed. No one knew what would happen if Congress failed to certify by March 4, when the new president was to be inaugurated. (The date mandated by the Constitution was actually March 3, but in 1877 that date fell on a Sunday, and inaugurations never took place on the sabbath.) Across the nation, the sense of impending danger continued to grow. There were persistent rumors that Hayes would be kidnapped if he attempted to travel to Washington, and that Tilden would be installed by force. Joseph Pulitzer, editor of the *New York World* and a Democratic partisan, called for 100,000 Tildenites to come to the capital armed and ready to fight, while the Louisville *Courier-Journal* incited 10,000 Kentuckians to swarm the Capitol: "Less than this will be of no avail." Some predicted that former General George B. McClellan, a conservative Democrat, would come out of retirement to lead troops in a march on Washington. The slogan "Tilden or blood" was heard in Democratic strongholds, and Tildenite "Minute Men" enrolled in eleven states, declaring themselves ready to go to war. Even saner heads feared that there could be two separate inauguration ceremonies, with both men claiming the powers of commander in chief. Tilden, to his credit, dampened the fervor, telling his agents that having just emerged from one civil war, the nation couldn't survive another. Privately, however, he seemed broken in spirit. The wife of his secretary, Mrs. G. W. Smith, later confided, "The result was a distinct shock to him, and from that time on, *paralysis agitans* grew on him."

Unknown to the public, driven by the urgency of the moment, secret talks were taking place among batteries of pragmatic Republicans and Democrats in the last days of February at different venues around Washington, from committee rooms at the Capitol to secluded suites in downtown hotels. In different configurations, they included Sherman and Garfield, several personal friends of

Hayes, former Indiana Republican Governor and now Senator Oliver P. Morton, fanatically pro-Southern Louisville *Courier-Journal* owner Henry Watterson, the former Confederate General and now Georgia Senator John B. Gordon, William Levy, a lame-duck Democratic congressman from Louisiana, and others. Gradually, the contours of a compromise—a "bargain," as it sometimes was disdainfully put—began to take shape.

Certain political facts were now clear: There was no public or congressional appetite for yet another military intervention in the South, and although few were prepared to say so openly, most Republicans understood that the government was no longer going to exert itself to protect Black Southerners. (When Louisiana Republican Governor-Elect Stephen Packard warned Grant that if troops were pulled out of New Orleans the White League "would leave no Republican state government for your successor to recognize," Grant coolly replied, via his commander in the city, "I would let the two governors work out their own precedence for Executive recognition.") At the same time, Democrats recognized that the commissions' rulings had severely weakened if not destroyed their hopes of putting Tilden in the White House. Democrats continued to demand ironclad concessions in favor of Southern home rule, which Republicans had been instructed by Hayes, albeit rather obliquely, not to give. However, Hayes had intimated in his elliptical way that he was ready to embrace a more conciliatory policy toward the South. As vague as this was, Hayes's representatives strongly advised their Democratic counterparts that they should understand it as an imminent change of policy in their favor, and that they would not get anything better.

When the members of Congress gathered for their final session, on March 1, it seemed to most that despite the herculean labors of past months, compromise still lay tantalizingly beyond reach. Hayes was already en route to Washington from Columbus with an entourage carried in two special cars provided by Tom Scott, with no certainty that he would be accepted as president. The mood on the floor of the House was stormier than anyone could remember, the tone of debate vicious. John Goode of Virginia, a former member of the Confederate Congress, fulminated that Wade Hampton was being kept out of the governor's office in South Carolina only by "the power of the federal bayonet." William Terry of Virginia, a former commander of the Confederacy's Stonewall Brigade, charged that the Republican Party had become "so flagrant in its frauds" that "I not only feel myself free to interpose every lawful impediment in the way of the inauguration of Governor Hayes but I should be derelict in duty if I failed to do so." Ignoring the commission's conclusions, or dismissing them as fraud, their allies objected to the counts in Michigan, Wisconsin, Nevada, Pennsylvania, Oregon, and Vermont, where Tildenites had baselessly submitted an alternate set of returns. The atmosphere was chaotic and deafening, with dueling cries for "order!" and hammerings of the Speaker's gavel. Members climbed onto desks demanding recognition. Visitors hooted from the galleries and pushed onto the floor. Revolvers were drawn and women fled in fear. Accused of wasting the body's time, an angry Democrat from Ohio inveighed, "When fraud is law, filibustering is patriotism."

To the relief of the vast majority of Americans, and no doubt himself, Hayes arrived safely at Union Station at the foot of Capitol Hill around 9:30 on the morning of March 2, to be greeted by John Sherman and his grizzled brother William Tecumseh. Fortunately, the kidnapping that he had been warned of never materialized. Nor did mobs of insurrectionary Democrats. That evening, Hayes was quietly sworn in as president by Chief Justice Morrison Waite at John Sherman's home, in hope of preventing a perilous daylong interregnum on Sunday with no president at all.

On Capitol Hill, the hours ticked away in sterile debate through the rest of March 2 and then through March 3, and on into March 4, as tempers further frayed, until bespectacled William Levy of Louisiana, until now a zealous obstructionist, emerged amid the mayhem to signal that he had something momentous to say. Fresh from the latest conference with Republican negotiators, he announced that he would no longer object to completing the count and urged other Democrats to join him. "Thoroughly convinced of the injustice wrought by the decision of the Electoral Commission," Levy said, "I feel that sound policy and the paramount consideration of the salvation of the state and people of Louisiana require that their representatives in this House should abstain from a futile attempt to nullify that decision and thereby postpone the redemption which is essential to their very existence." He said that he had received "solemn, earnest, and, I believe, truthful assurances" from prominent members of the Republican Party that Hayes was prepared to allow the Southern people to settle political matters in their own way. "Satisfied that his accession to the office is well-nigh an accomplished fact, I do not hesitate to declare that, actuated by a sense of duty to Louisiana, I shall throw no obstacle in the way of completion of the electoral count." He called upon his friends and allies to join him. Twenty-three Democrats would do just that. Tilden himself wired his loyalists that he wanted the count to end. Levy's speech was a watershed. Although some die-hards continued to raise dilatory points of order and demand time-consuming roll call votes, the stalemate was over.

At 4 a.m. on March 2, the members of the Senate marched into the House chamber. Senator Ferry took a seat next to the House Speaker, Democrat Samuel J. Randall of Pennsylvania, an enemy of Reconstruction who had also abandoned confrontation for pragmatism. State by state the tallies of electoral votes were read off with each disputed one being added to Hayes's column, inexorably providing him at last with the single-vote majority, 185 to 184, that the Republicans had anguished over for the past four months. At 4:10 a.m., Ferry declared, "Rutherford B. Hayes of Ohio, having received a majority of the whole number of electoral votes, is duly elected President of the United States." Politics had prevailed over insurrection.

The turbulent forty-fourth Congress came to its exhausted end at noon on March 4, in one final spasm of rancor. Its last piece of business was funding for the army for the next fiscal year. Democrats demanded an explicit ban against paying, transporting, or feeding any federal troops used to support the "claims" of Republican officials in Louisiana, or to support the activities of federal marshals in the state, under punishment of up to ten years in prison at hard labor. To its credit, the Republican-controlled Senate refused to countenance such oppressive measures, although more conciliatory Republicans in the House offered to slash the army's appropriation by half as a compromise. But they were scornfully howled down by Democrats shouting, "not a dollar!" Reported *The New York Times,* "Both sides seemed satisfied to have the 44th Congress expire in an angry struggle over providing means for carrying on the proper functions of government."

EPILOGUE

1877, PITTSBURGH

★ ★ ★ ★ ★

The problem of the future of America
is as dark as it is vast.

—WALT WHITMAN

With the outcome of the election uncertain until just days before, the customary pomp of Hayes's presidential inauguration failed to match that of years past. The cavalcade that marched along Pennsylvania Avenue had a thrown-together feel, composed as it was with but a few companies of soldiers hurried from area forts, Pennsylvania militia companies, local firemen, and Republican clubs from nearby states. Still, 30,000 spectators, half of them Black, lined the avenue, waving handkerchiefs, tossing their hats in the air, and cheering from perches on lampposts and trees as the carriage bearing Grant and Hayes rolled by. Hayes bore an expression of reassuring good nature, people said; Grant looked relieved to be done with Washington.

Hayes's inaugural address was reassuring and optimistic. He touted civil service reform, hard currency, healing the economy, and his desire for a constitutional amendment that would limit presidents to a single six-year term, to diminish the abuse of patronage that attended contests for reelection. But he devoted the core of his remarks to the South, which he said had yet to recover from the "calamitous effects of a tremendous revolution," that is, the overthrow of slavery. Immeasurable benefits must follow "sooner or later," he promised, even though "deplorable complications and perplexities" still existed with respect to the two races and their "peculiar relations" with each other. Once Southern state governments had submitted themselves "heartily" to the U.S. Constitution, by fully accepting the new postwar amendments, surely then bitter partisanship would fade into insignificance. The nation had a moral duty to former slaves, as he had so often said, but the "evils" that afflicted the South could ultimately be remedied only by the "united and harmonious efforts of both races, actuated by motives of mutual sympathy and regard." With that in view, he assured the white people of the South that he cherished their interests as he did those of the "colored" people. To that end, he promised to do his utmost to banish sectional distinctions so "that we may have not a merely united North or a united South, but a united country."

Hayes was signaling that a new era had begun, and that he was determined to shed the political detritus of the past. Outside Washington, some unforgiving Democrats draped flags with black crepe or flew them upside down to protest Hayes's ascent. But they missed the point. Southerners who understood Hayes liked what they heard. "Mighty good," remarked one congressman who had battled for Tilden until the end. There were many more. Hayes infuriated the more radical wing of his own party by appointing D. M. Key of Tennessee, a Democrat and former Confederate officer, as his postmaster general, overseeing the largest pot of patronage jobs in the federal government. He further riled power brokers like Blaine, Conkling, and Logan by ignoring pressure to name their friends to the cabinet. When they threatened to block his appointments, including Key's, Southern Democrats including Senators John Gordon of Georgia and L. Q. C. Lamar of Mississippi, both linked to the Ku Klux Klan, stepped in to save them.

Hayes's election did not result from a clear-cut quid pro quo, as some historians have asserted. But he was willing to accommodate Democrats for their acquiescence in the electoral count. He was also sincere in his belief that compromise would lead to stability, to a split between hard-line and more flexible whites, and finally to the achievement of a new reformed, biracial politics in the South. As early as mid-March he privately confided, "My policy is trust, peace, and to put aside the bayonet." For months, so-called Liberal Republicans like Carl Schurz, now his interior secretary, and former Ohio Governor Jacob Cox had urged him to curry favor with whites by moderating "the new kindled ambition of the colored people to fill places which neither their experience nor their knowledge of business or of the laws fits them for." Hayes was prepared to take the risk. He had three options: calling for new elections in the divided states; continuing to support the remaining Republican administrations; or pulling out federal troops and letting the Republican governments collapse. He chose the third option: "If this leads to the overthrow of the *de jure* government in a state, the *de facto* government must be recognized." Of the three states whose electoral votes had won Hayes the election, Florida was a lost cause, since the Democrats had already secured control of the state government. South Carolina and Louisiana still had Republican governors, but both hung by a thread.

Black Republicans had no role in the negotiations that brought Hayes to power, helping to ensure that his high-mindedness would not inhibit a deal that surrendered their rights to those who wished them harm. To put it in the most charitable way, Hayes had convinced himself that the Southerners would deal fairly with Blacks. What really lay in store for them was obvious to those who had eyes to see. The *St. Louis Globe-Democrat* editorialized on March 31, "Let us admit that the untiring hate of the Southerners has worn out our endurance, and that though we staked everything for freedom under the spur of the rebellion, we have not enough of principle about us to uphold the freedom, so dearly bought." Former Attorney General Amos Akerman, who had led Grant's campaign against the Ku Klux Klan, had no illusions, caustically noting that the new Republican policy was merely combating "lawlessness by letting the lawless have their own way."

At the end of March, South Carolina's desperate Republican governor, Daniel H. Chamberlain, and his Democratic rival, Wade

Hampton, both traveled separately to Washington to confer with Hayes. Hampton fulsomely promised to respect Black South Carolinians' constitutional rights and to advise his friends in Congress to support Republican James A. Garfield for Speaker of the House. Chamberlain, who had risked his life to run for reelection, warned Hayes that ending federal protection against Hampton's Red Shirts would seal the fate of his administration. Hayes had a lot in common with Chamberlain. Both were veteran Union officers, Harvard-trained lawyers, and prewar abolitionists. But Hampton had a massive popular, and ruthless, movement at his back, unlike the embattled Chamberlain. Hampton also struck Hayes as a man of his word, who could ensure the stability that Hayes wanted to see. "Everything is satisfactorily settled," Hampton happily telegraphed to his followers in South Carolina. Hayes decreed that the last federal troops must leave the statehouse on April 10. South Carolina would finally be rescued from biracial democracy.

Hampton's return was met by rallying Red Shirts, marching bands, and thousands wildly cheering from balconies and rooftops, some flaunting banners that read "Redeemed, thank God." Hoarse of voice, Hampton declared he would send fire companies to wash down the statehouse and teams of convicts to scrub what remained of "vermin and filth," perhaps the literal mess left by Chamberlain's garrison, but doubtless understood by most whites to also mean the Blacks and Yankee "carpetbaggers" who had governed the state. "The clouds have passed, the dark night is over, and the dawn has come," editorialized one South Carolina newspaper. "The people"—whites, that is—"feel like freemen again. Their state is their own once more, and there is no power on earth that can wrest it from their hands." South Carolina Republicans were aghast at Hayes's ingratitude for their sufferings and sacrifices. Senator John Patterson was heard to exclaim, "He has sold us out!"

Chamberlain's last bitter message to his supporters fairly vibrated with dashed hopes. He had held office for two of the most difficult years that any American governor had ever faced; now he, and they, had been abandoned by the government, by their party, by the president they had fought to elect in the face of massive fraud and intimidation. To the Black voters who had risked their lives to vote for him and for Hayes, he said, "You were denied employment, driven from your homes, robbed of the earnings of years, hunted for your lives like wild beasts, your families outraged and scattered for no offense except your peaceful and firm determination to exercise your political rights." Now by the order of the president "whom your votes alone rescued from overwhelming defeat," Black citizens were being handed over wholesale to their enemies. The North was all too clearly sick of the South's troubles. He added scathingly that "if a majority of the people of a state are unable by physical force to maintain their rights they must be left to political servitude. Is this a doctrine ever before heard in our history?" He would willingly have fought on, he said. But he could no longer ask the state's Republicans to fight with him, because no relief would come. "I cannot ask you to follow me further."

On April 10, the last nineteen men and two officers defending the statehouse mustered at 11:55 a.m. Then at 12:00 sharp a bell tolled the hour and their lieutenant cried, "Shoulder arms! Forward march!" As they left the building, the last vestige of Republican government in South Carolina went with them.

LOUISIANA'S DEMOCRATS lacked a leader with Hampton's unifying appeal. But the end was the same, the conclusion foregone. Hayes appointed a blue-ribbon federal commission to negotiate a political solution to the state's divided government, with its rival legislatures and governors. (The commission included, among others, the former president of the Centennial, Joseph R. Hawley, and future Supreme Court Justice John Harlan.) He also put a finger on the scales: He made clear that he intended to remove federal protection from the state's teetering Republican government, as he had done in South Carolina. He just wanted to be assured that the rights of the freed people would be protected. But the commission was blunt, telling local Republicans not to hope for a bailout: "If there is any member of the legislature who entertains the most lingering idea that the troops are going to remain, for God's sake disabuse him of that idea, for they are going to be removed."

By now, the Republican administration was little more than

a shell holed up in the St. Louis Hotel, which served as the seat of government. Many public officials had defected from the deeply unpopular Governor Stephen Packard and had either openly or tacitly acknowledged the Democrats' self-proclaimed chief executive, Francis T. Nicholls, a former general who had lost an eye, an arm, and a foot in Confederate service, and ran the Democrats' government from the Odd Fellows Hall. Nicholls told the commission what Hayes wanted to hear and certified several dozen African Americans who had been elected to assorted offices in November. Meanwhile, the commissioners persuaded, or more likely bribed, five opportunistic Republicans to shift their allegiance to the Democrats' legislature, giving it a quorum with which to conduct business, and denying it to Packard, who now governed nothing at all. The last troops shouldered arms at noon on April 24, as cannon boomed in jubilation. *The New York Times*'s next-day headline tersely announced, "The Surrender Complete." *The Nation* predicted, "The negro will disappear from the field of national politics. Henceforth the nation, as a nation, will have nothing more to do with him."

Hayes considered the ouster of Chamberlain and Packard regrettable, but nonetheless a job well done. He wrote in his diary with relief, "I am confident this is good work." He knew that the old antislavery men would condemn him but decided not to scold them. "I know they mean well. It is a comfort to know that I also mean well. It will, I trust, turn out that I am right."

JULY 4, 1877, dawned breezy and sunny over Philadelphia. This year, no feminist provocateurs would disrupt official programs. The news from the South, as much as anyone cared any longer to follow it, was mostly inconsequential, devoid of riotous violence that would roil Northern consciences. Reports from the Far West were encouraging too. The war with the Plains tribes had sputtered to an end. For months, three armies had hunted Custer's conquerors across the prairies of Montana and the Dakotas without bringing them to decisive battle. Sitting Bull's band eventually eluded the federal grasp and slipped across the border to safety in Canada.

One by one, the other war bands eventually gave up, defeated more by starvation and lack of ammunition than by shrewd American generalship. In May, Crazy Horse, the last major holdout, surrendered with his depleted followers, just under a thousand emaciated men, women, and children. Despite guarantees for his safety, on September 5, he was murdered by a bayonet-wielding soldier at Camp Robinson, Nebraska.

Custer's defeat was the last, pyrrhic victory of the Plains tribes and the effective end of the major Indian wars. The Nez Perce War of late 1877 and later actions against the Apaches in the Southwest were but anticlimax. The Sioux, the commissioner of Indian affairs wrote, "must be aware that as long as they hold vast areas of valuable land, lying, and destined to lie as long as they hold it, an unprofitable and unimproved waste, the cupidity of tens of thousands of white men is thereby excited—a cupidity which, already uncontrollable will increase in intensity from year to year till it becomes irresistible." From this point on, the tribes would cease to be independent peoples and be reduced to "wards of the government," as federal law officially put it, hemmed in on shrinking reservations, dependent on government provisions, pressured to assimilate to white people's ways, and known to most Americans mainly as living relics like the totem poles and woven baskets they had seen on exhibit at the Centennial. Soon the state-of-the-art plows and harvesters and steam-threshers that visitors had admired at Fairmount Park would be tearing up the prairies that had been Indian Country.

Although Philadelphia's Independence Day celebrations were naturally much scaled down from the extravagant displays of the previous year, the city entertained itself with the traditional patriotic hoopla of tolling bells, firing skyrockets, firecrackers, and, as *The Philadelphia Inquirer* wryly expressed it, "the small cannon with which the progressive youth of the generation show their disregard for the nerves." Flags and bunting festooned homes, stores, and horsecars. Thousands flocked to Fairmount Park, where in the Main Building, one of the few halls still standing, an orchestra rousingly played marches and "The Star-Spangled Banner." Catholic benefactors dedicated a "total abstinence" water fountain. Governor Hartranft extolled the current generation for having extended freedom to "all men," shrinking "from no cost in lives or estate to preserve liberty or constitutional government." Then the eminent publisher and Republican stalwart John Forney summarized the historical moment. "We seem to have approached solid ground within the last six months," he said. "The clouds still hang heavily over our country, and not only ours alone. Yet I can see the silver lining growing brighter and brighter. A wise administration of the general government bravely presses for the restoration of tranquility between recently divided states. The people of the South will be blind indeed, and callous, if they should turn away from a purpose so honest and sincere." Yes, the depression still continued, but it was not without its uses, he suggested optimistically. "It compels a severe and resolute self-examination. It imposes upon government and people a rigid frugality and economy."

Meanwhile, Custer morphed from man into legend, the forerunner of modern media-driven celebrities whose manufactured magnetism far outpaces their actual accomplishments. Before 1876 was out, a 694-page biography of him, the first of many, adoringly painted him as a spotlessly brave Yankee cavalier, a "military genius of a very high order," and "one of the few really great men that America had produced." His death soon became a staple of frontier-themed entertainment in Buffalo Bill's Wild West Show, as the climactic episode in a thrilling live-action series titled *The Drama of Civilization.* His charmed afterlife found romantic renewal in novels and films, while the trope of the "Last Stand" became embedded in the popular lexicon. Prints of his death in heroic pose were still common décor on the walls of American barrooms through the mid-twentieth century.

FOLLOWING GOVERNOR HARTRANFT, the liberal-minded publisher John Forney sought to reassure Philadelphians that America was safe and secure in Hayes's hands—"A great man had come in time as the instrument of reform"—and well launched into its second century of glory. Barely a week later, the country exploded. Class warfare on a scale that Americans had never witnessed shattered the nation's self-confidence. On July 16, train crews began walking off their jobs in Baltimore and Martinsburg, West Virginia, eighty-five miles west. A manifesto issued by the workers warned that unless the Baltimore & Ohio Railroad rescinded its latest draconian pay cuts "we shall run their trains and locomotives into the river." The strike rapidly spread to the vast network of the Pennsylvania Railroad, and ultimately to workers in fourteen states in the first national strike, and the first Red Scare, in American history. A violent new language would soon take root as workers denounced "thieving monopolies" and "wage slavery," and conservatives charged that labor activists were all communists who deserved to be "swept out of existence with grape shot."

Years of hard-handed cost-cutting had pushed workers in a host of industries to the brink of rebellion. In 1876, fewer than one-fifth of American workers were regularly employed, and another two-fifths worked only about six months out of the year; there were said to be 90,000 homeless workers in New York alone, with entire families huddling overnight on benches in police stations for warmth. Even skilled workers came to feel like mere disposable tools as employers embraced short-term profitability at the expense of labor. Although travelers praised the Pennsylvania Railroad for its service and efficiency, the depression, overexpansion, and debilitating rate wars had sapped its profits, shrinking the value of its securities by one-third over three years. To satisfy investors, Tom Scott reduced wages by between 20 and 50 percent of pre-1873 levels with yet another 10 percent cut announced in May, while increasing workloads to ten-hour days and six-day weeks.

Walkouts spread to Jersey City, Harrisburg, Altoona, Johnstown, Buffalo, Cincinnati, Indianapolis, Terre Haute, Louisville, Chicago, St. Louis, Galveston, and other cities in between. Though coordination was tenuous, suddenly the country's entire industrial landscape seemed to be on strike, involving steelworkers, canal workers, cannery men, factory hands, and miners. (Schuylkill County remained sullenly quiet. Mine workers were cowed by the hanging of the eleven alleged Molly Maguires on June 19—"Pennsylvania's Day with the Rope," as the pro-business *Daily Miner* jauntily dubbed it. John Kehoe was not among them. Although convicted of the murder of John Langdon, the mine supervisor killed in 1862, he continued to trust that Governor Hartranft, whom he had helped elect, would issue him a pardon.)

Within days, most commercial rail traffic ceased as strikers derailed engines, burned boxcars, blockaded tracks, jammed switches, and threatened the scabs sent to replace them. Militia units mustered by state officials either refused to march or joined the strikers, proclaiming that it was not the job of working men to shoot other workers. Tom Scott called the crisis "almost as serious as that which prevailed at the outbreak of the Civil War." The *New York World* blamed escalating violence on "men dominated by the devilish spirit of Communism." In Baltimore, eleven civilians were killed and forty wounded. In Chicago, *The New York Times* reported, "communistic Bohemians and belligerent Poles" brought a halt to work on the waterfront, in steel mills, and the streetcar lines, leaving eighteen dead. At Reading, Franklin Gowen ordered out militia on his own initiative to crush the strike. When local men refused to obey, units from out of town shot down strikers, hapless bystanders, and city policemen who were trying to keep the crowds under control, killing ten and wounding scores.

Pittsburgh saw the nation's worst urban violence since New York's Draft Riots in 1863. Hostility to the Pennsylvania Railroad was already ingrained: Many resented its predatory fees and its unconcern for the many children who were killed every year on its open tracks through the city. Pittsburgh's mayor denounced the railroad's management as "imperious and dictatorial." When the trainmen struck, thousands of men, women, and children joined them, swarming the train yards and overwhelming the handful of city policemen sent to disperse them. Local militiamen sent to bring the strikers under control instead fraternized with them.

In the absence of Governor Hartranft, who was on holiday in Wyoming—traveling in Tom Scott's luxury railway car—Scott set up a command center at the railroad's West Philadelphia depot. Working sleeplessly day and night, he monitored attacks on the railroad's lines, ran its hour-to-hour operations, and in coordination with the state's adjutant general oversaw the deployment of militia units, and later federal troops. "Never did Mr. Scott appear to better advantage than during the riots of 1877, and never was there more need of the personal and moral courage which animated his whole nature," the friendly *Philadelphia Times* declared in his 1881 obituary. "With pressure upon all sides to yield to the demands of the strikers, he was the central figure controlling the situation over 5,000 miles of road and determined to yield nothing and discuss nothing until the lawless element had been put down." Andrew Carnegie, Scott's old ally and sometime partner, while no friend to labor unions, blamed the carnage to come on his old mentor's intransigence.

Scott determined to finish off the Pittsburgh revolt with Philadelphia militiamen who had no local ties there. By now, the strikers had swelled by thousands of mill workers, their families, and the unemployed. (Carnegie's steelworkers staged a sympathetic one-day walkout, but did not strike.) On the afternoon of July 21 six hundred Philadelphians arrived and with fixed bayonets marched under a superintendent of the Pennsylvania Railroad toward the main mass of strikers at Twenty-Eighth Street. They were greeted with hoots and jeers. An officer then ordered the soldiers to charge. They were hit by a hail of stones and bricks, then fired point-blank into the crowd. Men, women, and children began to fall, some brought down by bullets, others by bayonet thrusts, others trampled in the panic that ensued. At least twenty were killed and many more wounded. A later investigation declared the troops' actions to be "willful and wanton killing which the inquest can call by no other name than murder."

That night, the infuriated demonstrators turned into a mob, looting gun shops, burning boxcars, oil tankers, and the railroad's complex of workshops, cutting the hoses of the few firemen who showed up to deal with the blaze. Overwhelmed by the ever-growing crowd, the Philadelphians holed up in a brick roundhouse, then abandoned their artillery pieces and fled to safety, sniped at from roofs and doorways. The fires continued to spread until they had engulfed virtually every piece of railroad property, and finally nearby grain elevators and businesses, leaving a smoking landscape of charred boxcars and collapsed buildings that resembled the ruins of Atlanta and Richmond during the war. Conservatives demanded immediate action. Cried the pro-business *Chicago Inter-Ocean,* Pittsburgh had fallen to "the vicious classes: lawlessness must be crushed with a strong hand."

When J. P. Barr, the editor of the *Pittsburgh Post,* begged Scott to save lives by offering concessions to the workers, or at least agree to a board of arbitration, Scott tersely replied that anything short of the full restoration of law and order amounted to "temporizing with the worst evil the world has ever seen," adding that any criticism of his own leadership was an attack on the "best interests of the country." He pressured Hayes for massive military intervention, citing Lincoln's response to secession in 1861. Hayes briefly hesitated, professing sympathy for "sober, intelligent, and industrious" working men. But he regarded strikers ultimately as lawbreakers who prevented other men from doing their jobs and who, by seizing employers' property, invited "the dangerous criminal classes" to wreak yet more destruction. Four members of his cabinet were linked directly to railroad interests; not surprisingly, they argued for a tough response. Hayes overcame his qualms, such as they were, and issued a series of proclamations declaring the strike "insurrectionary," and sanctioned force to crush it.

Regular troops were ordered from garrisons in Boston, Providence, and New York, and stripped from the South. Marines and gunboats were put on standby on the East Coast. Trains furnished by Scott set out for Pittsburgh with more than 2,000 federal troops and state militia, with Gatling guns mounted in gondolas in front of the engines. Their gunners were ordered to shoot at any sign of danger. Hartranft, a former general, now back in Pennsylvania, directed the operation from one of Scott's business cars. By the twenty-eighth, Scott felt able to announce that the railroad's lines were being fully reopened since workers were "rapidly recognizing that the interests of the company and their own are identical." The strike was essentially over. Across the nation, at least 117 men, women, and children, and four soldiers, had been killed, and many hundreds wounded. More than 120 locomotives and about 1,400 railway cars had been destroyed. The Pennsylvania Railroad alone suffered losses of at least $2 million and possibly as much as $7.5 million in property destroyed. At its peak, the strike had tied up two-thirds of the country's 79,000 miles of track, and involved tens of thousands of state militia, their largest use in American history to that point, apart from the Civil War.

Hayes felt a kind of remorse. "The strikes have been put down by force; but now for the real remedy," he privately reflected in August. "Can't something be done by education of the strikers, by judicious control of the capitalists, by wise general policy to end or diminish the evil?" These were questions that were not easily answered. They would dog labor and business leaders alike through the next century and beyond.

John Kehoe was, in a way, the last fatality of the strike of 1877. In January 1878, Pennsylvania's Supreme Court rejected his final appeal. No matter what Hartranft may have felt personally, in the aftermath of the strike he wouldn't risk pardoning a man tarred as a labor terrorist. From his cell in Pottsville, Kehoe wrote to his lawyer, "I did not get Justice in eighther [*sic*] Courts there is no evidence in my Case that should Convict me. There was Good evidence, that Proved my innocence. But it was All Jug handled Justice." He was hanged on December 18, 1878. The *Daily Miner* blandly remarked, "The execution of a prominent Mollie is an old story now."

Kehoe's nemesis, Franklin B. Gowen, regarded his bloody suppression of the strike in Reading as a triumph. But the cumulative cost of his expansionist ambitions weakened what had once been a company widely admired for its financial restraint. His personal magnetism ebbing, his career in decline, he was finally ousted from the Reading's presidency. He died alone in a Washington hotel room in 1889, an apparent suicide. The *Daily Miner* reported that he had been seen talking to himself, and appeared to be "laboring under some great mental strain. It was supposed that he had been brooding."

The strike of 1877 compelled Americans to realize, with trepidation, that the revolt of working people against untethered capitalism was something bigger than random disorder. The more affluent began to view it as the radical edge of a general attack on America itself. Reverend Henry Ward Beecher of Brooklyn's Plymouth Church, the stentorian star of the evangelical pulpit, captured this transformative moment in a sermon delivered on July 22 that was tellingly titled "Communism Denounced." A former abolitionist, Beecher—the brother of novelist Harriet Beecher Stowe—had become deeply conservative in the new postwar political landscape. He told his affluent congregation that "the necessities of the great railroad companies demanded that there should be a reduction of wages," and that workers had no right to "tyrannize over their fellow men." A wage of one dollar a day might not be much to support a man and five children if he insisted on smoking and drinking beer, but it was enough to buy bread, and water was free, he declared to laughter, adding, astonishingly, "The man who cannot live on bread and water is not fit to live." He went on to lay out a set of moral principles that would underpin conservative politics for generations to come. He scoffed at the idea that the government should take care of the welfare of its citizens as fundamentally "un-American"—perhaps one of the earliest uses of an epithet that would long serve as a weapon against liberal causes. "'Hands off,' we say to the government; see to it that we are protected in our rights and our individuality. No more than that." To threaten private property was to contradict natural law and was antithetical to both individuality and liberty, he went on. "We are against communism," he thundered. "God intended the great to be great and the little to be little."

Beecher saw himself as an apostle of freedom. Before the Civil War, he had sometimes held mock auctions of former slaves from the pulpit of his church in an effort to shock white Americans into embracing abolition. The concept of freedom that had so potently served the antislavery movement now fed fear of the aspiring working class, couched though it might be in the loftiest moral terms. "It is an American doctrine that every man is to have the full ownership of himself, and the right to develop himself if he can do it," Beecher asserted. Slavery had been the only exception to that doctrine, and it was now swept away. Any infringement on man's individuality, he said, was just another odious form of tyranny. Inequality was a law of nature. The only way for working men to get ahead was not "by way of caucus" or "combinations"—by politics or unionization—but to "call on God and stop using tobacco and beer, subdue their passions, and try by self-denial to make homes for themselves and [their] families," not to "grunt and grumble" but to bear their situation unflinchingly. "The manly way to meet misfortune is to go down boldly to poverty."

To many middle-class Americans, who were the core of the Republican Party, the dystopia that Beecher feared seemed to have become reality in the bloody railyards of Pittsburgh: If America was to defend itself against cancerous ideologies imported from the Old World, it would have to change. As Southern conservatives were now curtailing the freedoms of Black citizens, Northern conservatives must now bring the "communistic Bohemians and belligerent Poles" and the "Molly Maguires" under control before they destroyed American industry. "The days are over in which this country could rejoice in its freedom from the elements of social strife which have long abounded in old countries," declared *The New York Times*. "We have dangerous social elements to contend with."

Tom Scott, who identified the national interest with that of the Pennsylvania Railroad—and for that matter with himself—warned that the forces unleashed by the strike threatened the very existence of the United States. The smoldering ruins of Pittsburgh showed that class warfare could destroy cities and wreck the national economy. "For the first time in American history," he said, "an organized mob [has] learned its power to terrorize the law-abiding citizens of great communities. We shall have only ourselves to blame if we leave ourselves unprepared to meet an issue which is only too likely again to be forced upon us." National security, he now argued, meant not only defense against foreign enemies and Native tribes, but also against revolutionary internal dissent that threatened the country from within. Before the Great Railroad Strike of 1877, federal troops had never been used in peacetime except to guard federal property. From now on, following the precedent set by Hayes and Scott, they would often act at the behest of corporations.

The suppression of the Great Strike represented the apogee of Tom Scott's power. In October of 1878, he suffered a stroke, the first of several. Partially paralyzed, he traveled to Europe and the Middle East for the first and last vacation of his life. In 1880, he resigned from the board of the Pennsylvania Railroad, to which he had devoted his life. He died a year later at the age of fifty-seven. His obituary in the *Philadelphia Times* declared, "A Matchless Career: He did good because he loved to do good." A reporter less beholden to the Pennsylvania Railroad damned him as "a Davy Crockett of corruption" who "has probably done more to corrupt legislation, debauch politics, make bribery a science, elevate it to the rank of profession and enshrine it among the fine arts, than any man in this country."

ALEXANDER GRAHAM BELL almost collided with the strikers in Buffalo during his honeymoon, on his way home from Niagara Falls. Preparing to defend his new bride, Mabel, at all hazards, Bell bought a revolver "with ammunition enough to kill a hundred men," he wrote, with a fillip of uncharacteristic cockiness. Fortunately he never had to use it, since the strikers didn't interfere with passenger trains. Not even a prospective gun battle could dismay him. He was on his way to becoming one of the most consequential men in America, and he had at last won the hand of his deaf former student and daughter of his most important financial backer, Gardiner Green Hubbard.

Interest in his invention was surging. "The power possessed by my new telephone is marvelous beyond belief!" he exclaimed. News of Bell's success at the Centennial had spread rapidly, first through New England, then across the country, then to Europe. In February, he had recited the first newspaper dispatch ever delivered by telephone. The *Springfield Republican* enthused that someday political campaigns would be conducted by telephone, and that music would be broadcast and Sunday sermons delivered to congregations over the wires. In March, he was elected to the American Academy of Arts and Sciences. At Salem, an audience of five hundred resoundingly applauded him conversing with an assistant in Boston, forty-three miles away. Requests for more demonstrations flowed in from Henry Wadsworth Longfellow and Oliver Wendell Holmes, and from potential investors from New York, to the Pennsylvania oilfields, to San Francisco.

The telephone was as much a product of American capitalism as it was of Bell's brilliance. Although he was personally driven more by the creative force of his mind than by a desire for wealth or power, he understood that innovation required capital to turn it into hardware, contracts, and companies. In April, the first private telephone line was installed, linking a shop in Boston with its owner's home in suburban Somerville. In July, the Bell Telephone Company came into being, with Gardiner Hubbard as its de facto president. By then, there were some two hundred phone lines in operation; by August nearly eight hundred. Blackface minstrels were even singing about the telephone in the music halls of New York, and Mark Twain, an early adopter, would soon become the first writer to put Bell's invention into a short story, "A Telephonic Conversation," satirizing two women's difficulty understanding each other over a wonky line.

When the Bells sailed for the British Isles, in August, he entertained his fellow passengers by stringing telephone wires between the wheelhouse and the parlor. Once ashore, they were taken in hand by William Thomson, Lord Kelvin, Bell's advocate at the Centennial, who introduced him to men of science in Scotland and England. He lectured to a hall packed with the scientific luminaries of London. He demonstrated that a phone call could be made even from the depths of a coal mine. And he so impressed Queen Victoria with a private showing that she ordered a line to be installed at her summer estate on the Isle of Wight. By the end of the year, British engineers in Dover were talking to Calais in France via a Channel cable and listening to Christmas carols sung by French children. Soon Bell and his backers were negotiating licensing rights in France, Belgium, Germany, and beyond.

THE TELEPHONE was no longer a novelty, and it would soon be a necessity. It would accelerate commerce, revolutionize the growth of cities, change the tenor of personal relations, and shrink humankind's sense of distance to the vanishing point. Wrote Bell's biographer Robert V. Bruce, "Without the telephone as its nervous system, the twentieth century metropolis would have been stunted by congestion and slowed to the primordial pace of messengers and postmen. And the modern age would have been born with cerebral palsy." Bell would continue to generate inventions for almost fifty more years, including the first microphone, the first metal detector, the first artificial respirator, the first air conditioner, the first hydrofoil, and a practical aircraft. When he died in 1922, he would be one of the most famous men in the world.

Among the technological marvels of the Centennial, the giant Corliss Engine may have drawn the most attention. But Bell's telephone stood out as a more emblematic example of America's arrival as a rising power. The superiority of American engineers, the dynamism of its industry, the richness of its resources would all matter increasingly to the rest of the world. As the astute French visitor Louis Simonin observed after two weeks at the Centennial, "America will learn to dispense more and more with Europe, [but] Europe cannot dispense with her." Capitalism was generating wealth and opportunity of a kind that antebellum Americans could not even have imagined. Although it was not yet fully evident to all, the Centennial had made clear to many Americans that women were steadily advancing in their ascent from near servitude, legally at least, toward the expanding opportunities that awaited them in the twentieth century. Standards of living were also beginning a climb that would continue into the twenty-first century. Americans whose parents had hacked farms from primeval forest now took for granted a cornucopia of labor-saving machines and cheap appliances, railway travel, and astonishing long-distance communication. "We stand, live, move, in the huge flow of our nation's materialism," Walt Whitman enthused.

The Centennial was a celebration of America as the country's industrial magnates wished it to be, an expansive vision of a glittering consumerist future at a time of industrial turbulence, political anxiety, and rapid change—an America from which racial stress and class conflict had been entirely expunged, and women included only on sufferance. Meanwhile, outside the gates of Fairmount Park, Americans were still struggling with difficult questions that would shape the nation's life and politics for generations to come: Could the political parties ever be cleansed of corruption?

What place would African Americans have in American society? Would Native Americans survive at all, and at what cost to their embattled cultures? Would working people have to fight to survive in the America of the future? Could labor and capital somehow be reconciled? Could republican institutions—the core machinery of American democracy—survive under pressure from big money and self-dealing capitalists?

The Centennial answered none of these questions. Of course, the great fair was created to highlight the nation's achievements, not to inventory its shortcomings. It was meant to educate and inspire, and to draw Americans together around the idealized hearthstone of independence. The fair's rendering of America did not lie: the great engines, the multifarious inventions, the alluring pyramids of new products, the aspiring artwork, all spoke truthfully enough of the nation's swelling economic and cultural muscle. Rather, it deceived by omission. The troubling fissures of race and class and gender, the consequences of transcontinental expansion, and the impact of ever-growing corporate power all had been almost completely excised from the past and future alike. Only the fierce protest of organized women had challenged the sanitized official narrative. Workers were ignored, Native Americans reduced to artifacts tainted by "savagery," and the nation's four and a half million Black citizens erased; their sole public monument at Fairmount Park, to the cleric Richard Allen, was a mere asterisk to the plight of a people under siege by those determined to tear away their newly achieved constitutional rights.

UNBRIDLED CAPITALISM was dividing Americans as nothing had before, except perhaps slavery. Its growing power seemed unstoppable. In the years to come, labor violence would become increasingly endemic, marked by boycotts, walkouts, mass picketing, private armies, and bloody confrontations, from the Haymarket police riot in Chicago in 1892, which left sixty citizens dead, to the massive strike at Andrew Carnegie's Homestead steel plant at Pittsburgh the same year, to silver mines in Idaho. Federal courts would effectively outlaw strikes, Pinkerton agents would become ubiquitous, and armories that resembled medieval fortresses would rise in every major city to stockpile weapons for use against restive citizens. Unions struggled to survive in the face of repression, but they continued to grow as more and more workers from steel mills to garment-trade sweatshops came to feel that there was something fundamentally wrong with the nation's industrial system. "The corporations have the law on their side," observed the *Reading Eagle*. "They own the legislatures, they retain the ablest lawyers, they control most of the newspapers, and manufacture public opinion." Yet it would still take decades, until the 1930s, for the labor movement to gain widespread, if never universal, acceptance.

Although the Democrats remained shackled to the descendants of Southern "Redeemers" for almost a century, the party welcomed left-wing populists and embraced—in the 1930s, under the sheltering wing of Franklin Roosevelt—big-government solutions to social problems, and (very gradually) the reentry of Black Americans into national politics. The labor crisis of the 1870s bluntly revealed the sway that plutocrats already exercised over the Republican Party, which had reinvented itself as a safe harbor for the country's aristocrats of wealth who, rhetoric aside, replaced the legacy of Lincoln with leaders like Scott, Blaine, and Conkling, for whom reformers stood as obstacles to the influence of self-interest.

Rutherford B. Hayes was, perhaps, too virtuous for his moment. He was respected, as his 1893 obituary put it, for "a distinct elevating of the tone and standard of public life." But his single term was not a success. His primary ambition, reform of the civil service and the dismantling of partisan patronage, was thwarted by both hostile Democrats and the machine men of his own party. He was never considered for renomination in 1880. His misplaced trust in the goodwill of white Southerners left the Fourteenth Amendment a dead letter and cost Black Americans almost a century of disenfranchisement and social ostracism. After 1877, white supremacy was no longer an aspiration but the institutionalized norm. In state after state, Democrats repealed fair election laws, disenfranchised Black voters, and permitted lynching to become a popular method of social control. Hayes never lost his personal sense of social concern. In retirement, he served as a trustee for two foundations that raised money to educate Black students in the South, and to support prison reform. He grew ever more uneasy at the concentration of immense wealth in few hands. Near the end of his life, he reflected, "The great problem is to rid our country of the conflict between wealth and poverty without destroying either society or civilization, or liberty and free government."

WALT WHITMAN would live another sixteen years after the Centennial, half-forgotten among the factories of Camden. By his sixties, he already seemed aged and frail, just a ghost of his lusty prime. He continued to write, but his best poetry was behind him. Still, no one felt more sensitively the pulse of America, or recognized its fierce contradictions. "It seems as if the Almighty had spread before this Nation charts of imperial destinies, dazzling as the sun," he had written in *Democratic Vistas*. Americans of the future, he predicted, were destined to be "a copious race of superb men and women, a nation of supple and athletic minds," who in time were destined to dominate the world. Yet, he lamented, "Never was there, perhaps, more hollowness at heart than at present." The United States was a nation "saturated with hypocrisy," infected with an "almost maniacal appetite for wealth." The "depravity of the business classes" was beyond description, its government steeped in corruption and falsehood. What would become of all those superb men and women? He warned, "The problem of the future of America is as dark as it is vast."

Yet, for all his generosity of spirit, Whitman found no space in the American future for either Black or Native peoples. In 1888, four years before he died, he told a friend, with respect to racial integration, "I don't believe in it—it is not possible." Blacks and Indians "will be eliminated: it is the law of history, races, what-not: always so far inexorable." Race was an area of darkness into which even he could not see.

EDMONIA LEWIS had once incarnated the kind of possibilities that lay open to Black Americans after the Civil War. Seizing opportunity and trusting in her talent, she largely succeeded in her defiance of both racial assumptions and the vagaries of the marketplace. The Centennial was the high point of her career. When Frederick Douglass encountered her in Rome, in 1887, she had lived so long in Italy that she spoke English with an Italian accent. The public's taste for neoclassicism and her work faded, and increasingly she specialized in figures of the Virgin Mary and other religious imagery, exhibiting at Catholic fairs and selling her work to churches. She was deeply disappointed that her masterwork *The Death of Cleopatra* failed to sell at the Centennial. She left it in Chicago, where it eventually passed through the hands of a saloon-keeper, presumably as an erotic attraction in his bar, and then those of a gambler, to adorn the grave of a racehorse he named Cleopatra. After that, it disappeared. It was rediscovered in a junkyard in the 1990s, and now occupies a prominent place, along with several of Lewis's smaller sculptures, in the Smithsonian American Art Museum, in Washington, D.C. Lewis died from kidney failure in 1907. She was interred in London, her home for the last years of her life, as simply "Mary Lewis." Her life was daring and original, but she could not live it in the land of her birth.

Acknowledgments

Many individuals and institutions both large and small helped me to turn what was the glimmer of an idea about the nation's 1876 Centennial into the book that you are holding in your hands. I must mention several authors whose work was of special value to me: Albert Churella, whose monumental history of the Pennsylvania Railroad provided fundamental insights into Thomas A. Scott and the corporate world of the Gilden Age; and Kirsten Pai Buick, and Harry and Albert Henderson, whose groundbreaking research on Edmonia Lewis helped to deepen my understanding of that elusive artist. Anne Flaherty, author of the only biography of the tragic labor leader John Kehoe, was exceptionally generous in answering my questions and pointed me toward additional sources in the Pennsylvania coalfields. My good friend Orville Vernon Burton helped—not for the first time—to illuminate the intricate racial history of Edgefield County, South Carolina; Bettis Rainsford was an invaluable interlocutor in Edgefield, while Milledge Murray and Robert Scott generously served as on-the-ground guides to the site of the Hamburg Massacre, where the nineteenth-century town has now disappeared beneath a golf course. Edwin Grosvenor, the president of American Heritage, encouraged me to see Alexander Graham Bell, his great-grandfather, as a much more sensitive man than his iconic image may suggest.

I am also grateful, as ever, to librarians and curators whose seemingly inexhaustible patience made my work much easier than it would otherwise have been. Among them, the staffs of the Library of Congress, especially its Manuscript Reading Room; the

David Rubenstein Manuscript Library at Duke University; the South Caroliniana Collection at the University of South Carolina, in Columbia; the South Carolina Historical Society Archives, at the College of Charleston; the Historical Society of Pennsylvania; the Library Company of Philadelphia; the Schuylkill County Historical Society, in Pottsville, Pennsylvania; the Pennsylvania State Archives, in Harrisburg; and the New York Public Library were all exceptionally helpful. The superbly organized online resources of the Rutherford B. Hayes Presidential Library, in Fremont, Ohio; and of the Hagley Museum and Library, in Wilmington, Delaware were also of immense value.

Finally, without the support and encouragement of my eagle-eyed and ever-encouraging editor Todd Portnowitz, my agent, Adam Eaglin, of Elyse Cheney Literary Associates, and—above all—my wife, Jean P. Bordewich, whose concern for the moral dimension of history has always inspired me to look with both greater sympathy and a less forgiving eye at our American forbears and their actions, this book would not exist.

Notes

ABBREVIATIONS

AGB: Alexander Graham Bell
AMB: Alexander Melville Bell
CG: *Congressional Globe*
CR: *Congressional Record*
CS: Carl Schurz
EB: Eliza Bell
HSP: Historical Society of Pennsylvania
JAG: James A. Garfield
JGB: James G. Blaine
JS: John Sherman
LCP: Library Company of Philadelphia
LOC: Library of Congress
MGB: Mabel Gardiner Bell, a.k.a. MGH: Mabel Gardiner Hubbard
NYH: *New York Herald*
NYT: *New York Times*
PI: *Philadelphia Inquirer*
PT: *Philadelphia Times*
RBH: Rutherford B. Hayes
SCHS: Schuylkill County Historical Society
SJT: Samuel J. Tilden
USG: Ulysses S. Grant
WH: Wade Hampton
WW: Walt Whitman

PREFACE

xii "Altho' the Form": Patrick Henry to James Monroe, January 24, 1791, in Charlene Bangs Bickford et al., eds., *Documentary History of the First Federal Congress,* Vol. 21, 518–19.

CHAPTER 1 ⋆ THE GREAT FAIR

4 *"Oh! Make thou": PT,* May 11, 1876.

4 *"Waken voice": PT,* May 11, 1876.

5 "One hundred years ago": USG Papers, Vol. 27, 107–8.

6 "The obedient looms": *PT,* April 11, 1876.

6 "appears for the nonce": Robert W. Rydell, *All the World's a Fair: Visions of Empire at American International Expositions, 1876–1916* (Chicago: University of Chicago Press, 1984), 10.

7 "Floating in Congressional waters": Kathryn Allamong Jacob, *King of the Lobby: The Life and Times of Sam Ward* (Baltimore: Johns Hopkins University Press, 2010), 100.

8 "The fact is": Mark Twain and Charles Dudley Warner, *The Gilded Age* (Orinda, CA: Seawolf Press, 2020 [originally published 1873]), 80, 108.

8 "soon be organized": JS to A. M. Burns, January 2, 1876, JS, *John Sherman's Recollections of Forty Years in the House, Senate and Cabinet,* Vol. 1 (Chicago: Werner Co., 1895), 522.

8 "strengthen the bonds": *CR,* 43rd Congress, 1st session, Appendix, 250–53.

9 "We are lost": Frederick Tozier, *Centennial Record,* diary, HSP.

10 *"Here shall you":* WhitmanArchive.org.

11 strangely equivocal essay: WW, *Democratic Vistas,* ed. Ed Folson (Iowa City: University of Iowa Press, 2010 [originally published 1871]), 60, 4, 12, 43, 35.

13 "The whole government": Joseph Hooker to SJT, June 26, 1876, in John Bigelow, *Letters and Literary Memorials of Samuel J. Tilden,* Vol. 2 (New York: Harper and Bros., 1908), 436.

14 "like a free horse": Matthew Josephson, *The Politicos, 1865–1896* (New York: Harcourt Brace, 1938), 167.

15 "hothouse capitalism": Richard White, *Railroaded: The Transcontinentals and the Making of Modern America* (New York: Norton, 2011), 17.

15 Amid the constellation: *PT,* May 22, 1881; *NYT,* May 22, 1881.

15 Under the leadership: Albert J. Churella, *The Pennsylvania Railroad,* Vol. 1, *Building an Empire, 1846–1917* (Philadelphia: University of Pennsylvania Press, 2013), 207–12, 346–47; William B. Sipes, *The Pennsylvania Railroad: Its Origin, Construction, Condition, and Connections* (Philadelphia: The [Pennsylvania Railroad] Passenger Dept., 1875), 17–18.

16 Tall, blond, and boyish-looking: *NYT,* May 22, 1881.

16 Scott's bitter rival: Churella, *The Pennsylvania Railroad,* 208.

17 The idea for: J. S. Ingram, *The Centennial Exposition Described and Illustrated* (Philadelphia: Hubbard Bros., 1876), 41–42; *CG,* 42nd Congress, 2nd session, 3814.

18 The commission confidently: Rydell, *All the World's a Fair,* 19, note 21; Bruno Giberti, *Designing the Centennial* (Lexington: University Press of Kentucky, 2002), 176–81.

18 "a popular museum": *PT,* November 9, 1876.

18 "Well, Moon": Louis Simonin, *A French View of the Grand International Exposition of 1876,* trans. Samuel H. Needles (Philadelphia: Claxton, Remsen & Hafflefinger, 1877), 120.

19 One week after: William Dean Howells, "A Sennight of the Centennial," *Atlantic Monthly,* July 1876.

CHAPTER 2 ⋆ THE BEAT CONVULSIVE

22 Howells was far: Howells, "A Sennight of the Centennial"; Simonin, *A French View of the Grand International Exposition,* 46; Rydell, *All the World's a Fair,* 35.

23 "The most striking feature": *Georgia Weekly Telegraph,* November 7, 1876.

23 "as entrancing as": Rydell, *All the World's a Fair,* 11.

24 Although vendors hawked: Howells, "A Sennight of the Centennial"; *PI,* April 25, 1876, April 25, 1876, June 5, 1876, August 2, 1876, August 15, 1876; *NYT,* May 12, 1876; *Philadelphia Press,* May 11, 1876.

24 "Columbia has got": Marietta Holley, *Samantha at the Centennial* (Hartford, CT: American Publishing Co., 1881), 496.

24 "Why, a hull": Holley, *Samantha at the Centennial,* 411–12.

25 "A newborn child": Robert J. Gordon, *The Rise and Fall of American Growth: The U.S. Standard of Living Since the Civil War* (Princeton, NJ: Princeton University Press, 2016), 4.

25 By the 1870s: Gordon, *The Rise and Fall of American Growth,* 33ff., 73, 173.

26 "It is wonderful!": AGB to MGH, June 21, 1876, AGB Papers, LOC.

26 "Do you love disorder?": Simonin, *A French View of the Grand International Exposition,* 16–17.

27 "voluptuous dances": Simonin, *A French View of the Grand International Exposition,* 53.

27 Howells extolled displays: Howells, "A Sennight of the Centennial."

27 Howells took pride: Howells, "A Sennight of the Centennial."

28 But they were perplexed: Rydell, *All the World's a Fair,* 31.

28 "Both are essentially": *NYT,* July 9, 1876.

29 "their very presence": *PI,* June 9, 1876.

29 "bedeviled arts": Howells, "A Sennight of the Centennial."

29 "I am surprised": AGB to MHB, June 21, 1876, AGB Papers, LOC.

29 "The bribes almost": Howells, "A Sennight of the Centennial."

30 "Hearin' that soul stirrin'": Holley, *Samantha at the Centennial,* 384–85.

32 The federal Patent Office: Simonin, *A French View of the Grand International Exposition,* 28.

32 "on every side": Howells, "A Sennight of the Centennial."

32 *"Thee in thy":* Online at poets.org/poem/locomotive-winter.

33 "jewelers a jewelin'": Holley, *Samantha at the Centennial,* 507.

33 Howells, the father: Howells, "A Sennight of the Centennial."

33 The ponderously named: *NYT,* June 5 and June 15, 1876; Ingram, *The Centennial Exposition Described and Illustrated,* 291–98.

34 The industrial star: Simonin, *A French View of the Grand International Exposition,* 20–24.

36 "Should I be able": AGB to AMB, October 20, 1874, AGB Papers, LOC.

36 "It is a neck": AGB to AMB, November 23, 1874, AGB Papers, LOC.

37 "that I have scarce": AGB to AMB, November 23, 1874, AGB Papers, LOC.

37 "The iron core": AGB to AMB, November 26, 1874, AGB Papers, LOC.

37 "I am disheartened": AGB to MGH, January 7, 1876, AGB Papers, LOC.

38 "I close my eyes": AGB to MGH, April 2, 1876, AGB Papers, LOC.

38 Mabel, who was deeply: Robert V. Bruce, *Bell: Alexander Graham Bell and the Conquest of Solitude* (Ithaca, NY: Cornell University Press, 1973), 175.

38 Bell described what: AGB to AMB, March 10, 1876, AGB Papers, LOC.

CHAPTER 3 ⋆ WILDFIRE

41 "They all had": Holley, *Samantha at the Centennial,* 429.

42 "peculiarly attractive": Ingram, *The Centennial Exposition Described and Illustrated,* 373.

42 Raved one viewer: *Alexandria People's Advocate,* July 1876, cited in Harry Henderson and Albert Henderson, *The Indomitable Spirit of Edmonia Lewis: A Narrative Biography* (Milford, CT: Esquiline Hill Press, 2012), 337.

42 One Black tourist: *People's Advocate,* July 1, 1876, cited in Philip S. Foner, "Black Participation in the Centennial of 1876," *Phylon* 39, no. 4 (Winter 1978).

43 "We have been": *Philadelphia Press,* May 14, 1872, cited in Foner, "Black Participation in the Centennial of 1876."

43 "nearly every one": *Chicago Inter-Ocean,* May 27, 1876.

43 "Although the chains": *Philadelphia Press,* reprinted in *People's Advocate,* July 1, 1876.

44 "A new and black": Rydell, *All the World's a Fair,* 29.

44 A popular satirical account: "Shortcut, Daisy" and "O'Pagus, Arry." (Satirical pseudonyms.) *One Hundred Years a Republic. Our Show. A Humorous Account of the International Exposition* (Philadelphia: Claxton, Remsen, and Haffelfinger, 1876), 38.

44 "Africa—stagnant": Cited in Foner, "Black Participation in the Centennial of 1876."

44 "a most offensively": Howells, "A Sennight of the Centennial."

46 If "Negroes" were: Walt Whitman, *Democratic Vistas,* xxix.

46 "almost grotesque exercise": Charles W. Calhoun, *The Presidency of Ulysses S. Grant* (Lawrence: University Press of Kansas, 2017), 479.

46 a "Magna Charta": Josephson, *The Politicos,* 50, note 59.

47 Pontificated *The Nation*: Robert J. Kaczorowski, *The Politics of Judicial Inter-*

pretation: The Federal Courts, Department of Justice, and Civil Rights, 1866–1876 (New York: Fordham University Press, 2005), 135.

48 "I intend to": In Naurice Frank Woods Jr., *Race and Racism in Nineteenth Century Art: The Ascendancy of Robert Duncanson, Edward Bannister, and Edmonia Lewis* (Jackson: University of Mississippi Press, 2021), 189.

48 In an editorial: Henderson and Henderson, *The Indomitable Spirit of Edmonia Lewis,* 321.

49 "Edmonia Lewis was": *How Edmonia Lewis Became an Artist,* pamphlet, Houghton Library, Harvard University.

50 Recent research by: Kirsten Pai Buick, *Child of the Fire: Mary Edmonia Lewis and the Problem of Art History's Black and Indian Subject* (Durham, NC: Duke University Press, 2010), 4ff., 111; *New National Era and Citizen,* July 25, 1872; *NYT,* December 29, 1878.

51 She told the author: *The Liberator,* February 19, 1864.

52 "She has wrought": Henderson and Henderson, *The Indomitable Spirit of Edmonia Lewis,* 71–72.

52 Although she never: Henderson and Henderson, *The Indomitable Spirit of Edmonia Lewis,* 2.

52 "My enthusiasm increased": Henderson and Henderson, *The Indomitable Spirit of Edmonia Lewis,* 89.

53 "I was practically": *NYT,* December 29, 1878.

53 Some expatriate sculptors: Nathaniel Hawthorne, *The Marble Faun* (New York: Oxford University Press, 2008), 104.

53 "She lives here": Margaret Farrand Thorp, "The White, Marmorean Flock," *New England Quarterly* 32, no. 2 (June 1959).

53 "strange sisterhood": Tana Wojczuk, *Lady Romeo: The Revolutionary Life of Charlotte Cushman, America's First Celebrity* (New York: Simon & Schuster, 2021), 198.

54 On stage, Cushman: Wojczuk, *Lady Romeo,* 83.

54 "What she undertakes": In Buick, *Child of the Fire,* 15.

54 "Colored Genius": *Philadelphia Christian Recorder,* March 31, 1866.

54 "strong evidence of": In Henderson and Henderson, *The Indomitable Spirit of Edmonia Lewis,* 304.

55 Visitors found her: Henry T. Tuckerman, *Book of the Artists* (New York: James F. Carr, 1867), 603.

56 "I have Indian blood": *San Francisco Chronicle,* August 26, 1873.

56 She sometimes referred: Online at EdmoniaLewis.org.

56 she "has something": *NYT,* December 29, 1878.

56 "In Italy, Miss Lewis": *New National Era and Citizen,* July 25, 1873.

56 "Some people praise": *The Liberator,* February 19, 1864.

57 "They treat me": *NYT,* December 29, 1878.

57 "God's gift to": *How Edmonia Lewis Became an Artist.*

58 "She had seen": *NYT,* December 29, 1878.

CHAPTER 4 ⋆ GLADIATORS

59 "If other fools": Ari Hoogenboom, *Hayes: Warrior and President* (Lawrence: University Press of Kansas, 1995), 260.

59 He would only: RBH to Guy M. Bryan, April 2, 1876, RBH Papers, LOC.

60 In the Gilded Age: *NYT,* June 15 and 16, 1876.

60 News from the convention: *NYT,* June 15, 1876; *PI,* June 14–17, 1876.

61 "a massive job-creating": Josephson, *The Politicos,* 136.

61 Under Conkling's regime: Josephson, *The Politicos,* 94, note 38.

61 "Not more truly": *Proceedings of the Republican National Convention* (Concord, NH: Republican Press Association, 1876), 71.

61 As early as 1871: CS to E. L. Godkin, March 31, 1871, Papers of Carl Schurz, LOC.

62 "a common sewer": Josephson, *The Politicos,* 37, note 38.

63 His mortal rival: Neil Rolde, *Continental Liar from the State of Maine: James G. Blaine* (Gardiner, ME: Tilbury House, 2007), 114–15.

63 "There has never been": David M. Jordan, *Roscoe Conkling of New York: Voice in the Senate* (Ithaca, NY: Cornell University Press, 1971), 230.

64 "I may say": Henrietta M. Larson, *Jay Cooke, Private Banker* (Cambridge, MA: Harvard University Press, 1936), 274–75.

64 Blaine was also known: *NYT,* June 12, 1876; Churella, *The Pennsylvania Railroad,* 445ff.; Rolde, *Continental Liar from the State of Maine,* 176–83; Jordan, *Roscoe Conkling of New York,* 235; Josephson, *The Politicos,* 207–10.

65 Hayes, who knew Blaine: Harry T. Williams, ed., *Hayes: The Diary of a President, 1875–1881* (New York: David McKay Co., 1964), 21.

65 "My eyes are almost": RBH to JGB, June 12, 1876, RBH Papers, LOC.

66 Everyone knew that: *NYT,* June 15 and 16, 1876.

66 Too many officeholders: *Proceedings of the Republican National Convention,* 16ff.

67 Next, Frederick Douglass: *Proceedings of the Republican National Convention,* 26–27.

67 Like all party platforms: *Proceedings of the Republican National Convention,* 56–57.

68 Sara J. Spencer: *NYT,* June 16, 1876.

68 "In this bright": *Proceedings of the Republican National Convention,* 32–34.

68 "the honest demands": *Proceedings of the Republican National Convention,* 57.

69 Catering to the unrest: *Proceedings of the Republican National Convention,* 57–63.

69 Tension mounted: *Proceedings of the Republican National Convention,* 67–77.

70 When the famous orator: *Proceedings of the Republican National Convention,* 74.

70 "His private life": *Proceedings of the Republican National Convention,* 78.

70 "It sobers me": Williams, *Hayes: The Diary of a President,* 26.

70 Although Hayes was born in: William Dean Howells, *Sketch of the Life and*

Character of Rutherford B. Hayes (New York: Hurt and Houghton, 1876), 4, 63ff., 98.

71 Black Americans, he declared: Howells, *Sketch of the Life and Character of Rutherford B. Hayes,* 144–45.

72 Although his contempt: Hoogenboom, *Hayes: Warrior and President,* 3.

72 "I now would be": RBH to Guy M. Bryan, April 2, 1876, RBH Papers, LOC.

72 "I do not feel": Howells, *Sketch of the Life and Character of Rutherford B. Hayes,* 116.

72 Three hundred and seventy-nine votes: *Proceedings of the Republican National Convention,* 84–87, 101–9; *NYT,* June 17, 1876.

73 "It for a few": Williams, *Hayes: Diary of a President,* 26.

73 "was not the pluckiest": *NYT,* June 17, 1876.

74 "I cannot help": Hoogenboom, *Hayes: Warrior and President,* 265.

74 "there can be no": Howells, *Sketch of the Life and Character of Rutherford B. Hayes,* 126.

74 "Is he a figurehead": *NYH,* July 5, 1876.

74 There was Thomas Edison: Edmund Morris, *Edison* (New York: Random House, 2019), 522ff.

75 "When I saw how pale": AGB to EB, June 18, 1876, AGB Papers, LOC.

75 "I shall feel far": AGB to MGH, June 18, 1876, AGB Papers, LOC.

75 "If I can't": AGB to MGH, June 19, 1876, AGB Papers, LOC.

76 Nevertheless, he remained: AGB to AMB, June 22, 1876, AGB Papers, LOC.

76 With relief, Bell found: AGB to AMB, June 27, 1876, AGB Papers, LOC.

76 Bell surmised that Gray's: AGB to AMB, June 27, 1876, and AGB to MGH, June 21, 1876, AGB Papers, LOC.

77 He offered to transmit: Bruce, *Bell,* 190–97; AGB to AMB, June 27, 1876, AGB Papers, LOC.

78 "I have made": AGB to AMB, June 27, 1876, AGB Papers, LOC; Charlotte Gray, *Reluctant Genius: Alexander Graham Bell and the Passion for Invention* (New York: Arcade, 2006), 138; Bruce, *Bell,* 197.

78 "the greatest marvel": Edwin S. Grosvenor and Morgan Wesson, *Alexander Graham Bell* (Middletown, CT: New Word City, 2016), 88.

78 "before long friends": Bruce, *Bell,* 198.

CHAPTER 5 ⋆ THE DEMOCRATS RESURGENT

79 Compared to the: *Official Proceedings of the Democratic National Convention* (St. Louis: Woodward, Tiernan, & Hale, 1876), 1ff.; *NYT,* June 28, 1876; *St. Louis Globe,* June 28, 1876.

80 "In this Centennial": *Official Proceedings of the Democratic National Convention,* 19.

80 The platform: *NYH,* June 29, 1876; *Official Proceedings of the Democratic*

National Convention, 19; Alexander Clarence Flick, *Samuel Jones Tilden: A Study in Political Sagacity* (New York: Dodd Mead & Co., 1939), 288.

80 Declared the convention's: *Official Proceedings of the Democratic National Convention,* 62–64.

81 Senator Francis Kernan: *Official Proceedings of the Democratic National Convention,* 30ff.

81 During breaks between: *PI,* June 27, 1876; *New York Tribune,* June 29, 1876; *St. Louis Globe,* June 28 and 29, 1876.

82 "Sammy has all": *NYT,* June 29, 1876.

83 Senator John Sherman: JS, *John Sherman's Recollections of Forty Years in the House, Senate and Cabinet,* 551.

83 In every era: Roy Morris Jr., *Fraud of the Century: Rutherford B. Hayes, Samuel Tilden and the Stolen Election of 1876* (New York: Simon & Schuster, 2003), 85, 93, 107; *NYT,* July 11, 1876.

83 Tilden had nothing: Oliver E. Allen, *The Tiger: The Rise and Fall of Tammany Hall* (New York: Addison-Wesley, 1993), 101–5, 128–31; Gustavus Myers, *The History of Tammany Hall* (New York: Boni & Liveright, 1917), 227; *Official Proceedings of the Democratic National Convention,* 128–30.

84 When informed that: *NYH,* June 29, 1876.

84 That evening, Tilden: Flick, *Samuel Jones Tilden,* 295.

84 In his letter: *Official Proceedings of the Democratic National Convention,* 180ff.

85 Isaac Bourne: Isaac Bourne to USG, USG Papers, 25, 187.

86 In May 1876: *Chicago Inter-Ocean,* May 25, 1876.

86 "Slavery was a": *NYT,* May 11, 1876.

86 At the same time: United States v. Cruikshank, 92 U.S. 542 (1875); Kaczorowski, *Politics of Judicial Interpretation,* 150.

86 Even the: *New York Tribune,* October 31, 1874.

88 Marietta Holley's fictional: Holley, *Samantha at the Centennial,* 535–36.

89 No one worried: *Chicago Inter-Ocean,* May 27, 1876.

89 By contrast: Kimberly Orcutt, *Power and Posterity: American Art at Philadelphia's 1876 Centennial Exhibition* (University Park: Pennsylvania University Press, 2017), 93.

89 the Centennial's most: Rydell, *All the World's a Fair,* 28.

89 And one of the Centennial's: *NYT,* October 20, 1876.

89 Nevertheless, many Southerners: *Montgomery Advertiser,* March 17, 1875; *Bristol (TN) Democratic News,* May 23, 1876; *Richmond Examiner,* June 4, 1876; *Philadelphia Press,* November 3, 1876; Jack Noe, "'Everybody Is Centennializing': White Southerners and the 1876 Centennial," *American Nineteenth Century History* 17, no. 3 (2016); Mitch Kachun, "Before the Eyes of All Nations: African American Identity and Historical Memory at the Centennial Exposition of 1876," *Pennsylvania History* 65, no. 3 (Summer 1998).

90 Southerners claimed: *Mobile Register,* May 21, 1876; *Richmond Enquirer,* June 4, 1876; Orcutt, *Power and Posterity,* 96ff.

91 A Black Washington lawyer: Henderson and Henderson, *The Indomitable Spirit of Edmonia Lewis,* 349; *Christian Recorder,* October 1876.

91 A reporter from: *Athens (OH) Messenger,* August 17, 1876.

92 Despite the abuse: Ingram, *The Centennial Exposition Described and Illustrated,* 327.

92 "The face wears": John T. Dale, *What Ben Beverly Saw at the Great Exposition* (Chicago: Moses Warren & Co., 1877), 269–70.

92 For Lewis, *Cleopatra*: Woods, *Race and Racism in Nineteenth Century Art,* 196.

93 Lewis told John Patterson: Henderson and Henderson, *The Indomitable Spirit of Edmonia Lewis,* 349.

93 A Black journalist: Henderson and Henderson, *The Indomitable Spirit of Edmonia Lewis,* 350.

CHAPTER 6 ⋆ INDEFATIGABLE WOMEN

95 "The Fourth of July": *NYH,* July 5, 1876.

96 After making a few: *NYT,* July 5, 1876; *NYH,* July 5, 1876.

97 No woman more: Kathleen Barry, *Susan B. Anthony* (New York: New York University Press, 1998), 8–11, 38, 237.

98 Stone's faction supported: Elizabeth Cady Stanton, Susan B. Anthony, and Matilda Joslyn Gage, *History of Woman Suffrage,* Vol. 2 (Rochester, New York; Charles Mann Publishing Co., 1881–1887) 341, also 354, 383.

99 Stanton, Anthony, and Gage: Barry, *Susan B. Anthony,* 277.

100 "While the nation is": *NYT,* July 5, 1876; Stanton, Anthony, and Gage, *History of Woman Suffrage,* Vol. 3, 31.

100 Anthony was here: Barry, *Susan B. Anthony,* 263, 274; Stanton, Anthony, and Gage, *History of Woman Suffrage,* Vol. 2, 439–41.

101 The Declaration further: *NYT,* July 5, 1876; Stanton, Anthony, and Gage, *History of Woman Suffrage,* Vol. 3, 31.

102 One male journalist: Simonin, *A French View of the International Exposition of 1876,* 31.

102 "The day is coming": WW, *Democratic Vistas,* 46, 32.

102 *"She planted homes": NYT,* July 5, 1876.

103 Gillespie first recruited: Elizabeth Duane Gillespie, *A Book of Remembrance* (Philadelphia: Lippincott, 1901), 270ff., 283ff.

104 The committee also: Elizabeth Duane Gillespie and the Women's Centennial Executive Committee, *The National Cookery Book* (Philadelphia: Henry B. Ashmead, 1876), 141–43, 272ff.

104 In return for: Gillespie, *A Book of Remembrance,* 311–15ff., 327, 282.

105 The pavilion's exhibits: generally, Dolores Pfeuffer-Scherer, "Remembrance and the American Revolution: Women and the 1876 Centennial Exhibition" (PhD dissertation, Temple University, 2016); Ingram, *The Centennial Exposition Described and Illustrated,* 344–46, 366–70; Gillespie, *A Book of Remem-*

brance, 321; *Women's Journal,* May 1, 1875, and January 8, 1876, in Mary Frances Cordato, "Toward a New Century: Women and the Philadelphia Centennial Exhibition," *Pennsylvania Magazine of History and Biography* 107, no. 1 (1983).

106 All in all: Holley, *Samantha at the Centennial,* 522–23.

107 The pavilion's most popular: Gillespie, *A Book of Remembrance,* 319–20; *The New Century,* June 10, 1876; Frank B. Norton, *1876 Centennial Exhibition: The Illustrated Enhanced Historical Register* (Pittsburgh: CGR Publishing, 2020 [originally published 1876]), 162.

107 Allison's engine: Gillespie, *A Book of Remembrance,* 319.

108 Declared one editorial: *The New Century,* May 13, 1876.

108 Neither visitors to: Foner, "Black Participation in the Centennial of 1876"; *Philadelphia Press,* April 5 and 17, 1873; *PT,* April 27, 1873; *New National Era and Citizen,* May 22 and June 5, 1873.

108 The official Fourth: *NYT,* July 5, 1876.

109 The Centennial's commissioners: *Philadelphia Press,* June 13, 1876; Kachun, "Before the Eyes of All Nations."

110 William Evarts stem-windingly: *NYT,* July 5, 1876.

111 Amid the day's: *NYH,* July 3, 1876.

CHAPTER 7 ⋆ THE LAW OF PROGRESS

113 On July 5: *NYT,* July 6 and 8, and August 18, 1876; *Chicago Tribune,* August 10, 1876.

113 "It seems almost": *NYT,* July 7, 1876.

115 Visitors would observe: Simonin, *A French View of the Grand International Exposition of 1876,* 56.

115 In 1873, Joseph Henry: Rydell, *All the World's a Fair,* 23–24, 244, notes 31 and 32.

115 "It is most unpleasant": Robert E. Bieder, *Science Encounters the Indian, 1820–1880: The Early Years of American Ethnology* (Norman: University Press of Oklahoma, 1986), 66–67.

116 Like many Americans: George Armstrong Custer, *My Life on the Plains, or, Personal Experiences with Indians* (Norman: University of Oklahoma Press, 1962 [originally published 1874]), 17–18.

116 Custer would have seen: James D. McCabe, *The Illustrated History of the Centennial Exhibition* (Philadelphia: National Publishing Company, 1975), 205–6; Norton, *1876 Centennial Exhibition,* 107–12, 207; Dale, *What Ben Beverly Saw at the Great Exposition,* 114–16.

116 "The red man": Howells, "A Sennight of the Centennial."

117 "In the sweat of": Henry Nash Smith, *Virgin Land: The American West as Symbol and Myth* (Cambridge, MA: Harvard University Press, 1970), 182.

117 Few Americans doubted: Richard Slotkin, *The Fatal Environment: The Myth*

of the Frontier in the Age of Industrialization, 1800–1890 (New York: Harper Perennial, 1994), 440.

117 Frederick Douglass, who: David W. Blight, *Frederick Douglass: Prophet of Freedom* (New York: Simon & Schuster, 2018), 486; Buick, *Child of the Fire,* 107.

117 "These people must die": Michael Paul Rogin, *Fathers and Children: Andrew Jackson and the Subjugation of the American Indian* (New York: Alfred A. Knopf, 1975), 116.

117 Such contradictions were: Buick, *Child of the Fire,* 81, 129.

118 Lewis's greatest work: Buick, *Child of the Fire,* 110–12.

119 "Edmonia is younger": Buick, *Child of the Fire,* 110.

119 "I do not believe": Calhoun, *The Presidency of Ulysses S. Grant,* 390.

119 Bands that refused: Francis Paul Prucha, *American Indian Treaties: The History of a Political Anomaly* (Berkeley: University of California Press, 1994), 291; Francis Paul Prucha, *The Great Father: The United States Government and the American Indian* (Lincoln: University of Nebraska Press, 1984), 167.

121 "If I were an Indian": Custer, *My Life on the Plains,* 22, 13ff.

121 As prospectors flooded: Slotkin, *The Fatal Environment,* 339; James D. Richardson, ed., *Compilation of the Messages and Papers of the Presidents, 1789–1897,* Vol. 7 (Washington, DC: Government Printing Office, 1898), 401; *NYH,* July 7, 1876.

121 Custer was initially: *NYT,* July 6, 7, and 8, 1876; *NYH,* July 7, 1876; T. J. Stiles, *Custer's Trials: A Life on the Frontier of a New America* (New York: Vintage, 2016), 432–35; Calhoun, *The Presidency of Ulysses S. Grant,* 546–47.

122 "An impetuous man": *NYH,* July 7, 1876.

123 The Battle of the Little Big Horn: *NYH,* July 7, 1876.

123 *"The fall of": New York Tribune,* July 10, 1876.

123 In the weeks that: *NYT,* August 12, August 14, August 22, and August 30, 1876; Frederick Whittaker, *A Complete Life of Gen. George A. Custer* (New York: Sheldon & Co., 1876), 520ff.

124 The Republican *Nation*: Cited in *NYT,* August 30, 1876.

124 "The denunciations expressed": *NYH,* July 7, 1876.

124 "Either our people": Slotkin, *The Fatal Environment,* 473.

125 Along with Custer's men: *Yankton Dakotian* (undated), cited in Slotkin, *The Fatal Environment,* 473; *NYH,* July 7, 1876.

125 "The Indians were cheated": *NYT,* August 30, 1876.

126 The bitterness of the helpless: *NYT,* September 22 and September 23, 1876.

CHAPTER 8 ⋆ THE SHOTGUN PLAN

127 In keeping with: RBH to JAG, July 27, 1876, RBH Papers, LOC; RBH to JS, June 23, 1876, RBH Papers, LOC; Hoogenboom, *Hayes: Warrior and President,* 266–67.

127 "If we lose it": RBH to W. K. Rogers, August 13, 1876, RBH Papers, LOC.

128 "When I am alone": RBH to Lucy Hayes, August 13, 1876, RBH Papers, LOC.

128 "Your letter of acceptance": CS to RBH, August 10, 1876, T. Harry Williams, ed., *Hayes: The Diary of a President, 1875–1881,* Vol. 3, 342.

128 "I hate assessments": RBH to William Henry Smith, August 10, 1876, RBH Papers, LOC.

129 A Tammany operative: *NYT,* August 15, 1876.

129 It inexorably seemed: Howells, *Sketch of the Life of Rutherford B. Hayes,* 121ff.; RBH to JAG, August 6 and 12, 1876, RBH Papers, LOC; Charles Nordhoff to RBH, June 26 and 28, 1876, in Hoogenboom, *Hayes: Warrior and President,* 269–70.

130 Opined the bitter: Adelbert Ames to Blanche Butler Ames, November 4, 1875, Blanche Butler Ames, *Adelbert Ames, 1835–1933* (New York: Columbia University Press, 1964), 249; John R. Lynch, *The Facts of Reconstruction* (New York: Neale Publishing Co., 1913), 68–70.

130 Public opinion even in: James S. Pike, *The Prostrate State: South Carolina Under Negro Government* (New York: Appleton and Co., 1874), 12.

131 Claimed Rep. S. S. Cox: *A Centennial Fourth of July Democratic Celebration: The Massacre of Six Colored Citizens of the United States at Hamburgh, S.C.,* pamphlet, American Pamphlet Collection, LOC.

131 Such ugly incidents: *NYT,* July 9, July 12, and July 14, 1876.

132 Benjamin Tillman, one of: Benjamin Tillman, *The Struggles of 76: How South Carolina Was Delivered from Carpetbag and Negro Rule,* speech, 1909, Benjamin Ryan Tillman Papers, South Carolina Historical Society.

133 "They have done a deed": *NYT,* August 17, 1876.

133 On the floor of Congress: *A Centennial Fourth of July Democratic Celebration: The Massacre of Six Colored Citizens of the United States at Hamburgh, S.C.*

133 White Southerners quickly: *A Centennial Fourth of July Democratic Celebration: The Massacre of Six Colored Citizens of the United States at Hamburgh, S.C.;* Barbara Seaborn, *Monumental Legacy: The Rise and Fall of Hamburg, South Carolina* (Bloomington, IN: iUniverse, 2021), 134–38; William Arthur Sheppard, *Red Shirts Remembered* (Atlanta: Ruralist Press, Inc., 1940), 89.

134 The monument's promoters: Kachun, "Before the Eyes of All Nations."

135 Gaily beribboned ladies: *PT,* October 20, 1876.

136 There was nothing: Benjamin R. Tillman, *Autobiographical Sketch,* Benjamin R. Tillman Papers, South Caroliniana Library, University of South Carolina.

136 like "singing Psalms": Rod Andrew Jr., *Wade Hampton: Confederate Warrior to Southern Redeemer* (Chapel Hill: University of North Carolina Press, 2008), 373.

136 A frightened Republican: L. Cass Carpenter to USG, August 19, 1876, USG Papers, Vol. 27, LOC, 205.

136 Based on a similar: Sheppard, *Red Shirts Remembered,* 46–51; circular dated

August 1, 1876, in otherwise undated copy of *Allendale Citizen,* Martin Witherspoon Gary Papers, David Rubenstein Manuscript Library, Duke University.

137 "Hamburg is only": Daniel H. Chamberlain to USG, July 22, 1876, USG Papers, Vol. 27, 202–3.

137 Desperate pleas flooded: William F. Simonton to USG, June 3, 1876, USG Papers, Vol. 27, LOC, 240; Jasper Starr to USG, September 13, 1875, USG Papers, Vol. 25, LOC, 16–17; Grenville Peirce to USG, February 17, 1876, USG Papers, Vol. 27, LOC, 238; *NYT,* July 14 and July 15, 1876.

137 Grant knew that: USG to Daniel H. Chamberlain, July 26, 1876, USG Papers, Vol. 27, LOC, 199; Richard Zuczek, *State of Rebellion: Reconstruction in South Carolina* (Columbia: University of South Carolina Press, 1996), 164ff.

138 South Carolina Democrats: Francis Butler, *Gov. D. H. Chamberlain's Administration in S.C.,* unpublished manuscript dated May 6, 1918, Matthew Calbraith Butler Papers, David Rubenstein Manuscript Library, Duke University.

138 Hampton looked the part: Andrew, *Wade Hampton,* 371.

139 The state Democratic convention: *NYT,* August 18, 1876.

139 In 1871, with no reason: *Report of the Joint Select Committee to Inquire into the Condition of Affairs in the Late Insurrectionary States,* Vol. 1 (Washington, DC: Government Printing Office, 1871), 1236; *NYT,* August 18, 1876.

140 In fact, Gary's: *Abbeville (SC) Press and Banner,* August 16, 1876; Sheppard, *Red Shirts Remembered,* 97–103.

140 Chamberlain was swarmed: L. Cass Carpenter to USG, August 19, 1876, USG Papers, Vol. 27, 205; Sheppard, *Red Shirts Remembered,* 127.

140 "A small cannon": Robert W. Shand, unpublished memoir, South Caroliniana Collection, University of South Carolina.

140 After Abbeville: J. C. Grant to USG, August 26, 1876, USG Papers, Vol. 27, 207.

141 In Louisiana, which lacked: *Proceedings of the Returning Board of the State of Louisiana, Election of 1876, published by New Orleans Republican,* "compliments of W. R. Fish," 1876; JS to RBH, November 23, 1876, JS, *John Sherman's Recollections of Forty Years in the House, Senate and Cabinet,* Vol. 1, 558.

141 On August 19: Tillman, *The Struggles of 1876.*

CHAPTER 9 ⋆ THE MOLLIES

143 "It rises loftily": Howells, "A Sennight of the Centennial."

144 In a series of trials: Marvin W. Schlegel, *Ruler of the Reading: The Life of Franklin B. Gowen, 1836–1889* (Harrisburg, PA: Archives Publishing Co., 1947), 32ff.; *Lancaster Intelligencer-Journal,* July 26, 1876.

145 Walt Whitman wrote: WW, *Democratic Vistas,* 71.

146 A rare divergent voice: Heather Cox Richardson, *West from Appomattox: The Reconstruction of America after the Civil War* (New Haven, CT: Yale University Press, 2007), 72.

146 "Let the factories": Philip S. Foner, *History of the Labor Movement in the United States,* Vol. 1, *From Colonial Times to the Founding of the American Federation of Labor* (New York: International Publishers, 1998), 458.

147 "Every man is capable": Slotkin, *The Fatal Environment,* 340.

147 Like his rival: Walter J. Colman, "Labor Disturbances in Pennsylvania, 1850–1880" (PhD dissertation, Catholic University of America, 1936); Churella, *The Pennsylvania Railroad,* 501–2, 514; Schlegel, *Ruler of the Reading,* 186ff.

148 "Had an unfortunate accident": David Nasaw, *Andrew Carnegie* (New York: Penguin, 2007), 178.

149 Gowen liked to portray: Schlegel, *Ruler of the Reading,* 62ff.; Kevin Kenny, *Making Sense of the Molly Maguires* (New York: Oxford University Press, 1998), 170–71; *Argument of Franklin B. Gowen Before the Joint Committee of the Legislature of Pennsylvania to Enquire into the Affairs of the Philadelphia and Reading Coal and Iron Co. and the Philadelphia and Reading Railroad Co., July 29–30, 1875* (Philadelphia: Press of Helfenstein, Lewis & Co., 1875), report, SCHS; *NYT,* April 14 and May 14, 1876.

149 Gowen fostered: Anne Flaherty, *The Passion of John Kehoe and the Myth of the "Molly Maguires"* (Saint Leonard, MD: Hibernian Press, 2023), 6ff., 235; Kenny, *Making Sense of the Molly Maguires,* 146.

151 By the late spring: Colman, "Labor Disturbances in Pennsylvania, 1850–1880," 79–80; Schlegel, *Ruler of the Reading,* 69–73; *Miners' Journal,* June 11, 1875.

151 *"Well, we've been"*: Kenny, *Making Sense of the Molly Maguires,* 181.

151 "The union is Broke up": Shenandoah *Evening Herald,* October 2, 1875.

152 In December 1875: Shenandoah *Evening Herald,* December 11, 1875.

152 Influenced by Gowen: *NYH,* May 8, 1876.

152 On May 19, 1876: Pottsville *Daily Miner,* August 14, 1876; *New York Sun,* July 29, 1876; Flaherty, *The Passion of John Kehoe and the Myth of the "Molly Maguires,"* 145–47; *Report of the Case of the Commonwealth vs. John Kehoe et al., Members of the Ancient Order of Hibernians, Commonly Known as "Molly Maguires,"* pamphlet (Pottsville, PA: Miners' Journal Book and Job Rooms, 1876), SCHS.

153 "Their mouths are closed": Flaherty, *The Passion of John Kehoe and the Myth of the "Molly Maguires,"* 126.

153 One judge explicitly: Foner, *History of the Labor Movement in the United States,* Vol. 1, 459.

153 "a harvest of death": *PI,* May 20, 1876.

153 Even *The New York Times*: *NYT,* September 8, 1875.

154 Gowen stage-managed: *Report of the Case of the Commonwealth vs. John Kehoe;* Colman, "Labor Disturbances in Pennsylvania, 1850–1880," 150.

154 Gowen's attack on: *Argument of Franklin B. Gowen, Esq., in the Case of the Commonwealth vs. Thomas Munley et al.,* pamphlet (Pottsville, PA: Miners' Journal Book and Job Rooms, 1876); Pottsville *Daily Miner,* July 13–16, 1876.

154 He blamed the Hibernians: *Argument of Franklin B. Gowen, Esq. in the Case of the Commonwealth vs. Thomas Munley et al.*

155 *The Nation*, a leading: Slotkin, *The Fatal Environment,* 490.

155 Gowen cast John Kehoe: *Report of the Commonwealth vs. John Kehoe et al., Members of the Ancient Order of Hibernians, Commonly Known as "Molly Maguires"* (Pottsville, PA: Miners' Journal Book and Job Rooms, 1876), SCHS; *Argument of Franklin B. Gowen, Esq., in the Case of the Commonwealth vs. Thomas Munley et al.;* Flaherty, *The Passion of John Kehoe and the Myth of the "Molly Maguires,"* 237ff.; Shenandoah *Evening Herald*, October 17, 1876; Pottsville *Daily Miner,* January 13, 1877.

156 Kerrigan, a wholly unreliable: Patrick Butler statement to George R. Kaercher, August 16, 1876, in Kaercher Papers, SCHS; Flaherty, *The Passion of John Kehoe and the Myth of the "Molly Maguires,"* 161.

156 Not allowed to put: *Report of the Commonwealth vs. John Kehoe et al.*; Colman, "Labor Disturbances in Pennsylvania, 1850–1880," 142–43, 152.

157 One miner, Thomas King: Pottsville *Daily Miner,* July 22, 1876.

158 In letters prominently published: Pottsville *Daily Miner*, July 26, 1876; *PI,* July 18, 1876, and September 8, 1876.

158 "Now all are safe": Gowen, *Argument of Franklin B. Gowen, Esq., in the Case of the Commonwealth vs. Thomas Munley et al.*

158 "with one hand reaches": Scranton *Times,* cited in Schlegel, *Ruler of the Reading,* 68.

CHAPTER 10 ⋆ THE CONSTITUTIONAL ABYSS

159 On September 21: *PT,* September 22, 1876; *NYT,* September 22, 1876.

160 Tilden had some reason: *Harrisburg (PA) Patriot News,* August 9, 1876; *NYT,* July 11 and September 22, 1876; *Harper's Weekly,* November 11, 1876; *Brooklyn Eagle,* July 22, 1876; *Buffalo Courier,* July 27, 1876.

160 A month after Tilden: *PT,* October 27, 1876.

161 In his diary: Williams, *Hayes: The Diary of a President,* Vol. 33, October 29, 1876.

161 President Grant was inundated: USG Papers, Vol. 28, 26–27; *NYT,* November 6 and 7, 1876; "Affidavit" dated November 9, 1876, Gary Papers, Rubenstein Manuscript Library, Duke University; unpublished memoir, Shand Papers, South Caroliniana Collection, University of South Carolina.

162 "It is impossible": *NYH,* November 9, 1876.

162 "NECK AND NECK": *NYH,* November 9, 1876.

162 "We must, I now think": Williams, *Hayes: The Diary of a President,* Vol. 34, November 12, 1876, 380.

162 "In the heated state": JS, *John Sherman's Recollections of Forty Years in the House, Senate and Cabinet,* Vol. 1, 553.

163 "At no hour": Ward Lamon to USG, November 13, 1876, USG Papers, Vol. 28, 21.

163 Valedictory speeches attempted: *The New Century,* November 11, 1876; Annie Britton scrapbook, HSP; *Closing Ceremonies of the International Exhibition, 1876,* pamphlet (Philadelphia: U.S. Centennial Commission, 1876), HSP; *Public Sale of the Centennial Buildings, December 1, 1876,* auction catalog, HSP.

163 "The Corliss engine": Francis A. Walker, *The World's Fair, Philadelphia 1876: A Critical Account* (New York: A. S. Barnes, 1878).

164 The nation teetered: Edward B. Foley, *Ballot Battles: The History of Disputed Elections in the United States* (New York: Oxford University Press, 2016), 125–27; John Tyler Jr. to USG, January 6, 1877, USG Papers, Vol. 28, 146; William Tecumseh Sherman to Winfield Scott Hancock, November 21, 1876, USG Papers, Vol. 28, 37; William Tecumseh Sherman to Philip H. Sheridan, November 16, 1876, USG Papers, Vol. 28, 37.

165 As indignation flooded: Flick, *Samuel Jones Tilden,* 328–31.

166 The contested returns: Paul Leland Haworth, *The Hayes-Tilden Contested Election of 1876* (Cedar Rapids, IA: Burrows Bros. Co., 1906), 57ff., 223ff., 331; Foley, *Ballot Battles,* 134–35.

166 In South Carolina: Haworth, *The Hayes-Tilden Contested Election of 1876,* 150–56; WH to USG, November 27, 1876, USG Papers, Vol. 28, 49; USG to James D. Cameron, November 26, 1876, USG Papers, Vol. 28, 49ff.

167 Virtually everyone was: *New York Tribune,* December 6, 1876; Robert Shand, unpublished manuscript, Shand Papers, South Caroliniana Library, University of South Carolina.

167 "Unless you reach": USG to JS, November 12, 1876, in JS, *Forty Years in the House, Senate and Cabinet,* 554.

167 "We are not to allow": RBH to JS, November 27, 1876, Williams, *Hayes: The Diary of a President,* Vol. 34, 381; JS, *Forty Years in the House, Senate and Cabinet,* 554, 558–59.

167 The canvassing board: *New York Tribune,* December 6, 1876.

168 Grant, with just weeks: Cited by Hamilton Fish, USG Papers, Vol. 28, 107; USG message to U.S. Senate, January 29, 1877, USG Papers, Vol. 28, 143ff.

168 "We must rely": RBH to Samuel Shellabarger, January 3, 1877, Williams, *Hayes: The Diary of a President,* Vol. 34, 387.

168 It would mean: December 7, 1876, Williams, *Hayes: The Diary of a President,* Vol. 34, 387.

168 A subtle shift: November 11, 1876, and November 23, 1876, Williams, *Hayes: The Diary of a President,* Vol. 34, 378–80.

169 "Too much politics": RBH to William Henry Smith, December 24, 1876, Williams, *Hayes: The Diary of a President,* Vol. 34, 393.

169 "My anxiety to do": RBH to CS, February 4, 1877, Williams, *Hayes: The Diary of a President,* Vol. 34, 412.

169 "It has always seemed": RBH to JS, December 25, 1876, Williams, *Hayes: The Diary of a President,* Vol. 34, 393.

170 Conclusive evidence that Scott: Churella, *The Pennsylvania Railroad,* 424–25; White, *Railroaded,* 118ff.

170 One well-connected journalist: Hoogenboom, *Hayes: Warrior and President,* 283.

171 This would entail: Churella, *The Pennsylvania Railroad,* 424.

171 The Electoral Commission: Haworth, *The Hayes-Tilden Disputed Election of 1876,* 220ff., 238ff.; Foley, *Ballot Battles,* 135–36.

172 There were persistent rumors: USG Papers, Vol. 28, 24–25, 35–36, 128–30; Anne E. Marshall, *Creating a Confederate Kentucky: The Lost Cause and Civil War Memory in a Border State* (Chapel Hill: University of North Carolina Press, 2010), 72; Flick, *Samuel Jones Tilden,* 331, 407–9.

172 "The result was": Flick, *Samuel Jones Tilden,* 409.

173 Grant coolly replied: USG to James D. Cameron, March 3, 1877, USG Papers, Vol. 28, 165.

173 The mood on the floor: *CR,* 44th Congress, 2nd session, 2004ff., 2012, 2032–38.

174 On Capitol Hill: *CR,* 44th Congress, 2nd session, 2046ff.

175 At 4 a.m.: *CR,* 44th Congress, 2nd session, 2068; *NYT,* March 2, 1877.

176 "Both sides seemed satisfied": *NYT,* March 5, 1877.

EPILOGUE ⋆ 1877, PITTSBURGH

177 Hayes's inaugural address: Williams, *Hayes: The Diary of a President,* Vol. 34, 421.

178 "Mighty good": *NYT,* March 6, 1877.

179 "My policy is trust": March 16, 1877, Williams, *Hayes: The Diary of a President,* Vol. 35, 427.

179 For months, so-called: Ari Hoogenboom, *The Presidency of Rutherford B. Hayes* (Lawrence: University of Kansas Press, 1988), 61.

179 "If this leads to": March 20, 1877, Williams, *Hayes: The Diary of a President,* Vol. 35, 428.

179 "Let us admit": *St. Louis Globe-Democrat,* March 31, 1877.

179 Former Attorney General: Hoogenboom, *The Presidency of Rutherford B. Hayes,* 68.

180 "Everything is satisfactorily settled": Andrew, *Wade Hampton,* 418.

180 Hampton's Return: *Newberry (SC) Weekly Herald,* April 11, 1877; *NYT,* April 11, 1877.

180 Chamberlain's last bitter message: *NYT,* April 11, 1877.

180 On April 10: *NYT,* April 11, 1877.

181 "If there is any member": *NYT,* April 20, 1877.

182 "The Surrender Complete": *NYT,* April 25, 1877.

182 "The Negro will disappear": *The Nation,* April 5, 1877.

182 "I am confident": April 22, 1877, Williams, *Hayes: The Diary of a President,* Vol. 35, 430.

182 "I know they mean well": RBH to William D. Bickham, April 22, 1877, also RBH to Bickham, May 3, 1877, Williams, *Hayes: The Diary of a President,* Vol. 35, 431–32.

183 Custer's defeat was: John Q. Smith to Zachariah Chandler, December 19, 1876, USG Papers, Vol. 28, 97.

183 Although Philadelphia's: *PI,* July 5, 1877.

183 Governor Hartranft extolled: *PI,* July 5, 1877.

184 Custer morphed: Slotkin, *The Fatal Environment,* 502ff.

184 His death soon: Louis S. Warren, *Buffalo Bill's America: William Cody and the Wild West Show* (New York: Alfred A. Knopf, 2005).

184 Following Governor Hartranft: John W. Forney, "Oration, July 4, 1877, at Fairmount Park," pamphlet (Philadelphia: Valette, Haslam & Co., 1877).

184 Barely a week later: Michael B. Bellesiles, *1877: America's Year of Living Violently* (New York: New Press, 2010), 151, 166–67.

185 Schuylkill County remained: Pottsville *Daily Miner,* June 22, 1877; *PI,* July 27, 1877.

186 Within days, most: *NYT,* July 23 and July 25; *Pittsburgh Post,* July 24, 1877; Churella, *The Pennsylvania Railroad,* 476ff.

186 Tom Scott called: Churella, *The Pennsylvania Railroad,* 490.

186 The *New York World:* Churella, *The Pennsylvania Railroad,* 490.

186 In Chicago: *NYT,* July 26, 1877.

186 "Imperious and dictatorial": Churella, *The Pennsylvania Railroad,* 482.

186 "Never did Mr. Scott": *PT,* May 22, 1881.

187 Scott determined to: *Report of the Committee Appointed to Investigate the Railroad Riots in July 1877* (Harrisburg, PA: Superintendent of Public Printing, 1878), 135, 179, 213ff; *NYT,* July 22, 1877; Churella, *The Pennsylvania Railroad,* 484–85; Philip S. Foner, *The Great Labor Uprising of 1877* (New York: Pathfinder, 1977), 81ff.

188 Cried the *Chicago: Chicago Inter-Ocean,* July 23, 1877.

188 Scott tersely replied: *PI,* July 27, 1877.

188 Hayes briefly hesitated: August 2, 1877, Williams, *Hayes: The Diary of a President,* Vol. 35, 440; Richardson, *Compilation of the Messages and Papers of the Presidents, 1789*–1897, Vol. 7, 448–49.

188 Regular troops were ordered: *NYT,* July 29, 1877; Churella, *The Pennsylvania Railroad,* 488–89; Bellesiles, *1877: America's Year of Living Violently,* 175–76; *Report of the Committee Appointed to Investigate the Railroad Riots in July 1877,* generally.

189 Hayes felt a kind: August 2, 1877, Williams, *Hayes: The Diary of a President,* Vol. 35, 440.

189 "I did not get Justice": John Kehoe to Ramsey Potts, 1878 (otherwise undated), SCHS.

189 He was hanged: Pottsville *Daily Miner,* December 19, 1878.

189 Kehoe's nemesis: Pottsville *Daily Miner,* December 14, 1889.

189 Reverend Henry Ward Beecher: *NYT,* July 23, 1877.

190 "It is an American doctrine": *NYT,* July 30, 1877.

191 "The days are over": *NYT,* July 25, 1877.

191 Tom Scott, who identified: Thomas A. Scott, "The Recent Strikes," *North American Review,* September 1877.

191 The suppression of: *NYT,* May 22, 1881; *PT,* May 22, 1881; Churella, *The Pennsylvania Railroad,* 491; White, *Railroaded,* 103.

192 Preparing to defend: Bruce, *Bell,* 234.

192 "The power possessed": AGB to AMB, January 21, 1877, AGB Papers, LOC.

193 "Without the telephone": Bruce, *Bell,* 234.

194 "America will learn": Simonin, *A French View of the Grand International Exposition of 1876,* 68.

194 "We stand, live": WW, *Democratic Vistas,* 55.

196 "The corporations have": Bellesiles, *1877: America's Year of Living Violently,* 175.

196 "a distinct elevating": *NYT,* January 18, 1893.

197 "The great problem": Hoogenboom, *Hayes: Warrior and President,* 494.

197 Walt Whitman would: WW, *Democratic Vistas,* 71, 39, 28–29, 4, 44, 12.

197 "The problem of": WW, *Democratic Vistas,* 71.

197 "I don't believe in it": WW, *Democratic Vistas,* xlviii.

Selected Bibliography

BOOKS

Allen, Oliver E. *The Tiger: The Rise and Fall of Tammany Hall.* New York: Addison-Wesley, 1993.

Andrew, Rod, Jr. *Wade Hampton: Confederate Warrior to Southern Redeemer.* Chapel Hill: University of North Carolina Press, 2008.

Barry, Kathleen. *Susan B. Anthony: A Biography.* New York: New York University Press, 1998.

Beatty, Jack. *Age of Betrayal: The Triumph of Money in America, 1865–1900.* New York: Vintage, 2008.

Bellesiles, Michael B. *1877: America's Year of Living Violently.* New York: New Press, 2010.

Berkhofer, Robert F., Jr. *The White Man's Indian: Images of the American Indian from Columbus to the Present.* New York: Vintage, 1978.

Bigelow, John. *Letters and Literary Memorials of Samuel J. Tilden.* Vols. 1 and 2. New York: Harper and Bros., 1908.

Blight, David W. *Frederick Douglass: Prophet of Freedom.* New York: Simon & Schuster, 2018.

Bogen, Jules I. *The Anthracite Railroads: A Study in American Railroad Enterprise.* New York: The Ronald Press Co., 1927.

Brands, H. W. *American Colossus: The Triumph of Capitalism, 1865–1900.* New York: Anchor, 2010.

Brown, Dee. *The Year of the Century: 1876.* New York: Scribner's, 1966.

Bruce, Robert V. *1877: Year of Violence.* Indianapolis: Bobbs-Merrill, 1959.

———. *Bell: Alexander Graham Bell and the Conquest of Solitude.* Ithaca, NY: Cornell University Press, 1973.

Buick, Kirsten Pai. *Child of the Fire: Mary Edmonia Lewis and the Problem of Art History's Black and Indian Subject.* Durham, NC: Duke University Press, 2010.

Calhoun, Charles W. *The Presidency of Ulysses S. Grant.* Lawrence: University Press of Kansas, 2017.

Churella, Albert J. *The Pennsylvania Railroad*. Vol. 1, *Building an Empire, 1846–1917*. Philadelphia: University of Pennsylvania Press, 2013.

Coleman, J. William. *The Molly Maguire Riots: Industrial Conflict in the Pennsylvania Coal Region*. Richmond, VA: Garrett & Massie, Inc., 1936.

Crown, H. T. *A Molly Maguire on Trial: The Thomas Munley Story*. Frackville, PA: Bread Mountain Publishing Co., 2002.

Custer, George Armstrong. *My Life on the Plains, or, Personal Experiences with Indians*. Norman: University of Oklahoma Press, 1962. Originally published in 1874 by Sheldon and Company, New York.

Dale, John T. *What Ben Beverly Saw at the Great Exposition*. Chicago: Moses Warren & Co., 1877.

Dippie, Brian W. *The Vanishing American: White Attitudes and U.S. Policy*. Middletown, CT: Wesleyan University Press, 1982.

Flaherty, Anne. *The Passion of John Kehoe and the Myth of the "Molly Maguires."* St. Leonard, MD: Hibernian Press, 2023.

Flick, Alexander Clarence. *Samuel Jones Tilden: A Study in Political Sagacity*. New York: Dodd, Mead & Co., 1939.

Foley, Edward B. *Ballot Battles: The History of Disputed Elections in the United States*. New York: Oxford University Press, 2016.

Foner, Philip S. *The Great Labor Uprising of 1877*. New York: Pathfinder, 1977.

———. *History of the Labor Movement in the United States*. Vol. 1, *From Colonial Times to the Founding of the American Federation of Labor*. New York: International Publishers, 1998.

Giberti, Bruno. *Designing the Centennial: A History of the 1876 International Exhibition in Philadelphia*. Lexington: University Press of Kentucky, 2002.

Gillespie, Elizabeth Duane. *A Book of Remembrance*. Philadelphia: Lippincott, 1901.

Goodman, Susan, and Dawson, Carl. *William Dean Howells: A Writer's Life*. Berkeley: University of California Press, 2005.

Gordon, John Steele. *An Empire of Wealth: The Epic History of American Economic Power*. New York: Harper Perennial, 2004.

Gordon, Robert J. *The Rise and Fall of American Growth: The U.S. Standard of Living Since the Civil War*. Princeton, NJ: Princeton University Press, 2016.

Gray, Charlotte. *Reluctant Genius: Alexander Graham Bell and the Passion for Invention*. New York: Arcade, 2006.

Gross, Linda P., and Snyder, Theresa R. *Philadelphia's 1876 Centennial Exhibition*. Charleston, SC: Arcadia, 2005.

Grosvenor, Edwin S., and Wesson, Morgan. *Alexander Graham Bell*. Middletown, DE: New Word City, 2016.

Hamilton, Gail. *Biography of James G. Blaine*. Norwich, CT: Henry Bill Publishing Co., 1895.

Haworth, Paul Leland. *The Hayes-Tilden Disputed Election of 1876*. Cedar Rapids, IA: Burrows Bros. Co., 1906.

Henderson, Harry, and Henderson, Albert. *The Indomitable Spirit of Edmonia Lewis: A Narrative Biography.* Milford, CT: Esquiline Hill Press, 2012.

Hiltzik, Michael. *Iron Empires: Robber Barons, Railroads, and the Making of Modern America.* Boston: Houghton Mifflin, 2020.

Holley, Marietta. *Samantha at the Centennial.* Hartford, CT: American Publishing Co., 1881.

Hoogenboom, Ari. *Hayes: Warrior and President.* Lawrence: University Press of Kansas, 1995.

———. *The Presidency of Rutherford B. Hayes.* Lawrence: University Press of Kansas, 1988.

Howells, William Dean. *Sketch of the Life and Character of Rutherford B. Hayes.* New York: Hurt and Houghton, 1876.

Huffard, R. Scott, Jr. *Engines of Redemption: Railroads and the Reconstruction of Capitalism in the South.* Chapel Hill: University of North Carolina Press, 2019.

Ingram, J. S. *The Centennial Exposition Described and Illustrated.* Philadelphia: Hubbard Bros., 1876.

International Exhibition, 1876: Official Catalogue. Sponsored by United States Centennial Commission. Philadelphia: John R. Nagle & Co., 1876.

Jacob, Kathryn Allamong. *King of the Lobby: The Life and Times of Sam Ward.* Baltimore: Johns Hopkins University Press, 2010.

James, Henry. *Collected Travel Writings.* New York: Library of America, 1993.

Jordan, David M. *Roscoe Conkling of New York: Voice in the Senate.* Ithaca, NY: Cornell University Press, 1971.

Josephson, Matthew. *The Politicos, 1865–1896.* New York: Harcourt Brace, 1938.

Kaczorowski, Robert J. *The Politics of Judicial Interpretation: The Federal Courts, Department of Justice, and Civil Rights, 1866–1876.* New York: Fordham University Press, 2005.

Kenny, Kevin. *Making Sense of the Molly McGuires.* New York: Oxford University Press, 1998.

Larson, Henrietta M. *Jay Cooke, Private Banker.* Cambridge, MA: Harvard University Press, 1936.

Lemann, Nicholas. *Redemption: The Last Battle of the Civil War.* New York: Farrar, Straus & Giroux, 2006.

Licht, Walter. *Industrializing America: The Nineteenth Century.* Baltimore: Johns Hopkins University Press, 1995.

Maass, John. *The Glorious Enterprise: The Centennial Exhibition of 1876 and H. J. Schwarzmann, Architect-in-Chief.* Watkins Glen, NY: American Life Foundation, 1973.

McCabe, James D. *The Illustrated History of the Centennial Exhibition.* Philadelphia: The National Publishing Company, 1975.

Merrill, Lisa. *When Romeo Was a Woman: Charlotte Cushman and Her Circle of Female Spectators.* Ann Arbor: University of Michigan Press, 1999.

Montgomery, David. *Beyond Equality: Labor and the Radical Republicans, 1862–1872.* New York: Knopf, 1967.

———. *The Fall of the House of Labor.* New York: Cambridge University Press, 1987.

Morris, Edmund. *Edison.* New York: Random House, 2019.

Morris, Roy, Jr. *Fraud of the Century: Rutherford B. Hayes, Samuel Tilden, and the Stolen Election of 1876.* New York: Simon & Schuster, 2003.

Munsell, W. W. *History of Schuylkill County.* New York: W. W. Munsell Co., 1881.

Myers, Gustavus. *The History of Tammany Hall.* New York: Boni & Liveright, 1917.

Nasaw, David. *Andrew Carnegie.* New York: Penguin, 2007.

Noe, Jack. *Contesting Commemoration: The 1876 Centennial, Independence Day, and the Reconstruction-Era South.* Baton Rouge: Louisiana State University Press, 2021.

Norton, Frank B. *1876 Centennial Exhibition: The Illustrated Enhanced Historical Register.* Pittsburgh: CGR Publishing, 2020. Originally published in 1876.

Orcutt, Kimberly. *Power and Posterity: American Art at Philadelphia's 1876 Centennial Exhibition.* University Park: Pennsylvania University Press, 2017.

Parker, Watson. *Gold in the Black Hills.* Lincoln: University of Nebraska Press, 1966.

Pike, James S. *The Prostrate State: South Carolina Under Negro Government.* New York: Appleton and Co., 1874.

Polakoff, Keith Ian. *The Politics of Inertia: The Election of 1876 and the End of Reconstruction.* Baton Rouge: Louisiana State University Press, 1973.

Prucha, Francis Paul. *American Indian Policy in Crisis: Christian Reformers and the Indian, 1865–1900.* Norman: University of Oklahoma Press, 1976.

———. *The Great Father: The United States Government and the American Indians.* Lincoln: University of Nebraska Press, 1984.

Rehnquist, William H. *Centennial Crisis: The Disputed Election of 1876.* New York: Knopf, 2004.

Richardson, Heather Cox. *West from Appomattox: The Reconstruction of America After the Civil War.* New Haven, CT: Yale University Press, 2007.

Richardson, James D., ed. *Compilation of the Messages and Papers of the Presidents, 1789–1897.* Vol. 7. Washington, DC: Government Printing Office, 1898.

Rolde, Neil. *Continental Liar from the State of Maine: James G. Blaine.* Gardiner, ME: Tilbury House, 2007.

Rydell, Robert W. *All the World's a Fair: Visions of Empire at American International Expositions, 1876–1916.* Chicago: University of Chicago Press, 1984.

Schlegel, Marvin W. *Ruler of the Reading: The Life of Franklin B. Gowen, 1836–1889.* Harrisburg, PA: Archives Publishing Co., 1947.

Seaborn, Barbara. *Monumental Legacy: The Rise and Fall of Hamburg, South Carolina.* Bloomington, IN: iUniverse, 2021.

Sheppard, William Arthur. *Red Shirts Remembered.* Atlanta: Ruralist Press, Inc., 1940.

Sherman, John. *John Sherman's Recollections of Forty Years in the House, Senate and Cabinet: An Autobiography*. Vol. 1. Chicago: Werner Co., 1895.

Simkins, Francis Butler. *Pitchfork Ben Tillman: South Carolinian*. Baton Rouge: Louisiana State University Press, 1944.

Simon, John Y., ed. *The Papers of Ulysses S. Grant*. Vol. 27, *January 1–October 31, 1876*, and Vol. 28, *November 1, 1876–September 30, 1878*. Carbondale: Southern Illinois University Press, 2005.

Simonin, Louis. *A French View of the Grand International Exposition of 1876*. Translated by Samuel H. Needles. Philadelphia: Claxton, Remsen & Haffelfinger, 1877.

Sipes, William B. *The Pennsylvania Railroad: Its Origin, Construction, Condition, and Connections*. Philadelphia: The (Pennsylvania Railroad) Passenger Dept., 1875.

Slap, Andrew L. *The Doom of Reconstruction: The Liberal Republicans in the Civil War Era*. New York: Fordham University Press, 2006.

Slotkin, Richard. *The Fatal Environment: The Myth of the Frontier in the Age of Industrialization, 1800–1890*. New York: Harper Perennial, 1994.

Smith, Henry Nash. *Virgin Land: The American West as Symbol and Myth*. Cambridge, MA: Harvard University Press, 1970.

Spruill, Marjorie S. *One Woman, One Vote: Rediscovering the Woman Suffrage Movement*. Tillamook, OR: NewSage Press, 2021.

Stanton, Elizabeth Cady, Susan B. Anthony, and Matilda Joslyn Gage. *History of Woman Suffrage*. Vols. 2 and 3. Rochester, NY: Charles Mann Printing Co., 1881–87.

Stiles, T. J. *Custer's Trials: A Life on the Frontier of a New America*. New York: Vintage, 2016.

Summers, Mark Wahlgren. *The Era of Good Stealings*. New York: Oxford University Press, 1993.

Thirtieth Annual Report of the Board of Directors of the Pennsylvania Railroad Co. Philadelphia: E. C. Markley & Son, 1877.

Tuckerman, Henry T. *Book of the Artists*. New York: James F. Carr, 1867.

Twain, Mark, and Charles Dudley Warner. *The Gilded Age*. Orinda, CA: Seawolf Press, 2020. Originally published in 1873 by the American Publishing Company.

Walker, Francis A. *The Indian Question*. Boston: James R. Osgood and Co., 1874.

———. *The World's Fair, Philadelphia, 1876: A Critical Account*. New York: A. S. Barnes, 1878.

Ward, James A. *Railroads and the Character of America, 1820–1887*. Knoxville: University of Tennessee Press, 1986.

Warren, Louis S. *Buffalo Bill's America: William Cody and the Wild West Show*. New York: Knopf, 2005.

White, Richard. *Railroaded: The Transcontinentals and the Making of Modern America*. New York: Norton, 2011.

———. *The Republic for Which It Stands: The United States During Reconstruction and the Gilded Age, 1865–1896.* New York: Oxford University Press, 2017.

Whitman, Walt. *Democratic Vistas.* Edited by Ed Folsom. Iowa City: University of Iowa Press, 2010. Originally published in 1871.

Whittaker, Frederick. *A Complete Life of Gen. George A. Custer.* New York: Sheldon & Co., 1876.

Williams, T. Harry, ed. *Hayes: The Diary of a President, 1875–1881.* New York: David McKay Co., 1964.

Wojczuk, Tana. *Lady Romeo: The Revolutionary Life of Charlotte Cushman, America's First Celebrity.* New York: Simon & Schuster, 2021.

Woods, Naurice Frank, Jr. *Race and Racism in Nineteenth-Century Art: The Ascendancy of Robert Duncanson, Edward Bannister, and Edmonia Lewis.* Jackson: University of Mississippi Press, 2021.

Zuczek, Richard. *State of Rebellion: Reconstruction in South Carolina.* Columbia: University of South Carolina Press, 1996.

ARTICLES, PAMPHLETS, MANUSCRIPTS, AND REPORTS

Anonymous. *All About the Telephone and Telegraph.* London: Ward, Lock, & Co. 1878. LCP.

Anonymous. *How Edmonia Lewis Became an Artist.* Pamphlet. Philadelphia: John Spence, 1876.

Argument of Franklin B. Gowen Before the Joint Committee of the Legislature of Pennsylvania to Enquire into the Affairs of the Philadelphia and Reading Coal and Iron Co. and the Philadelphia and Reading Railroad Co., July 29–30, 1875. Pamphlet. Philadelphia: Press of Helfenstein, Lewis & Co., 1875. SCHS.

Argument of Messers. John Q. Lane, and Silas W. Pettit, Showing the Illegality and Criminal Conspiracy of the Anthracite Coal Monopoly, Before the Investigating Committee of the Pennsylvania Legislature, July 28th–31st 1875. Pamphlet. Philadelphia: A. T. Zeising & Co., 1875. LCP.

Bailey, David. *"Eastward Ho!" or Leaves from the Diary of a Centennial Pilgrim.* Highland, OH: Highland County Post Office, 1877. HSP.

Ball, W. W. *A Boy's Recollections of the Red Shirt Campaign of 1876 in South Carolina.* Pamphlet. Columbia, SC: The State Co., 1911.

Bell, Alexander Graham. *The Telephone: Researches in Electric Telephony.* Pamphlet. London: E. and F. N. Sons, 1878.

Britton, Annie. Scrapbook, 1876. HSP.

Brums, J. Dickson. *Address to the White League of New Orleans, September 14, 1875.* Pamphlet. New Orleans: W. Hyatt, 1875.

Buick, Kirsten P. "The Ideal Works of Edmonia Lewis: Invoking and Inverting Autobiography." *American Art* 9, no. 2 (Summer 1995).

Butler, Francis. *Gov. D. H. Chamberlain's Administration in S.C.* Unpublished manuscript dated May 6, 1918. Matthew Calbraith Butler Papers, David Rubenstein Research Library, Duke University.

A Centennial Fourth of July Democratic Celebration: The Massacre of Six Colored Citizens of the United States at Hamburgh, S.C. Pamphlet. African American Pamphlet Collection, LOC.

The Centennial: The Interests of the Great West and the Atlantic-Southern States: Extract from the Coming Event and Centennial Gazette. Pamphlet. HSP.

Closing Ceremonies of the International Exhibition, 1876. Pamphlet. Philadelphia: U.S. Centennial Commission, 1876. HSP.

Colman, J. Walter. "Labor Disturbances in Pennsylvania, 1850–1880." PhD dissertation. Catholic University of America, 1936.

Cordato, Mary Frances. "Toward a New Century: Women and the Philadelphia Centennial Exhibition, 1876." *Pennsylvania Magazine of History and Biography* 107, no. 1 (1983).

Democratic Party platform of 1876. At https://www.presidency.ucsb.edu/documents/1876-democratic-party-platform.

Falke, Wayne. "Samantha at the Centennial." *Hayes Historical Journal* 1, no. 3 (Spring 1977).

Foner, Philip S. "Black Participation in the Centennial of 1876." *Phylon* 39, no. 4 (Winter 1978).

Forney, John W. *Oration: July 4, 1877, at Fairmount Park.* Pamphlet. Philadelphia: Valette, Haslam & Co., 1877.

Gowen, Franklin B. *Argument of Franklin B. Gowen, Esq., in the Case of the Commonwealth vs. Thomas Munley et al.* Pamphlet. Pottsville, PA: Miners' Journal Book and Job Rooms, 1876.

Hartley, Gilbert. *Diary of a Trip to the Centennial.* Unpublished manuscript. HSP.

Hounshell, David. "Elisha Gray and the Telephone: On the Disadvantages of Being an Expert." *Technology and Culture* 16, no. 2 (April 1975).

Howells, William Dean. "A Sennight of the Centennial." *Atlantic Monthly*, July 1876.

Kachun, Mitch. "Before the Eyes of All Nations: African American Identity and Historical Memory at the Centennial Exposition of 1876." *Pennsylvania History* 65, no. 3 (Summer 1998).

Kelley, William D. *The Pecuniary and the Political Value of the Proposed International Exhibition.* Speech, May 5, 1874. Pamphlet. Washington, DC: Government Printing Office, 1874.

Kent, Patrick Den. "Red Shirts Revisited: The Politics of Martin Gary, 1868–1881." Master's thesis, 2015, Clemson University.

Kingsbury, Theodore Bryant. *The International Exhibition Guide for the Southern States.* Pamphlet. Raleigh: R. T. Fulghum, 1876.

Leighton, George R. "Shenandoah, Pennsylvania: The Story of an Anthracite Town." *Harper's Monthly*, January 1937.

Moore, James. *Thoughts Connected with the Great Centennial Exhibition of 1876.* Pamphlet. Philadelphia: Allen, Lane & Scott's Printing House, 1876.

Noe, Jack. "'Everybody Is Centennializing': White Southerners and the 1876 Centennial." *American Nineteenth Century History* 17, no. 3 (2016).

Official Proceedings of the Democratic National Convention. St. Louis: Woodward, Tiernan, & Hale, 1876.

Peremptory Sale in the Main Building of the International Exhibition Co., October 12th and 13th, 1881. Auction catalog. HSP.

Pfeuffer-Scherer, Dolores. "Remembrance and the American Revolution: Women and the 1876 Centennial Exhibition." PhD dissertation, Temple University, 2016.

Pomilio, Daniele. "The American Literary Sculptors: A Map of the Roman Studios." *European Journal of American Studies* 17, no. 3 (2022), journals.openedition.org/ejas/18843.

Proceedings, Convention of Colored Newspaper Men, Cincinnati, August 4, 1875. Pamphlet.

Proceedings of the Republican National Convention. Concord, NH: Republican Press Association, 1876.

Proceedings of the Returning Board of the State of Louisiana, Election of 1876. New Orleans Republican, published "compliments of W. R. Fish," 1876.

Public Sale of the Centennial Buildings, December 1, 1876. Auction catalog. HSP.

Recollections of Annette H. Kaercher. Typescript. SCHS.

Recollections of the Molly Maguire Era. Scrapbook. SCHS.

Report of the Committee Appointed to Investigate the Railroad Riots in July 1877. Harrisburg, PA: Superintendent of Public Printing, 1878.

Report of the Commonwealth vs. John Kehoe et al., Members of the Ancient Order of Hibernians, Commonly Known as "Molly Maguires." Pottsville, PA: Miners' Journal Book and Job Rooms, 1876. SCHS.

San Diego: The California Terminus of the Texas and Pacific Railway. Pamphlet. San Diego: San Diego Union, 1872. LCP.

Scott, Thomas A. "The Recent Strikes." *North American Review*, September 1877.

Small, George G. ("Bricktop"). *Going to the Centennial.* Pamphlet. New York: Collin & Small, 1876.

"The Studios of Rome." Anonymous. *The Art Journal*, Vol. 32 (March 1870).

Thorp, Margaret Farrand. "The White, Marmorean Flock." *New England Quarterly* 32, no. 2 (June 1959).

Tillman, Benjamin F. *The Struggles of 1876: How South Carolina Was Delivered from Carpetbag and Negro Rule.* Speech delivered in Anderson, S.C., to the Red Shirt Reunion, 1909. South Carolina Historical Society.

Townsend, Belton O'Neal. "The Political Condition of South Carolina." *Atlantic Monthly*, Vol. 39 (February 1877).

Index

A NOTE ABOUT THE AUTHOR

Fergus M. Bordewich is the author of nine previous nonfiction books, including *Klan War: Ulysses S. Grant and the Battle to Save Reconstruction; The First Congress: How James Madison, George Washington, and a Group of Extraordinary Men Invented the Government* (winner of the 2019 D. B. Hardeman Prize in American History); *America's Great Debate: Henry Clay, Stephen A. Douglas, and the Compromise That Preserved the Union* (named best history book of 2012 by the *Los Angeles Times*); and *Bound for Canaan: The Underground Railroad and the War for the Soul of America.* He lives in Washington, D.C., and Greensboro, North Carolina, with his wife, Jean Parvin Bordewich, the president of Guilford College and a playwright.

A NOTE ON THE TYPE

The text of this book was set in Century Schoolbook, one of several variations of Century Roman to appear within a decade of its creation. The original Century Roman face was cut by Linn Boyd Benton (1844–1932) in 1895, in response to a request by Theodore Low De Vinne for an attractive, easy-to-read typeface to fit the narrow columns of his *Century Magazine*.

Century Schoolbook was specifically designed for school textbooks in the primary grades, but its great legibility quickly earned it popularity in a range of applications. Century remains the only American face cut before 1910 that is still widely in use today.

Composed by North Market Street Graphics, Lancaster, Pennsylvania
Designed by Anna B. Knighton